CONSCIENCE: AN INTERDISCIPLINARY VIEW

THEORY AND DECISION LIBRARY

General Editors: W. Leinfellner and G. Eberlein

> Series A: Philosophy and Methodology of the Social Sciences
> Editors: W. Leinfellner (Technical University of Vienna)
> G. Eberlein (Technical University of Munich)
>
> Series B: Mathematical and Statistical Methods
> Editor: H. Skala (University of Paderborn)
>
> Series C: Game Theory, Mathematical Programming and Mathematical Economics
> Editor: S. Tijs (University of Nijmegen)
>
> Series D: System Theory, Knowledge Engineering and Problem Solving
> Editor: W. Janko (University of Vienna)

SERIES A: PHILOSOPHY AND METHODOLOGY OF THE SOCIAL SCIENCES

Editors: W. Leinfellner (Technical University of Vienna)
G. Eberlein (Technical University of Munich)

Editorial Board

M. Bunge (Montreal), J. S. Coleman (Chocago), M. Dogan (Paris), J. Elster (Oslo), L. Kern (Munich), I. Levi (New York), R. Mattessich (Vancouver), A. Rapoport (Toronto), A. Sen (Oxford), R. Tuomela (Helsinki), A. Tversky (Stanford).

Scope

This series deals with the foundations, the general methodology and the criteria, goals and purpose of the social sciences. The emphasis in the new Series A will be on well-argued, thoroughly analytical rather than advanced mathematical treatments. In this context, particular attention will be paid to game and decision theory and general philosophical topics from mathematics, psychology and economics, such as game theory, voting and welfare theory, with applications to political science, sociology, law and ethics.

CONSCIENCE:
AN
INTERDISCIPLINARY VIEW

*Salzburg Colloquium on Ethics in
the Sciences and Humanities*

Edited by

GERHARD ZECHA

and

PAUL WEINGARTNER

*Institute for Theoretical Science,
Salzburg International Research Centre,
and Department of Philosophy,
University of Salzburg, Austria*

D. REIDEL PUBLISHING COMPANY

A MEMBER OF THE KLUWER ACADEMIC PUBLISHERS GROUP

DORDRECHT / BOSTON / LANCASTER / TOKYO

Library of Congress Cataloging in Publication Data

Salzburg Colloquium on Ethics in the Sciences and Humanities (1984)
    Conscience: an interdisciplinary view.

    (Theory and decision library. Series A, Philosphy and methodology of the
social sciences)
    Includes indexes.
    1. Conscience–Congresses.   I.   Zecha, Gerhard.   II.   Weingartner,
Paul.   III.   Title.   IV.   Series.
BJ471.S18   1984   171.6   87–4343
ISBN 90–277–2452–0

Published by D. Reidel Publishing Company,
P.O. Box 17, 3300 AA Dordrecht, Holland.

Sold and distributed in the U.S.A. and Canada
by Kluwer Academic Publishers,
101 Philip Drive, Assinippi Park, Norwell, MA 02061, U.S.A.

In all other countries, sold and distributed
by Kluwer Academic Publishers Group,
P.O. Box 322, 3300 AH Dordrecht, Holland.

Printed in The Netherlands

TABLE OF CONTENTS

PART 3 / CONSCIENCE: SPECIAL TOPICS

PREFACE

Value change and uncertainty about the validity of traditional moral convictions are frequently observed when scientific research confronts us with new moral problems or challenges the moral responsibility of the scientist. Which ethics is to be relied on? Which principles are the most reasonable, the most humane ones? For want of an appropriate answer, moral authorities often point to conscience, the individual conscience, which seems to be man's unique, directly accessible and final source of moral contention. But what is meant by 'conscience'? There is hardly a notion as widely used and at the same time as controversial as that of conscience.

In the history of ethics we can distinguish several trends in the interpretation of the concept and function of conscience. The Greeks used the word συνείδησις to denote a kind of 'accompanying knowledge' that mostly referred to negatively experienced behavior. In Latin, the expression *conscientia* meant a knowing-together pointing beyond the individual consciousness to the common knowledge of other people. In the Bible, especially in the New Testament, συνείδησις is used for the guiding consciousness of the morality of one's own action.

St. Augustine described the Golden Rule as 'written conscience' and as *lex naturalis*. Since God has written this law into the heart of man, 'conscience' can be understood as 'the voice of God'. St. Thomas Aquinas distinguished, as it was usual in medieval times, between *synderesis* as a natural habitual knowledge of general principles of action and *conscientia* as the application of knowledge to a special act. He described three functions of *conscientia* in control and decision procedures and explained the logic of judgments of conscience in detail. Immanuel Kant typically identified 'conscience' as consciousness which is duty in itself; he also called it 'the law within us', and was sharply criticized by Arthur Schopenhauer, who rejected this concept of conscience as a *forum internum* and instead preferred to view conscience as 'moral self-determination'.

In the twentieth century three main trends can be identified:

(1) Conscience as natural consciousness of values either rooted in value emotions (Max Scheler, Nicolai Hartmann) or pointing to some transcendental authority (Viktor Cathrein, Viktor Frankl). This means that conscience does not create values autonomously but rather presupposes them.

(2) Contrary to this, existential philosophers point to a very self-conscious type of conscience, e.g. Karl Jaspers, 'In conscience a voice speaks to me which is myself' ['Im Gewissen spricht eine Stimme zu mir, die ich selbst bin'] or Martin Heidegger, 'In conscience Dasein calls itself' ['Das Dasein ruft im Gewissen sich selbst'].

(3) Still another theory of conscience is conceived by Sigmund Freud. The values and norms of the society or culture embodied in the authority of the father on the one hand and the desire to identify oneself with the simultaneously feared and beloved father on the other originate an ideal in the unconscious. Freud called this ideal Super-Ego, and it plays the role of a very strict judge and causes, therefore, the so-called 'qualms of conscience'.

In this rich but also somewhat perplexing tradition experts of many disciplines are now working on a new understanding of the concepts, contents, and functions of conscience. To ascertain the present status of research, an international colloquium was organized on the topic with the title 'Conscience: An Interdisciplinary View' and took place on 30 July - 1 August 1984 at the Institut für Wissenschaftstheorie of the International Research Center Salzburg, Austria. Scholars from various disciplines were invited to report on their work on conscience and to compare and discuss their results with colleagues from other disciplines. The present volume contains not only all the papers that were read at the colloquium, all of which are original contributions, but also the discussions that followed immediately after the presentation of each paper. These discussions are very important as they contain additional information and useful clarifications; they point to open questions and sometimes critically even to problematic suggestions.

The collection is divided into three parts:
Part 1: Conscience: Foundational Aspects
Part 2: Conscience: Social and Educational Aspects
Part 3: Conscience: Special Topics

In Part 1, Lawrence Kohlberg, after commenting on the question why moral psychology needs moral philosophy, describes the philosophical implications of his famous Six Stage Theory of cognitive moral development to the effect that each higher stage is a better stage in both a psychological and a philosophical sense. The philosophically most challenging Stage 6 is connected with the concepts of principle, reversibility, respect for persons, and judgments of conscience. Kohlberg expounds these concepts and their interrelations by illustrating the moral point of view, the dialogue condition and ideal consensus with a Stage 6 example that also makes clear the motivational force of responsibility at this stage of moral thinking.

Josef Fuchs SJ distinguishes two fundamentally different aspects of conscience: the subject-orientation and the object-orientation. Conscience is, above all, subject-related in the sense of having an inner knowledge, a self-consciousness that is existent in every person's life. In this respect, the primary interest of conscience is the moral goodness of the subject, whereas moral rightness is a secondary element, belonging to conscience but mainly connected with practical reason. Here the normative and evaluative functions of conscience are at stake. What is morally right often depends on personal interests and dispositions, hence opinions and moral judgments may differ. Dialogue and consensus nourish the hope of acquiring moral truths, leaving untouched the conscience's subject-orientation. Finally, a series of traditional problems (e.g., universal norms and the conscience in a concrete situation) are discussed in the light of this distinction.

Part 2 addresses various social sciences, especially social and educational aspects of conscience.

Gerhard Zecha is concerned with the crucial role that conscience may play in the moral responsibility of the social scientist. Many social scientists pursue as responsible scientists strict objectivity, which entails value-neutrality. But there are also other thinkers who argue for an elimination of value-neutrality from the social sciences. Referring to these controversial views, Zecha first clarifies the notions of value-neutrality and responsibility. He then describes and critically analyzes two suggestions for introducing norms and value-judgments into the object-language of the social scientist. In this connection he alludes to some of the so-called discipline-oriented values and finally proposes a normative concept of conscience which supports a general framework for justifying valuations and recommendations in his field.

This is in a way illustrated by Georg Lind's paper, which views conscience in the context of society and education. The main question, 'Do institutions of education in our societies foster moral judgment competence?', he answers positively after reviewing an impressive body of research findings related to this problem. With respect to these empirical data he argues for a series of requirements to the effect that extraordinary value-conflicts and difficulties with norms and principles call for a development of extraordinary moral competency. Improving the moral cognitive development may be achieved by fostering general education as well as the moral atmosphere of schools and colleges, Lind concludes.

This is, indeed, exactly what Ann Higgins shows in her contribution: that judgments of responsibility can be taken as one manifestation of the idea of conscience and that certain social environments and educational institutions do have an influence on the ability to make such judgments of responsibility. In this project, three alternative democratic high schools using the just community idea of education and three traditional high schools were studied. The students were asked to respond to moral dilemmas. Their responses were analyzed and compared with one another. The democratic school students turned out to be more socially responsible than their regular high school comparison students in favoring prosocial responsibility, in making judgments of responsibility and in their stage of judgment. This is - according to Higgins - the effect of a different moral atmosphere of the democratic schools where a strong sense of collective prosocial norms and a strong sense of community have a considerable impact on the development of conscience in students.

Part 3 is devoted to specific aspects of several concepts of conscience and their consequences in social life and social science. Günter Virt starts with a dilemma: on the one hand we nowadays quite often find our conscience in conflict with various ideologies, with laws of the state, with traditional norms, with practical interests. On the other hand, society is increasingly shifting the responsibility of moral decisions onto the individual's conscience. Virt views this intricate situation from a Christian moral perspective. He suggests interpreting the concept of conscience as an all-encompassing analogous symbolic notion for a basic trust which has its source in God, the creator and absolute goodness. It is, therefore, the firm foundation upon which every person has to build his/her identity. In the light of this notion, Virt discusses several practical questions; he finally formulates a set of rules that are designed to determine the decisions of conscience proper.

Paul Weingartner analyzes the logical structure of Thomas Aquinas' theory of conscience. Basically it satisfies all the conditions of the Hempel-Oppenheim-Scheme of scientific explanations and predictions. There are, however, several special features in this theory which Weingartner interprets in the light of recent investigations in the logic of scientific explanations. He distinguishes sharply between *synderesis*, the habitual knowledge of general principles of action, and *conscientia*, the application of knowledge.

In this sense, 'conscience' is to be understood as a very general logical inference-form that occurs in two different modes. One mode can be described in terms of the teleological explanation, the second mode sometimes in terms of a normative explanation, sometimes in terms of an evaluative explanation. In view of this analysis, Weingartner also explains Thomas' theory of error in conscience and illustrates frequent confusions about moral decisions with characteristic examples.

Heinrich Scholler uses the notions of relaxation of conscience and of intensification of conscience to describe the relationship between the law and freedom of conscience. In particular, he points out a certain ambivalence of the legal system towards phenomena of conscience. After a brief historical review, Scholler studies in detail the case of the conscientious offender, i. e., the problem of dissident religions. Here the intensification of conscience as provided by German law seems as problematic as the role of conscience in the legal system is ambiguous. Scholler discovers a 'continuing process of equalization' between the freedom of conscience and the state authority that is necessary to avoid conflicts with the right of others.

Hans Strotzka deals with two problems: the contribution of psychoanalysis to ethics and the moral aspects of psychotherapy. He starts with a description of shame pointing to so-called shame cultures as opposed to guilt cultures. The polarization of shame and guilt creates the dichotomy of egoism and altruism which psychoanalysis tends to transcend. With this knowledge of the origin of values together with the experience of a working psychiatrist Strotzka offers a new moral concept, a psychoanalytic ethics, that proved useful in treating his patients where traditional as well as philosophical moral principles were of no real help. - The ethics of psychotherapy, however, views the conflict between a patient-centered approach and a theory-centered approach. Again, Strotzka sketches a solution out of his personal experience as both a psychoanalytic theoretician and therapist.

We want to thank all authors for their active participation in discussing these papers and for their unflagging cooperation on preparing this volume. We also wish to acknowledge with thanks the generous sponsoring of the colloquium by the International Research Center Salzburg. Finally, we are most grateful to Professors Eberlein and Leinfellner, the editors of the Theory and Decision Library, for adopting the volume for their series.

Gerhard Zecha, Paul Weingartner, editors

THE PARTICIPANTS OF THE COLLOQUIUM

Front row (l. to r.): *Werner Stark, Hans Strotzka, Günter Virt, Thomas E. Wren, Ann Higgins, Lawrence Kohlberg, Heinrich Scholler, Georg Lind* .
Back row (l. to r.): *Paul Weingartner, Fr. Josef Fuchs SJ, Gerhard Zecha, Jean-Luc Patry* .

PHOTOGRAPH BY *Rudolf Stranzinger*

LIST OF PARTICIPANTS

FUCHS, JOSEF SJ - Pontificia Università Gregoriana, I-00187 Roma, Italy.

HIGGINS, ANN - Harvard University, Graduate School of Education, Cambridge, Massachusetts 02138, USA.

KOHLBERG, LAWRENCE - Harvard University, Graduate School of Education, Cambridge, Massachusetts 02138, USA.

LIND, GEORG - Universität Konstanz, Sozialwissenschaftliche Fakultät, Forschungsgruppe Hochschulsozialisation, D-7750 Konstanz 1, FRG.

SCHOLLER, HEINRICH - Universität München, Institut für Politik und öffentliches Recht, D-8000 München 22, FRG.

STARK, WERNER - Fordham University, New York, USA, and Universität Salzburg, Institut für Kultursoziologie, A-5020 Salzburg, Austria.

STROTZKA, HANS - Universität Wien, Institut für Tiefenpsychologie und Psychotherapie, A-1090 Wien, Austria.

VIRT, GÜNTER - Universität Salzburg, Institut für Moraltheologie, A-5020 Salzburg, Austria.

WEINGARTNER, PAUL - Institut für Wissenschaftstheorie, Internationales Forschungszentrum Salzburg, and Universität Salzburg, Institut für Philosophie, A-5020 Salzburg, Austria.

WREN, THOMAS E. - Loyola University of Chicago, Department of Philosophy, Chicago, Illinois 60626, USA.

ZECHA, GERHARD - Institut für Wissenschaftstheorie, Internationales Forschungszentrum Salzburg, and Universität Salzburg, Institut für Philosophie, A-5020 Salzburg, Austria.

PART 1

CONSCIENCE: FOUNDATIONAL ASPECTS

LAWRENCE KOHLBERG

CONSCIENCE AS PRINCIPLED RESPONSIBILITY: ON THE PHILOSOPHY OF STAGE SIX

I thought I might take one minute to deal with the question Dr. Strotzka[1] raised: While the history of Aquinas is of great interest and my own history is of none, I think sometimes it's helpful to have a very short historical background to my own thinking. I left high school and went into the Navy and the merchant Marines at the end of World War II, and then I was involved in bringing displaced persons and Jewish refugees through the British blockade and through Palestine, what later became Israel, for a number of years. At that time I was quite convinced I was acting out of conscience, but I became more and more confused about the justice or rightness of what I was doing since as a side effect of these things people were being killed in combat, in connection with bringing these ships in. So, when I went back to start college at the University of Chicago, I was very interested in the question of justice and some cognitive approach to ethics which would go beyond my own confused intuitions. Chicago at the time was a very unusual place, of course dominated by Hutchins and the Great Books, but also by a very strong pragmatic tradition of Dewey and G. H. Mead.

In any case I studied particularly under Charles Morris who represented the American pragmatic tradition, and was the editor and heir to George Herbert Mead's works. I decided to go into clinical psychology for a variety of reasons, but I retained my interest in philosophy. I came to Piaget's work through George Herbert Mead's work on the constitution of the moral self through communication. Mead's theory loosely corresponds to Piaget's notion of the construction of morality through cooperation, both seeing these constructions as going through stages. My own work has focussed pretty much on the right, on the deontological approach to morality. Coming from the pragmatic tradition in America, which starts with Charles Peirce's idea of truth as the ideal limit of inquiry I have been sympathetic

3

G. Zecha and P. Weingartner (eds.), Conscience: An Interdisciplinary View, 3–25.
© *1987 by D. Reidel Publishing Company.*

to what could be phrased as the "Consensus Theory of Rightness". That is, that rightness is the ideal limit of dialogue. In any case it seemed to me very important that we have a focus upon rightness because this is an area where there's a requirement to reach a consensus about rightness, where there isn't a requirement to reach a consensus about the good, the ideals of the good and their basis perhaps in ontology or religion. That is, that regardless of the varying ideals of the good, we still need to have a consensus on issues of justice, that is where individuals' competing ideals of the good come into conflict with one another. There needs to be some resolution of this problem.

1. THE RELATION BETWEEN PHILOSOPHY AND PSYCHOLOGY

Now, I'd like to go a little bit to my general notion of the relation between philosophy and psychology. I had originally not planned to talk about Stage 6, which is the most controversial part of my work and the most uncertain and unsettled; but perhaps it is philosophically the most interesting part of it. I think one has to make a few statements about the relation between philosophy and psychology. I think it's clear enough to people though, not to some of my behavioristic and socially relativistic psychological colleagues in America why moral psychology needs moral philosophy. This, I don't think, would be considered to require justification here. The actual carrying it out in terms of the Stage 6, that is some characterization which has to be philosophic in the highest stage of development is obviously controversial. But it's obviously necessary for psychology, at least the kind of psychology that I do, because in some sense this ideal stage is a rational reconstruction of ontogenetic development that presupposes in some sense an endpoint in a set of categories of morality from which one can eventually derive the sequence of stages.

Now I think it's less clear how psychology can help the philosopher and I've been involved in that controversy and said different things since I wrote a paper in 1972, "From 'Is' to 'Ought': How to Commit the Naturalistic Fallacy and Get Away with It" (Kohlberg 1981a). Nobody agreed that I had gotten away with it, though I denied that I had committed the naturalistic fallacy. I think in the most simple terms one can say that at least from the standpoint of the project of the modern normative moral philosophy, going from Sidgwick to Hare or to Rawls, to name some figures, that they take as their task the systematization and the justification of the moral judgments of competent moral judges or competent moral speakers. There is some sense that the philosopher can't rely on his own intuitions in order to systematize a moral philosophy. His own intuitions may be in error; he can't really trust them. If you're Rawls you say you can trust the intuition of the readers. His book is a dialogue between himself and the reader, he can only convince the reader, if from the readers' intuitions you can construct his system. But obviously many readers of Rawls have failed to be convinced by his argumentation and it may be that one of his problems, which I've discussed with him, is that perhaps his notion of a competent moral judge is limited to someone at Stage 5 or Stage 6 or some higher stage (Kohlberg 1981c). That is, we're not talking about the majority here, clearly as necessarily morally competent speakers. We don't take an opinion poll to determine the intuitions which should be reconstructed by the philosopher, but only, the morally developed judge, whoever that might be. At least this is one framework for why Developmental Psychology is possibly important to the philosopher.

The second point I would make is that my own approach has been bootstrapping, that is, it goes back and forth between descriptive moral psychology and philosophy in the sense that, for instance, when I started my work back in 1958 I took a few rather loose notions and used them for *a definition of the highest stage:*

Reference to judgments of conscience was one necessary condition. Another was the sanctity of life as revealed in my different dilemmas. Another was a sense of categorical duty in the sense of Kant. And then I found such characteristics in some of my subjects, not many but some at the end of high school. But as I followed these subjects along, some of them went into

college and became cynical egoists and relativists that said,
"Morality is nothing but the mores, and my responsibility is to
myself; there is no such thing as right or wrong, it's all totally
relative". These same subjects talked about conscience in high
school. So then I interpreted their high school responses as reflecting conventional understanding of conscience and moral
principles. When they questioned the world of their family, their
school, their neighborhood, their society, they adapted cynical
relativism. Their actions often changed as a result. One of these
subjects I call "Raskolnikov" because from being a moral leader
in the high school he embezzled from his fraternity, stole from
his friends and told me all sorts of things that he was doing,
because there was no such thing as morality. So then we
followed his progress and many years later he finally reached
stage five-principled thinking. In any case, my following along
over 25 years the development of my subjects led to revisions of
the notions of the stages and even of the moral philosophic assumptions necessary to be built into this.

2. SIX STAGES: THE HIGHER THE BETTER

I will briefly go over some responses to the Heinz dilemma that
indicate the sense in which each higher stage is a better stage in
a philosophic sense as well as a psychological sense. I might
point out that the dilemmas I did use because of my focus did
tend to these deontic issues of justice, like whether you should
steal to save a life, the *Heinz dilemma:*

In Europe, a woman was near death from a very bad disease,
a special kind of cancer. There was one drug that the doctors
thought might save her. It was a form of radium that a druggist
in the same town had recently discovered. The drug was ex-
pensive to make, but the druggist was charging ten times what
the drug cost him to make. He paid $ 200 for the radium and
charged $ 2,000 for a small dose of the drug. The sick woman's
husband, Heinz, went to everyone he knew to borrow the
money, but he could get together only about $ 1,000 which was
half of what it cost. He told the druggist that his wife was

dying, and asked him to sell it cheaper or let him pay later, but the druggist said, "No, I discovered the drug and I'm going to make money from it." Heinz got desperate and broke into the man's store to steal the drug for his wife.

The same subject Tommy is followed every three years. In each three years, he moves from one stage to the next. At age 10 and *Stage 1* he says, "Heinz shouldn't steal; he should buy the drug. If he steals the drug, he might get put in jail and have to put the drug back anyway." This shows some concern about obedience to law and justifying this obedience in terms of punishment. This is a sign that the law is right. Then he goes on to say how he qualifies it "but maybe the wife is an important woman like Betsy Ross who made the American flag," then it would be alright to steal for her. Underneath it, there would be an "egocentric perspective" that is a confusion of the self-perspective with the perspective authority. These aren't really differentiated. And there isn't a differentiation between psychological and physical values. I went on and asked him when he should start talking about important people, "Which is better, save the life of one important person or the lives of many unimportant people?" He said, "Maybe the unimportant people because they might have more furniture than the one important person". In any case a value of life was confused with the value of property.

At *Stage 2* he has moved away from that. He says, "Heinz should steal the drug to save his wife's life. He might get to jail, but he will still have his wife." This is a rather individual, egoistic conception that he values his wife's life more than he values going to jail for a while. The concrete egoism of his logic is indicated by when he is asked, "Why is life so valuable?", he said, "If it was a pet he could get a new pet, but it's not so easy to get a new wife". This is a kind of rationalism of an egoistic variety. This is also a sense of justice based on a rather simple notion of equality and concrete reciprocity. Asked "How about stealing for a friend?", he said, "That's going too far, he could be in jail while his friend is alive and free. I don't think a friend would do that for him". So we call these two stages preconventional. There is still a morality, still a justice there, but it's not one that is recognizable as a social morality in a certain sense.

At sixteen and *Stage 3* he says, "If I was Heinz, I would have stolen the drug for my wife. You can't put a price on love, no amount of gifts make love, you can't put a price on life either". Here he is taking what I call a third-party perspective, that is on a small group; the dyad, the marriage, the family. There are shared norms here, like care, love, trust which are mutually shared and morally valuable. They aren't reducible to the egoistic interests or exchanges as they were at Stage 2.

This third-party perspective is one point that I would emphasize. The second is the use of the *Golden Rule*. In a sense, the greater normative adequacy of each stage, one can think of perhaps by asking a moral question of the subject and judging, "Can he answer this question?" So, Stage 3 can to some extent answer the question: How do you feel in the other person's place? A question that really can't be answered at Stage 2.

At *Stage 4* Tommy says, "When you get married, you take a vow, love and cherish your wife. Marriage is not only love, it's an obligation like a legal contract"; he goes on to say, "but it's also a contract before God". So, he has a notion of now a religious and legal order which is obligatory and in which you have a defined place, a role, and that you've entered into this role and this commits you to certain rules. This, we would say, represents what in George Herbert Mead's terms would be called "The Generalized Other Perspective". The perspective of any other member of a similar religious society. It's recognized that society is not just small groups which can conflict with one another, but one must meet the expectations of the generalized other.

Here comes the *criterion of universalizability* for the first time. That is, at Stage 4 you can answer the question, "What if everyone did it?" This question is spontaneously asked and performatively in moral dialogues, we have with these people in moral education, so we have this question. And it's a meaningful question at Stage 4. It's unanswerable at Stage 3 and not thought of at Stage 2.

Moving on to *Stage 5*, Kim who went from Stage 2 at age 10 to Stage 5 at age 25 responsed to the Heinz dilemma, "I think he was justified in breaking in because there was a human life at stake. I think that transcends any right that the druggist had to the drug". Asked, "What does the word 'morality' mean to you?" he answers, "I think it is presumably recognizing the rights of the individual, the rights of other individuals, not interfering with the rights of others, act as fairly and honestly" and "I think these rights are first basically to preserve the human beings' rights to existence. I think that's most important. Secondly, the human being's right to do as he pleases, that is the right to liberty; again, as long as it doesn't interfere with somebody else's rights."

This way of thinking is oriented to natural rights and social contract, but more generally there is an awareness of a prior-to-law or society-perspective, which in this case stresses natural rights. And an understanding of law is to protect a hierarchy of rights: life and liberty in this case, so laws conceived as a social contract to protect individual rights. There is also rule-utilitarian thinking at this stage. This is the highest stage that we've gotten very full empirical data on, and one which is reasonably non-controversial, because I think it could be fitted to almost any normative philosophy. That is, the problems of philosophy, we call it post-conventional in a sense, involved the reconstruction of laws, both civil laws, but more particularly moral obligations on a rational basis prior to the consensus of the society.

To go on to *Stage 6*, to some extent in a very loose sense Kantian ideas are somewhat useful here. First, the notion that Stage 6 is principled, even that there's a single principle. Now the conception of a *principle* is a little problematic, but I'll try to develop it. Kant stressed one formal quality of principles, the "principle of universalizability" in his Categorical Imperative. In my own thinking I've stressed much more that universalizability is really derivative of what I call *reversibility*, which means the Golden Rule ideally (cf. Kohlberg 1981b). I take the Golden Rule in its most elaborate form to be what I call "*Ideal Role-taking*" or "Moral Musical-chairs". To give a simple example of what this might mean, say in this Heinz dilemma, I would ask the question, "Try to put yourself in the place of each of the actors who is concerned or involved in the dilemma and conceive each of the others to do likewise". Now at Stage 3, in the first order Golden Rule, there is no resolution of this in a strict sense, because if you take the role of the perspective of the wife, then you should steal. If you take the perspective of the druggist, then you shouldn't steal. Then there is a second order Golden Rule required, so to speak, in which each must take each other's role, so that the wife must imagine whether she could make her claim to the drug if she were in the perspective of the druggist; and can the druggist maintain his claim to the drug if he were to put himself in the perspective of the dying wife or the husband? And I would say, "No, the druggist can't really maintain his claim to property, if he puts himself in the perspective of the dying wife. The dying wife can still maintain her claim a right to the medicine if she puts herself in the role of the druggist".

You could formalize it by saying, "The druggist as a rational egoistic actor would prefer to save his own life over saving his property; and if he is to take a moral point of view, then he would have to recognize this as being a legitimate claim of the wife". I think Rawls has a different version of this notion of "Ideal Role-taking" or *the moral point of view*. But basically it's not the same, but it's loosely analogous in terms of his original position in the "Veil of Ignorance". That is, again the moral point of view from which one generates principles of justice for society is one in which you don't know who is going to be in the society rich or poor, Black or White, young or old, or so on. This is a way of defining a moral point of view.

As I say, the two ideas aren't exactly equivalent "Moral Musical-chairs" as I call it and the "Veil of Ignorance"; but I've written to show the parallelism between the two ideas.

3. PRINCIPLES, CONSCIENCE AND MORAL RESPONSIBILITY

Returning a little bit to *the notion of principle* again: The notion of principle has to be differentiated from the notion of a rule

because a priniciple is something that resolves primafacie obligations that rules or norms create. So, it's a method of choosing
between conflicted rules. As I say, I think I've stressed the
generality or universalizability of the Categorical Imperative of
Kant, which he treats as equivalent to a more substantive, less
formalistic way. That is, as I would see the principle of treating
each person as an end in himself and not merely as a means.
This introduces a notion of the good to a certain extent and not
strictly of the right. In order to treat the other as an end, you
must be concerned about active sympathy with the other. I see
respect for persons as a broader principle, which in some sense
loosely reconciles the good and the right in the very narrow
sense of the right as strict rights, what Kant called "perfect
duties". Of course, Kant held that it was right to tell the truth to
a murderer about the location of his victim because there was a
perfect duty to tell the truth by his universalizability criterion and
only an imperfect duty to save the life of another person. Now,
this strikes me as counter-intuitive and not something that I
would want to include in the principleness of Stage 6. As I say,
it's also not consistent with the notion of reversibility that I've
introduced.

The Principle of Respect for Persons while it considers the
good, avoids the utilitarian treatment in which there's a pater-
nalistic interpretation in which you don't have to respect the
autonomy of the will of the others in terms of promoting the
interest of either the individual other or the majority interest. I
would say that the formal properties of what today has come to
be called "a moral point of view" by a number of moral philosophers. They view the moral point of view as
  (a) a way of coming to principles,
  (b) a way of justifying principles,
  (c) a way of interpreting principles, and
  (d) I would stress particularly a way of coming to consen-
      sual agreement about the solution of conflicting claims.
That is, that it presupposes a dialogue; the moral point of
view is one in which people would consider each person's notions of what's right or just and can, by adopting the moral point
of view, hopefully come to ideal consensus. In this sense then,

as I say, the right is the ideal limit of dialogue. "Dialogue" - I would take it to be "communicative interaction about rightness" from the moral point of view, which includes premises such as respect for the other's person and his reason and autonomy.

To give an illustration, I'll go to a woman Joan whom I classified as Stage 6. In the Heinz dilemma the first question asked is, "What do you see as a problem in this situation?" She says, "I'd like to think there is a conflict for everybody here. As soon as more than one person knows about a situation there is a shared conflict, and the conflicts of each person sort of play off one another, and I think that conflicts can be resolved to some extent by kind of pooling. So that as soon as more than one person becomes aware of the conflict that there are automatically problems to be resolved by each, things to be considered by each. Each person, then, has the power to effect what happens in the conflict. If I were Heinz I would keep trying to talk with the druggist. I have a hard time thinking of any decision as being static. It seems to me the dialogue is very important and a continuing dialogue in this kind of situation." She tries to work out a dialogue solution of consensus, but then the interviewer presses her and says, "Still you must make a choice, the druggist isn't open to reason". Then she says, "I think it ultimately comes down to a conflict of duties. I don't think that Heinz should do anything he wouldn't be willing to say everyone should do and stealing is not something that one can be prescribed for humanity in general. On the other hand I think that Heinz just by virtue of being a member of the human race has an obligation, a duty to protect other people. When it gets down to conflict between these two, what I would call 'primafacie obligation', I think that the protection of human life is more important." And then she goes on to say, "It's not out of a sense of love even, it's out of a sense of responsibility meaning a recognition of the dignity on the part of every living being's responsibility that's entailed in that recognition. If I respect you as a creature with dignity in your own unique special being in recognizing that I won't intrude on you, I won't purposely harm you, there's also a whole series of positives and I have to preserve all that, preserve human life."

I'd like to show how this functions in terms of motivation in conscience and then conclude a little bit with a general approach to moral education.

She says, to go on, "What does 'conscience' mean to you? Well, I guess 'conscience' means to me the same thing as what I call 'moral responsibility', and that's the way I would interpret that, that he should act out of moral responsibility over a societal law in this case, again talking about responsibility to respect the dignity and preserve your life, and so on and so forth." Then she says, "I don't know how to explain it but expect that when I do things, particularly things that I don't really want to do very much, you know, but I really feel they're the right thing to do, usually what sort of sets me over the edge and makes a motivation enough for me to do it has to do with, well, how would I like to see people in general act in this case? What do I think is right in general? And that's what I would do." Then she gives a trivial example which again is not strictly in the realm of the right and the conscience. "Want a specific example? My ex-roommate calls a couple of weeks ago and I haven't seen her for a long time. She said, 'I really have a problem. I was supposed to borrow this typewriter and the friend copped out on me, and I've got this report to get typed, and you're the only person I know who's got a good typewriter, and so on. Can I come over and use your typewriter?' I was using the typewriter myself at that moment and I was really tired and I wanted to sleep but I thought about it and said 'Sure'. So she came over and used the machine. What I thought at the time was, 'Gosh, what I really want to do is now, I've got my own work to do and I'm tired, but on the other hand, would like to think of people who go out of their way to help other persons. I mean, that's a good way, that's a right way of being, to put other people's needs over your own when they come to you directly'. So I went along with them, let Kathy come over even though I don't want to do that." She then describes another more pragmatic kind of moral action which she interprets in a similar way.

4. CONCLUSION

I'd just like to conclude then in terms of our approach to the motivational basis for our approach to moral education. On the one hand we have to develop the competence of moral judgment which we interpret primarily as a stage increase in judgments of justice. And second, to develop the capacity and motivation for moral action, which we view primarily as acting responsibly. Like Piaget we assume the motivation for the development of making judgments themselves is largely based on the internal cognitive moral conflict, and to adapt to the world by role-taking or taking into account the moral or social perspective of others, that this is a taken-for-granted tendency, to take the point of view of others and it's also, there's a need to resolve "disequilibrium" as Piaget would call it, within or conflict within one's own point of view. There's a conflict within each stage, a latent conflict which predisposes to moving to the next stage. On this basis we developed "Classroom Moral Education" in more than a hundred classrooms in different studies. We've done this type of Socratic moral discussion or argumentation in which these children and the students argued with one another about real or hypothetical moral dilemmas. In these studies, the result is in general that in a year there's half a stage upward movement. In classrooms which do not engage in this kind of moral discussion, there is no such change during the year. Now such a discussion approach doesn't deal directly with either conscience or moral action as usually considered. Accordingly we have developed our "*just-community-approach*".

There are *two basic motivational principles* here. The *first* is that, again, the student is capable of *self-criticism*. When there is a contradiction between his judgment what he's agreed upon and his action. There is a long process of democratic discussion about norms of rightness for each of the particular schools. If the student deviates from this norm which he has agreed to then he is subject not only to group criticism of course as having violated the agreements he has made with the community but he is subject also to self-criticism as having been irresponsible in his conduct.

The *second* motivational principle which Ann Higgins discusses is really the notion that moral motivation involves *membership in a moral community*. The school becomes a moral community in which people care about one another and the welfare and solidarity of the school itself. When they conform to the agreements that they have made, this is seen as contributing to the welfare of the community and increasing the solidarity of the community, the moral community. This kind of education really has the aim that eventually people should reach the position of Joan, in which she has the sense of not only a moral community bounded by the school but a universal human community to which she is responsible, as well as having a sense of justice which involves the notion of universal respect for human dignity.

Harvard University, Graduate School of Education

NOTE

1 Here Dr. Kohlberg is referring to a remark of Dr. Strotzka's in the discussion of Dr. Weingartner's paper, see p. 225f of this volume. [G.Z., P.W.]

BIBLIOGRAPHY

Kohlberg, L.: 1981a, 'From *Is* to *Ought*: How to Commit the Naturalistic Fallacy and Get Away with It in the Study of Moral Development' in L. Kohlberg: *Essays on Moral Development. Vol. One: The Philosophy of Moral Development*, Harper & Row, San Francisco, pp. 101-189.
Kohlberg, L.: 1981b, 'Justice as Reversibility: The Claim to Moral Adequacy of a Highest Stage of Moral Judgment' in L. Kohlberg, *op. cit.*, pp. 190-226.
Kohlberg, L. and C. Power: 1981c, 'Moral Development, Religious Thinking, and the Question of the Seventh Stage' in L. Kohlberg, *op. cit.*, pp. 311-372.

DISCUSSION

Ann Higgins, Lawrence Kohlberg, Georg Lind,
Heinrich Scholler, Hans Strotzka, Günter Virt,
Paul Weingartner, Thomas E. Wren, Gerhard Zecha

<u>KOHLBERG</u>: I will paraphrase Frankena, a textbook on *Ethics* (1963). He asked, "How can we justify judgments of actual duty general or particular, second, how can we justify principles of primafacie duty?" The same answer will do for both: First, we must take the moral point of view. We must also be free, impartial, willing to universalize, conceptually clear, and informed about all possibly relevant facts. Then we are justified in judging that a certain act of a kind is right, wrong, or obligatory. In claiming that our judgment is objectively valid, at least as long as no one who is doing likewise disagrees, our judgment or principle is really justified.

Suppose we encounter someone who claims to be doing this but comes to a different conclusion. Then we must do our best through reconsideration and discussion to see if one of us is failing to meet the conditions in some way. If we can detect no failing on the other side, and still disagree, we may, and I still think, must each claim to be correct. But if what is said about relativism, we cannot both be correct. Both of us must be open-minded and tolerant.

If this line is thought as acceptable, then we may say that a basic moral judgment, principle, or code is justified or valid, if it is or will be agreed to by everyone who takes a moral point of view, and is clear-headed and logical and knows all that is relevant about himself, mankind, and the universe. The fact that moral judgments claim a consensus on the part of others does not mean that the individual thinker must bow to the judgment of the majority in a society. He's claiming an ideal consensus that transcends majorities and actual societies. Here enters the autonomy of the moral agent. He must judge for himself. He may be mistaken but, like Luther, he cannot do otherwise. I wanted at least to clarify this idea of a moral point of view which seems to be not present at Stage 5, there's a moral point of view in that sense but this explicit awareness of a point of view by which a dialogue can insure a consensus on the right in the form of a way of coming to consensual agreement about a particular situation in which there are conflicting claims only found at Stage 6. Of the various formal properties of this point of view, I have particularly stressed this one of reversibility, implied by the Golden Rule which a moral philosopher calls the 'folk-wisdom of the world'; but it's a little bit more than the folk-wisdom of the world.

WEINGARTNER: First I want to comment on the principle of reversibility. If one can exchange the roles then the principle of reversibility is satisfied. This is not identical with the simple principle of universalizability, because Kant's view was always: not only to exchange my role with one particular arbitrarily chosen person but at the same time with all of them, to make the maxim a law for all of them. Therefore, the Categorical Imperative does not work, as Scheler has shown, for individual decisions.

Well, a logician would say, we have two types of general propositions: the one which says, 'for all', and the one which says, 'an arbitrary one'. Both are general. So, it seems your reversibility principle is general, in the sense that you can take an arbitrary one. I think, this is important because it takes into account also individual decisions, whereas Kant's idea does not.

Second, you said that on Stage 6 you would not allow certain conflicts. Here I have a couple of questions. Do such conflicts not arise anymore if one is already at this stage? Is it always so that on Stage 6 you can solve them? And if so, what is, so to speak, a higher value and what is a lower value which we need as ordering principles?

KOHLBERG: I'm not sure that the role-reversal is with the simply arbitrary other that in some sense it has to be any individual other or all the others who are involved in the particular situation. So that there would be some necessity of actually sympathetic or empathetic role-taking involved.

The next question, what is the hierarchy of values? It seems to me in principle to be given by the notion of a single general moral principle, which interpreted in light of this moral point of view; that is, it would be characteristic at the 5th Stage to have a number of discrete hierarchies of values: the easiest one to talk about is life and property. When I talked about the consensus theory of rightness, I might have added the notion of constructivism, that in some sense the purpose of principles of justice and of a moral point of view is to come to consensus about conflicts, moral conflicts, and it would be nice to entertain the possibility to say at least that ultimately this is what "rightness" means. That's the ideal limit of the concept of rightness.

STROTZKA: It's certainly legitimate to study moral development with typical dilemma stories but with the Heinz story I have the greatest difficulties. If I would be confronted with this story, I would say, first: "Stealing is a more realistic alternative for me because I need certain qualities to steal (probably the drug is in a safe or something)". The first part of the story sounds to me very strange. It's obviously a profit-sharing gang of the doctor and the druggist because there is only one drug which helps, only one pharmacist who is producing it. Probably the drug is totally ineffective besides the profit for the two people. But if it is the moral dilemma, which frequently happens, then there would be a lot of possibilities to solve the problem without a moral dilemma.

KOHLBERG: Which makes you very autonomous and on a high stage to refuse to answer the dilemma. But this dilemma is unrealistic. In America we set it in Europe, in Europe you'd have to set it in America, then maybe it's more believable. The other dilemmas are a little less unrealistic but were created to try to force one to make a choice between two very strong primafacie obligations. You just engaged in some very practical, rational reasoning, I would call it.

WREN: Why is it that you, Professor Strotzka, or let us say, an arbitrarily taken subject, refuses to consider this hypothetical dilemma? I just always wonder whether it's just a hard-headed realism or whether it's something deep in the structure of personality that refuses to allow people in certain cases to consider hypothetical moral situations.

HIGGINS: I don't think we will ask Professor Strotzka to give an immediate answer. I think in terms of this issue there is this idea of the hypothetical dilemma as a research tool of getting at the competency of people's thinking. What we want is their best moral thinking and none of their other kind of thinking. It's an attempt to isolate the moral issues.

KOHLBERG: Or discriminate, as we say, between content and structure of reasoning. So that familiarity with some children or subjects might have greater familiarity with certain dilemmas. Therefore they would apparently have greater competence to structure them than others. So in general we prefer to use unrealistic dilemmas on the grounds that there aren't given cultural, school or family pre-set solutions to these dilemmas.

LIND: I think what you have told us helps to make sense of a developmental order of consciousness. This idea is appealing to me. Another idea that is appealing to me are some of your criteria for judging on the morally right; it's point (d) especially when you say, "Ways of coming to consensual agreement upon what is right and just". I think this criterion of consensual agreement is very important to guard against what one might call "moral imperialism".

A third critical point that I would like you to comment on: I miss a general sociological perspective: If you speak of a wrong consciousness or inadequate consciousness, that is one thing. The other is when you explain your stages you say, "This is a way of just reasoning and reciprocity which has its value". Could that mean: If you have a particular social context or social dilemma and a particular type of social tasks, then this type or moral reasoning, Stage 2, say, is adequate and we solve all problems. So you come to a theory of types of moral tasks which require different types of moral reasoning. In order to complement your kind of psychological theory of moral development you have to complement it by a sociological theory of the types of social or moral tasks which you implicitly refer to when you speak of an adequate or inadequate moral consciousness.

KOHLBERG: I would agree. Some of this comes down in the cross-cultural data that is reassuring for me to know that in East and West we still find Stage 5 and Stage 6. But Stage 5 reasoning we find in the Asiatic - India, Taiwan, and Turkey and many other places, it's not only in the Western or Judaeo-Christian culture. But it does not seem to be found in simple moral societies. There we don't find any Stage 5 thinking. I think you could say the problems in a small folk village don't require Stage 5 reasoning. To have Stage 5 reasoning there must be a conflict between groups in which institutional systems are somehow different. It is this conflict between them that forces one to move to Stage 5, but if you are in a small society where there is a consensus reached on a more face-to-face village basis, then there is perhaps no need for that. If I just elaborate one thing that the claim that these stages of reasoning and judgment are progressively moral adequate by no means allows you to make a judgment that the possessor of that reasoning is a moral worthy person. Sometimes people make this mistake what I call abuse of my moral stages to use them in that sort of way.

VIRT: I want to go back to the Golden Rule and the book by Bruno Schüller, *The Foundation of Moral Judgments* (1980). He gives four interpretations of the Golden Rule and it would be interesting to relate them to your stages of moral development. The first is a rule of naive egoism: "By experience I know why I do unto others in this way". The second, "Do unto others as you would like to be treated by the others".

KOHLBERG: That's Stage 2 at least.

VIRT: The third interpretation points to reversibility in this sense: "I am obliged to treat the other as the other is obliged to treat me." For instance, parents have to treat their children as the children are obliged to treat their parents. Is this the correct sense of reversibility? That's the problem, because there are so many interpretations of the Golden Rule in the literature.

KOHLBERG: Right, I think there are, however, that doesn't mean we should despair about it, but only we need a bit more moral philosophy and analytic clarification of what the meaning of the norm is. I think it really presupposes a notion of rationality to a certain extent, you see? This isn't clarified at Stage 3 interpretation of the Golden Rule. For instance, in Stage 3 when it is confused, "Shall I act to treat the other in the way in which I would want to be treated if I were in his place" with the one "Act in the way in which he wants to be treated where what he wants is something different than what I want in his place". This is the problem then: It says to require some degree of a construction of a rational actor in order to resolve this problem.

LIND: All these examples were not beyond Stage 2 or beyond preconventional reasoning: And they always treat exchange or reciprocity in a very concrete manner: "Parents should not hit the children, because they do not want to be hit by the children". Stage 3 would mean: This exchange has to go in a more indirect manner over a level of social unit of a family, that is: "Be a good parent!", whatever that means completely, because you want your children to be good children, whatever that means. It could mean something quite different, but it implies, "Every member of the family should do what he is supposed to do: Be a good member of the family", because he wants the others also to be good members of the family, in order to hold up the family. The Golden Rule, hence, has to be translated differently on each stage.

VIRT: This interpretation becomes more and more formal, when you go to higher stages. As a truly moral rule it could mean that what is a moral obligation for one man has to be a moral obligation for all the other members of a human society. I think that's the true meaning of the Golden Rule, but in the formal sense.

KOHLBERG: This is Kant in a certain way, but my suggestion is that the true formal equivalence that Kant was pointing to was between the substantive principle of respect for human personality and the formal principle of reversibility in the Golden Rule rather than universalizability. This is a more adequate equation. We say that each of us wants others to treat us as ends and not as a mere means. This is more or less the content of reversibility in the Golden Rule.

SCHOLLER: I have four questions.

First, you said there is a relationship between legal development and the moral stages, but if we go back to legal anthropology then there is, I suppose, not a linear development, but there is a kind of co-existence of different phases.

In archaic society you have Stages 1, 2 and 3, but no 6. And in the early modern state, we have stage 4, mainly 4 and no 6. And only in the late modern state you have Stage 5 and Stage 6. So I suppose it's more complicated.

Second question: We have also a kind of co-existence of different levels of moral development in the modern state: we have Stage 5 and 6, but with regard to penal law also 4. And with regard to public international law we have Stage 2.

Point three: It would be interesting now to have interviews with lawyers, legal people, let's say policemen, people of the administration or judges. We might then see that the policeman will belong to Stage 4, whereas judges would fit into 6: So we have another kind of co-existence.

Last question: I think it could be very interesting for a law-suit to find decisions of which we have a first instance, a second and third instance and may therefore have different types of reasoning and you could relate them to your stages.

KOHLBERG: Well, you raise several questions. You indicated there has been some socio-cultural legal evolution. I relied partly on the work of the English sociologist Leonard Hobhouse (1906) who has a stage scheme somewhat similar to my own. Some of my students did some cross-cultural studies. There are some societies on Stage 1 where murder simply calls for a murder in return by the family of the murderer. There are other societies where there is a mechanism of restitution which we would call Stage 2. You pay back the family for the murder. Then you have a Stage 3-system, which might be roughly called "kadi justice" or something like that. And on Stage 4 you might say that a definite judge with definite procedures that he has to follow to come to a decision. On Stage 5 there is a procedural protection of the rights of each of the disputants.

As far as the interviewing of judges: One of my students has just started such a study and he's not only interviewing judges in Massachusetts, but hopefully he will be interviewing some of the American Supreme Court-Justices, as a couple have given permission for this, which will be very interesting. Finally in terms of use of actual legal decisions, we did a little bit of that in this volume of mine *The Philosophy of Moral Development*: Capital punishment, for instance, where we discuss different jurisprudential opinions on capital punishment that we can represent with different stages (Kohlberg/Elfenbein 1981).

ZECHA: I think I can understand why, say, Stage 3 is higher than Stage 2 or Stage 6 is higher than Stage 4 from a psychological point of view. But you also claimed that they are better in a moral sense: why is this so?

The second question: You are doing cognitive moral psychology and I wonder whether this implies in some sense cognitive moral philosophy. I have certain doubts about this, because you frequently appealed to the idea of a consensus-theory - the model of consensus - which is quite common today (we know that from Habermas and other people in different versions).

In scientific matters we do not appeal to consensus but in moral questions there is a very strong tendency to find a decision with a majority or consensus. What is your point of view on this question?

KOHLBERG: Well, we can mean 'consensus' in the sense of majority agreement, but I meant it only in the sense of a limiting ideal, as I said: justice. Peirce meant that the limiting ideal in science is the ideal of the community of scientific inquirers. I think, 'ideal consensus' is very different than 'democratic consensus'. So, that would be one point of view but I think these are all, as I say, maybe personal meta-ethical preferences of mine. Certainly, the psychologist is typically interested in explaining, "Why is it that you go from, say, Stage 3 to 4?" And they try to give some explanation of that, but that explanation has - it seems to me - within it as a part (not as a whole) a normative claim that all of the conditions that we lay out in the psychological work presuppose a normative claim that 4 is more morally adequate than Stage 3 or none of these things would work.

It's very difficult to understand that without some postulates that the child perceives that Stage 4 is more adequate otherwise there wouldn't be such movement. This is not proven in any sense, but if the adequacy could be disproved - I don't think it can be proved empirically, but I think it can be disproved empirically.

ZECHA: To me 'adequate' is a relation term, so: adequate to what?

KOHLBERG: Aha - not necessarily morally adequate. Well, one has to introduce some notion of a moral point of view into this discussion. Dialogue and consensus talk - if I engage in a dialogue with a subject strictly remaining within a framework of what philosophers would consider 'moral argumentation', one ought to be able to help moving subjects from one moral decision or stage to the next. As I say, to give an illustration: If you keep with somebody on Stage 3, if you keep asking him the question, "What if everybody did it?" or "What about the responsibility to this person that you haven't considered, because you are not considering everybody?" These things can be forms of moral argument and by engaging in this form of open moral argument asking questions that in fact you do get movement from one stage to the next seems to me an argument.

ZECHA: Thank you.

WEINGARTNER: I want to comment once again on reversibility because this principle is an interesting interpretation of the Golden Rule. And this interpretation has two new features as far as I can see: The one feature points out a difference between this interpretation of the Golden Rule and Kant's Categorical Imperative, because it does not require a maxim holding as a law for all independent of being in a particular situation, but just the possibility of exchanging the role with someone of those "others" mentioned in the Golden Rule. Therefore it's also applicable, as I said, to individual situations.

The second point is - in my view - this: that it holds only conditionally. Why? Because it holds only if one can exchange the "arbitrary person" on the condition that he (she) plays the same role. So, the exchange must be role-invariant, and this is the interesting and new feature in this interpretation. Finally I have a short comment on Zecha's point about the consensus. In the area of knowledge I would not agree completely that we have never a consensus. In very difficult situations, if there is a crucial experiment in physics, for example, very important physicists have to repeat it. Or think of the famous proof of the independence of the Continuum Hypothesis by Cohen, where the referees of the journal didn't know whether the proof was correct and only after Kreisel and Gödel both said that it was correct, the paper was accepted for publication. But on the ethical side, one thing is very interesting: Remember what Plato wrote in the *Protagoras*: By order of Zeus, Hermes distributed shame and justice equally among men, not like the special abilities for mathematicians or musicians. So Plato makes understandable what the jury in the lawcourt says: "We accept anyone - not necessarily an expert, but just someone who is mature enough." This, I think, is also an interesting point concerning consensus, especially in ethics.

HIGGINS: Thank you all, thank you.

End of discussion.

BIBLIOGRAPHY

Frankena, W.K.: 1963, *Ethics*, Prentice-Hall, Englewood Cliffs, N.J.

Kohlberg, L. and D. Elfenbein: 1981, 'Capital Punishment, Moral Development, and the Constitution' in L. Kohlberg: *Essays on Moral Development. Vol. I: The Philosophy of Moral Development*, Harper & Row, San Francisco, pp. 243-293.

Schüller, B.: [2]1980, *Die Begründung sittlicher Urteile.*, Patmos, Düsseldorf.

JOSEF FUCHS

THE PHENOMENON OF CONSCIENCE:
SUBJECT-ORIENTATION AND OBJECT-ORIENTATION

There is no doubt that conscience is connected with the sphere
of ethics; a closer study of the phenomenon of conscience leads
into the field of psychology as well. Now that I, as a Catholic
moral theologian, am to say something about the conscience
phenomenon, I would like firstly to refer to two extremely di-
verging statements made recently by two Catholic moral theologians. In the foreword to his Fundamentalmoral (1977)[1] F.
Böckle says that he is dispensing with a chapter on conscience
as he cedes this subject to the competency of the psychologists
and will apply himself to the problems concerning justified ethical judgment. Contrary to this, A. Molinaro identifies moral
conscience and moral norm in his most recent article on conscience (1983)[2] and understands them as being "the constitution
of the ethical subject or person". In the following an attempt will
firstly be made at grasping the conscience-phenomenon to a certain extent[3] in order to be able to study the primary subject-
orientation and the merely secondary object-orientation more
closely afterwards.

1. THE PHENOMENON OF CONSCIENCE: VARIOUS ASPECTS

It is not possible here to expound and analyze the extremely
complex phenomenon of conscience in its entirety. The intention
is rather to call attention to only a few aspects of this phenomenon in order to come to some sort of common understanding
and so prepare the ground for discussion.

1.1 Conscience and the Orientation for the Conduct of Life

One generally tends to look upon conscience somehow as an authority of the way of leading a wordly life; in concreto it determines personal obligation and, thereby, the goodness and right-

27

G. Zecha and P. Weingartner (eds.), Conscience: An Interdisciplinary View, 27–56.
© 1987 by D. Reidel Publishing Company.

ness of actual behavior and of freely performed life. The conscience is, consequently, throughout understood as being an authority governing the conduct of life.

Today we are more aware than in the past of the fact that the conscience is not the only authority governing the way life is conducted. There are other authorities which determine our conduct in life and which do not call on the freedom of the human being. Behavioral research shows, for instance, that certain behavior in humans and animals is based on biological factors[4] which pretend to be something of an ethical order but which are not ethical orientation; astonishing cases of 'selfless' behavior within personal relationships and society are not necessarily ethical and conscientious acts - certainly not with animals, and also not with human beings. Social conduct and personal behavior can be a spontaneous reaction prompted by accepted rules of *social* behavior and are, therefore, not necessarily caused by morality. *Psychology* investigates how certain types of psychological motivation determine the behavior of young children, who undoubtedly lack moral conscience, and also often that of juveniles and adults. The Freudian Super-Ego can play a predominant part in the way we conduct our lives and is far too often in danger of being mistaken for moral conscience. L. Kohlberg's studies on moral maturity and immaturity clearly show that not all orientation for life is the call of moral conscience. We usually consider the adult and mature person - contrary to animals - as that living being which is able to reflect on himself and his behavior: he has a moral conscience which affords him orientation for life.[5] He is also able, at least partly, to reflect on biological, sociological and psychological impulses and orientation and to evaluate their goodness and rightness and eventually to either accept or reject them at will. It can be supposed that people's good and right conduct is sometimes based on both ethical and non-ethical orientation *simultaneously*. Who is able to judge to what extent their conduct is based on spontaneous reaction or on moral motivation and decision?

1.2 *Conscience and Practical Reason*

Morality thus presupposes that human action is not a spontaneous reaction but follows decisions based on insight of conscience. Such insight is, in a formal sense, the result of that
which is generally termed in practical reason. As already mentioned, F. Böckle emphasizes the fact that he is exclusively interested in the problem relating to practical reason which determines, *in abstracto* and *in concreto*, the ruling as to good and
right that practical reason and conscience are not one and the
same. The question as to whether one can separate the two, and
be it only theoretically, remains problematic. In other words, is
there such a thing as practical reason outside the conscience or
not?

This question has a double meaning in accordance with the
double meaning of the concept of conscience. 'Conscience'
means - particularly in Catholic Moral Theology - in a narrower
sense the authority which determines good and right conduct in
a concrete situation. Another conception of conscience conversely does not limit the authority of conscience to the assessment of a *concrete situation*, but extends its competency to include *theoretical* moral evaluation and formulation of norms.

It should not be overlooked by both meanings, and most im-
portantly by the first and narrower meaning, that the isssue is
never one of 'pure' practical reason. What is that supposed to
mean? Practical reason is, on account of the many facets constituting human existence, subject to diverse influence, but does
not, however, lose its own identity. For moral judgment based
on practical reason is carried out under the powerful influence
exercised by tradition, custom and environment, and also under
biological, sociological and psychological influences as well as
individual tendencies, interests and dispositions. Judgment based on practical reason is truly *its own* judgment and is, nevertheless, a result of influences exercised by the diverse elements comprised in human reality as a whole. In this sense, it is
true that practical reason proves itself to be not pure a-priori
speculation, and that it comes closer to the much richer concept

of conscience, which always pervades man in his personal entirety.

This becomes even clearer if one asks on what grounds and with what justification judgments that are based on practical reason are termed 'moral judgments'? This indeed presupposes that one knows when making such judgments what morality means; young children, for instance, do not know this. Whoever talks about morality, also with respect to judgments based on practical reason, is only justified in doing so if he has personal experience of the phenomenon of morality, which is in fact nothing other than the irreducible phenomenon of moral conscience. And this means: the valuing and driving experience of the human person does exist - stemming from the innermost self-consciousness - to be participation in absolute freedom, that is to say not original and absolute freedom but an 'obligatory' freedom. Here freedom is understood as freedom of the *person as such* and for the means of self-realization and not necessarily as freedom to all concrete and particular action. This phenomenon can neither be explained in psychological categories nor is the subject, as the result of thought on the matter, compelled to freely acknowledge it or any definite explanation of the deepest part of the own being. It is not only considered as, and declared to be, a primary phenomenon by Christian but also by humanist and Marxist philosophers; compare, for instance, corresponding thoughts in philosophical circles in Poland.

Judgment of good and right conduct based on practical reason, therefore, always takes place as part of existential basic moral experience and deepest moral conviction. *Moral judgment and personal moral experience are always interlaced* . This becomes clearest when it is not only a case of abstract values and standardization, but of a concrete decision made by the subject in a concrete situation. Judgment based on practical reason qualifies as being 'moral' exclusively on account of the interconnected and ever-manifest conscience. Indeed, it may sometimes appear in the case of judgment based on practical reason that it is firstly a matter only concerning particular ethical questions, whereas it is in the last analysis a matter concerning the human being as such and its meaningful self-realization. This then makes it understandable that judgment based on practical reason, being judgment *in the conscience*, has above all else, but not exclusively, the characteristics of insight, while at the same time and to a certain extent, those of decision.

1.3 *Conscience and Religious Experience*

According to that which has already been mentioned, conscientious experience is of an absolute nature. This is not meant in the sense that the particular contents of judgment based on conscience guarantee absolute moral truths but in the other sense that the moral judgments, as long as they hold good, imply absolute personal commitment on the side of the subject. This then leads to the question of whether awareness of conscience is not basically a religious experience and, furthermore, whether an awareness of conscience lacking *religious* sense is possible at all.

Many humanists, both agnostic and atheistic, would answer this question in the negative. They would explain the experience of morality and with it the experience of conscience as an *absolutum* and, perhaps, as a mystery. They would, hence, reject the explanation of the conscience-phenomenon as being a religious one and, at the same time, as being a pure psychological or social phenomenon. Is one not obliged to say that the human being at its deepest level experiences himself as he in reality is : that is as an 'obligated' being and not as an *absolutum*? He is not able to free himself from this experience, not even by way of explicit reflection on the matter or by either denying it or trying to explain it as a pure fact, or else a purely psychological phenomenon, while at any rate, not as a religious one. The religious person might possibly understand the awareness of conscience, as it has just been described and discussed, as an *implicitly* or *virtually* religious experience *without* an explicit belief in God.

A creationist interpretation of the experience of conscience can talk of the deepest experience of the true relationship between, and *in*, the created person and his ever-present God of Creation and this in the sense that the person, every person, is at his deepest level always conscious of his own being and, thus, of his true reality as being related to God, and accordingly, is conscious of the ultimate significance of his reality; this applies even then when the person, on considering the matter, is not able to define this relationship. It may particularly be pointed out that a God who "imposes" or demands is neither expressly nor implicitly experienced within the conscience, but rather as a 'God' in whom everything has its base and, therefore, on whom everything is dependent and who provides a meaning to life. In accordance with this one can then define morality as an implicit religious dialogue. However, the religious person comprehends these facts according to his specific belief, be it Hinduism, Mohammedanism, Judaism, Christianity or his own individual religion. Belief of this sort qualifies the experience of conscience, and also when it has not been reached by way of reflection.

Here the question of the possible significance of a particular sort of belief determining the moral content of conscience has not been broached.

1.4 *Conscience - Super-Ego - Ethical Maturity (Immaturity)*

It has already been mentioned that there is also orientation for the conduct of life which does not in the least represent ethical judgment based on practical reason in the conscience. Additionally it should be remarked that there is also true moral orientation coming from the conscience which has, however, no reference to the actual values, but to ones which are, nevertheless, true, even though more obvious; the necessity of self-integration in a specific society, for instance. The question arises as to which *moral* significance should be bestowed on this kind of orientation for the conduct of life.

In an article several years ago (1971)[6] J. W. Glaser investigated the question of the moral significance of decisions which are not, or have obviously not been, based on true judgment stemming from the conscience, but on the authority of the Super-Ego. Glaser is above all interested in the question about whether decisions concerning the future, such as decisions that are taken for life, e. g., celibacy and priesthood, which clearly have been based not on true morality but on the authority of the Super-Ego, and also in the case of this happening unconsciously at the time of decision, represent a moral commitment if these should at any time be revealed as what they in reality are.

According to L. Kohlberg the question as to the significance of moral maturity, and immaturity, lies partly elsewhere, as relatively few people attain the full maturity necessary to arrive at moral valuations. There are many variations between these relatively few on the one side and the young children, who lack any sort of moral maturity, on the other side. Is it really true that these variations are all moral judgments? Should these decisions made according to such 'immature' motivation be considered as 'moral' decisions? This question must be answered in the positive. Whoever demands more than this does not recognize the peculiar manner in which human beings find their way and how they arrive at moral judgments; humans are social beings and not isolated islands. Judgment so reached is to be considered as true judgment stemming from the conscience and, likewise, as a binding authority. This, nevertheless, does not exclude the possibility of further experience of life and deeper insight into the true meaning of humanity leading to new and different moral judgments, which will then have binding validity. And, again, such possibilities for improvement are also not excluded in the case where moral judgment has been reached at a high level of moral maturity.

2. THE SUBJECT-ORIENTATION OF THE CONSCIENCE

The thoughts on various aspects of the conscience-phenomenon so far stated should now lead on to reflection on the fundamental difference between the conscience's primary subject-orientation and the secondary object-orientation. In earlier centuries also distinctions were made between the various functions of the conscience but the distinction at stake was not always arrived at by thorough methods and, above all, was not applied permanently. This led occasionally to long-standing vehement discus-

sions and friction, which up till the present day has not been
fully resolved.

2.1 *The Problem*

In the history of Moral Theology (and also of the problems connected with conscience in other sciences) the emphasis has been
laid on the object-orientation of the conscience. It is that which
tells one *what* one has to do, it provides ethical evaluations and
formulation of ethical norms, and it indicates the solution to
problematic situations. In theology these elements are often considered as being 'the Voice of God'; hence, there is a general
tendency to identify the conscience in many cases with practical
reason. The fact that the conscience, understood in such terms,
can also make mistakes - *per accidens* - has consequently been
the cause of harsh discussion through the centuries.

Also in the New Testament occasional passages are to be
found in which the conscience is understood as being object-re-
lated, e. g., Rom. 2, 14f, Rom. 14, 1 Cor. 8 & 10. However,
in the two latter texts, the fundamental subject-orientation of the
conscience also gains in importance. In other passages conscience is considered to be, above all, subject-related, as for instance in parts where the conscience is understood as having inner knowledge of the moral goodness of the Christian, and that
before God, and Christ and in the Holy Ghost. Or, also, where
it is emphatically stated that it is only on account of belief in the
works of Christ, and of the Holy Ghost which acts within us,
that there is such a thing as a 'good conscience', e. g., Rom.
13, 15, Rom. 9, 1, 2 Cor. 1, 12, Rom. 2, 15, Heb. 9, 14, 1
Pet. 3, 21.

The formulation 'follow your conscience', often heard in
connection with morality and pastoral matters, is basically subject-related. Nevertheless, it is often in fact concerned with object-orientation; it is after all about right conduct in the world of
the human being - the object. That is to say, that it is not possible to learn about objective morally right behavior and conduct
in the world only from external norms but also from one's own
convictions seated in the conscience.

Object-orientation is basically the tendency to more or less identify conscience with practical reason. Conversely, the formulation which grants that the moral subject is constituted in the conscience is clearly subject-orientated. This subject-orientation logically precedes the object-orientation.

2.2 Subject-Orientated Conscience - The Basic Phenomenon

In order to comprehend the true essence of the conscience-phenomenon one is obliged, as already indicated above, to return to the matter concerning the human being's deep-seated self-consciousness. This consciousness is existent in every person's life, even if not as the object of actual thought, but so that the matter is not only one of particular actions being carried out in this or that situation, but is rather, at the same time and very decidedly, a case involving the existence of the entire person. This is not intended to be taken as solely a psychological observation but rather in a deeper sense as a transcendental philosophical and theological reflection. This is also valid with regard to morality. A moral decision concerning conduct in any situation is at the same time decidedly - even if unreflected - a decision met by the Ego about itself. Decisions about concrete actions can only be understood as an expression and a symbol of an ethical decision about oneself (M. Luther: "Persona facit opera"; K. Wojtyla: "The Acting Person").

It has already been implied that the human being, at his deepest level of consciousness, which is never fully accessible by way of objective reflection, is aware of himself; he therefore is also aware of himself as to be an 'obligated' existence, which means a moral being. This is the deepest core of the conscience as personal subject. This deepest experience of conscience is at the same time, and to a certain extent, experienced as part of the categorial existence of the person, and, also even in the case of this having been reflected upon and denied; a considered denial is not able to suppress the existential experience.

The existential experience of the person at a reflected level is expressed in various ways: someone considers himself to be bound by obligations; one is aware of the personal responsibility for one's self-realization - in a state of freedom both granted and claimed; one holds oneself responsible for the furtherance of the 'good'; one professes to be faithful to true insight gained through the conscience; one feels required to remain receptive to all things that prove themselves to be either true or good or also as obliged to be open to one's neighbour, etc. All these definitions concern the moral reality of the personal subject. In accordance with this concept of oneself, morality basically deems *that the personal subject should accept itself as it is and realize itself as this self.* This is the genuine imperative made by the conscience in its fundamental subject-orientation.

In other words, the conscience's genuine and, therefore, primary interest is the moral goodness of the personal subject *as such*. And it is solely this personal morality that is morality in the true and original meaning of this word. Every other use of the word is analogous, e. g., 'moral rightness' in life, moral norms for acting, etc.

It is, on the other hand, true that the subject always only fulfils itself when it emerges from itself and steps into the categorial object world and becomes responsibly active there. And this is the reason why the conscience has to be *also* object-orientated. This is the case just because the subject, in the realization of the object world, expresses itself, symbolically, must on account of his goodness attempt with personal responsibility to act according to the proper meaning of the human object world. The reason why the subject takes pains as to the goodness of its significance in this world, in the interests of human society and as an extension of its own self, is anchored in its personal *morality*. It is exactly on account of this relationship between personal moral goodness and the rightness of the conduct in the world that this *rightness* is defined analogously as 'moral'. And it is also due to this same reason that makes one obliged to refer to 'primary' subject-orientation and 'secondary' object-orientation of the conscience.

It will then be clear to understand that the personal subject's own decisions are either moral or immoral not on account of the subject either *actually* accepting or rejecting the 'morally right' conduct of the object world, *but* because he either *takes the necessary pains* or fails to do so. Personal moral goodness is not a case of someone acting *morally right* in our human world, but of acting according to what the conscience *recognizes as being right*. Moral goodness as being personal, is exclusively something existing within the subject (conscience), as is likewise the 'moral truth' and the 'moral decision' which exist and take place internally; the latter refers not to a truth 'in itself' but to a truth 'in myself'. Thomas Aquinas agrees with Aristotle[7] when he says that the 'moral truth' with reference to personal decisions is not determined by the objective rightness of the action but by the right moral orientation applied by the acting subject ('appetitus rectus'). It is obvious that here Aquinas has in mind the concept 'moral truth' as personal goodness which exists exclusively in the person, i. e., in the decisions made in accordance with the conscience.

It is, therefore, understandable why there is a tendency in present-day Moral Theology to view conscience as being exclusively subject-orientated and purely concerned with personal moral goodness. The object-orientated 'knowledge within conscience' is thus eliminated from the concept 'conscience' and banished to the area of practical reason. It then follows, according to this, that the psychological question concerning moral maturity and immaturity (L. Kohlberg) in its proper sense does not primarily concern morality and conscience in a narrower sense. There is, of course, no obligation to acknowledge this concept of conscience as implied here. But in a broader sense of the concept 'conscience' a fundamental distinction (not separation) between moral goodness as the primary element and moral rightness as the merely secondary element belonging to conscience is imperative.

2.3 *Problems of Moral Theology in History*

An insufficient, or at least an inadequately accurate, differentiation between primary subject-orientated and secondary object-orientated conscience, and the likewise insufficient or inadequate differentiation between personal moral goodness and

moral rightness has caused considerable friction and debate in
the history of Moral Theology. And today it is not in the least as
if these difficulties have been simply overridden. A few brief
examples will have to suffice here as illustration.[8]

An allusion has already been made to the concept of 'moral
truth' in respect of the concrete personal situation as understood by Thomas Aquinas. As already mentioned, Aquinas relates this definition to the personal moral goodness, the primary
interest of conscience, above all else. It is, of course, possible
to interpret this same terminology in another way in that one
relates it to moral rightness, thereby leading the way to a judgment of moral rightness *in concreto* as opposed to general
norms.[9] There is certainly the danger of not differentiating the
two concepts adequately, which is the case if, on the one side,
one accepts strictly universal norms of moral rightness while,
however, allowing *in situatione* a 'moral truth', which is in
content different, and without defining it as moral truth and as
belonging to the sphere of moral goodness.[10]

It is well known that even as late as the 12th century St.
Bernard of Clairvaux' opinion on the so-called 'erring conscience' considered it to be still a sin (the contrary of moral goodness) if one acts morally incorrectly even though one is acting in
good faith. This opinion was in opposition to that of his contemporary Abélard. A century later Thomas Aquinas refuted the
opinion held by Bernard but did not go so far as to say that
whoever acts in this way is consequently morally good. It is
obvious that neither Bernard nor Thomas made a sufficiently
clear distinction between primary subject-orientation and secondary object-orientation of conscience. Moral goodness exclusively corresponds with subject-orientation, whereas the
'conscience's error', which occurs unintentionally, emerges
from the sphere of the conscience's object-orientation and consequently is not concerned with personal judgment in the conscience.

Discussion on the problematic nature of 'erring conscience'
has never been brought to a conclusion. Not only is it the case
that the emphasis is constantly laid on the primacy of the 'objective' moral norm as against the merely 'subjective' and,

consequently, its occasional erroneous application in the matter of concrete conscience, although in both cases the individual *subject* strives for *objective* rightness, be it *in abstracto* or *in concreto*; but, on the contrary, it is also not a rare occurrence for the following of erroneous judgment made by the conscience to be represented as justified only *per accidens*. Here one overlooks the fact that the justified compliance with the conscience's erroneous judgment has nothing to do with either rightness or incorrectness of the object-orientated function of conscience but that it only concerns the conscience's judgment as such and as an inner element of the conscience, and the compliance with that is assigned to the personal moral goodness and thus to the subject-orientated and, correspondingly, to the primary function of conscience. The fear that this leads to the primacy being granted to the 'subjective' conscience instead of the 'objective' moral norm is, unfortunately, often expressed; here one overlooks the fact that it has nothing to do with the *rightness* of a moral norm and the *rightness* of the content of judgment reached by conscience, but has to do with the *distinction between moral goodness and moral rightness*. One should say that *morally good* - in an objective sense - is personal fidelity in the conscience's judgment. The judgment which is *morally right* - in an objective sense - is that which corresponds to concrete human reality. The relationship between the abstract norm and the concrete judgment made by the conscience is in both cases a matter concerning the object; this will be discussed later

3. THE OBJECT-ORIENTATION OF THE CONSCIENCE

Even if the conscience's subject-orientation is also its primary characteristic, it would be here impermissible to omit speaking about its object-orientation; especially as the object-orientation is the one more likely to be dealt with in discussions on conscience. And even if this is referred to as 'merely' secondary, it is of considerable and crucial importance for the conscience-phenomenon as a whole. The question here is how conscience provides orientation for a right human behavior and conduct in this world; this means that it concerns the material content of the function of the conscience.

3.1 *The Evaluative and Normative Function of the Conscience*

The evaluative and normative function of the conscience is also part of the broader sense of the concept of conscience as the evaluative and normative authority for the human being, and also, in the narrower sense of this concept as the authority which expresses an orientation - contentwise - in moments when a concrete decision is to be made.

The individual is certainly not an *isolated island* within his object-orientated conscience. The pure a priori reason does not exist here. That, which one in a particular epoch and that, which an individual in his life considers as being humanly and morally justifiable, is also determined by longstanding traditions and accepted valuations. Whether one, as a member of a certain cultural society, considers that to take loving care of an aged person up till his very last breath satisfies the demands of piety, or whether, in another cultural society, one considers that it is not permissible according to the rules of piety to allow an aged person on his own as well as on the account of others, to suffer the burdens of old age, is in both cases understood as being explicitly based on practical reason. Differing moral convictions, even when they are the honest result of practical reasoning, are nevertheless to a great extent influenced by upbringing, family traditions, political affiliations and existing trends in particular groups and movements, etc. They *are*, nonetheless, often the result of rational insight within conscience and therefore partake of the conscience's subject-orientated and absolute nature.

The individual is thus in the object-orientation of his conscience also *not 'pure' reason*. It is possible that someone, on account of his moral immaturity, quite simply orientates himself according to 'convention', and consequently, *not* morally and in accordance with conscience. But it can also be the case that the decision in favour of conventional behavior is grounded on rational insight and the corresponding faith to conscience. Not only the reasons advanced to justify conduct grounded on traditional convention, but also the fact that one advocates and adjusts oneself to convention, can be understood as being rationally justified and, therefore, morally right, and consequently as being unconditional demands made by the conscience's subject-orientation. Moreover, it is possible that what someone considers and declares to be morally right is dependent on his personal interests - good or bad - or on his moral disposition and readiness to accept abstract norms and concrete insight; his interests and his disposition can lead him to judge that what suits his interests and readiness really is morally right.

On account of such considerations one should, nevertheless, not too readily subscribe to the opinion that nothing is practically definite and that nothing in human society is adequately equipped for a consensus. It is indeed true that there is nothing of metaphysical insight as regards practical judgment; but even so, a general scepticism would contradict broader experience. Where there is the possibility of discussing and considering differences of opinion and values, the hope of arriving at practically certain moral truths has not and should not be abandoned. The human being is fundamentally able to get insights of the practical reason.

3.2 Conscience in a Specific Situation

Judgment made by conscience in a specific situation, that is with respect to the person in a concrete situation, is exclusively judgment by the subject who has to reach some decision on the spot. Conscience's judgment on moral rightness, the conscience's subject-orientated assessment and the personal moral decision all take place simultaneously. There is neither a preceding nor a subsequent situation from the point of view of time, only from a logical point of view. This is the reason why the moral subject is quite alone with its conscientious decision; theologically speaking, with and before God.[11]

The statement as formulated above is extremely important for the *forming* of the moral judgment in the conscience, since in the personal situation it is not a matter of academic questions on the subject of moral rightness and not even only a matter of the personal interest afforded to the considerations which slowly lead up to the judgment in the conscience. The moment the conscience reaches an actual decision the fact becomes clear that it is also a matter concerning the moral person as a whole, and not only a particular action, but also the person's meaning of life and his fate as a person. This is, in any case, valid in those situations in which demands are made on a person's entire being and innermost existence.

How does concrete judgment - judgment about moral rightness - made by the conscience *in situatione* 'ensue'? The case of someone understanding completely himself in his concrete situatedness and directly, that is without referring to norms of moral acting, making a moral judgment on the right handling of a concrete situation is not an impossibility in itself.[12] Why should that be less possible than theoretical judgment of realities and, hence, assessment of moral norms by way of the human ratio? In fact, however, it is so that one does not begin making a concrete judgment in the conscience without any moral insight into the human way of acting. One lives permanently in contact with moral orientation and moral judgments, either assumed or self-formulated, and with moral experience and moral guidance. All this can influence moral rational judgment in the conscience. Nevertheless, this judgment is unique and one which has never been made by the subject in this particular situation before. It contains elements that have never before formed and defined the human being in exactly this way. It is in this sense that judgment in the conscience on concrete moral rightness must be considered as unique and as having been arrived at in a state of isolation.

3.3 *The Problem Concerning "Universal Norms and the Conscience in a Concrete Situation"*

As a result of what has just been said, the question arises as to the significance of general, normative authorities with regard to the contents of the subject-orientated conscience's judgments in concrete situations. Such normative authorities can possibly be so-called objective norms, which are perhaps also accepted in principle by the subject. Normative authorities can also, for example, be the habits of certain societies which are looked upon as being unalterable, or pieces of advice offered by people competent to do so, etc.

According to a long and not yet overcome tradition, it was taught that universal norms point to solutions in concrete situations, whereby the situation is obviously considered as being just a numerical case. The norms were considered 'simply applicable' to the case in question. It would seem that it is in fact possible to handle many concrete situations in this way; only seemingly however, since the suggested solution overlooks the fact that there are perhaps morally relevant qualitative peculiarities involved in concrete situations and not only numerical ones. This has been admitted indirectly somehow by several moralists who advocate the principle of a simple 'application' of norms to a single case. The formulation that deems the norms are to be 'applied, of course, in accordance with the concrete circumstances' makes it clear that the way in which the application is made *in situatione,* in respect of the particular circumstances, is still a matter of *moral judgment,* since this cannot be deduced from the 'objective norms' alone.

This means, briefly, that there are still moral judgments to be made that have so far been lacking to be pronounced. This may concern new problems which were overlooked by the community of the moralists, or it may concern judgments of conscience that are absolutely determined by the situation. Thus it follows for the object-orientated conscience that moral norms of right conduct and other normative authorities coming from outside offer basically nothing more than assistance - real assi-

stance, but nonetheless purely assistance - in the assessment of
morally right decisions made in the conscience.

All this concerns the hermeneutic problems involved in the
sphere of moral norms[13]; for wherever concrete norms present
themselves, be it in the conscience or elsewhere, the question
arises as to the actual truth (in the singular) of the moral rightness. On account of this, one must ask the following questions: from where do such norms come, which facts of human
nature are being presupposed in them, which ethical problems
(from historical point of view) are supposed to be thus solved,
and under what sort of human self-awareness of a particular
period or culture were these norms formulated? Possibly some
of the conditions referred to are, at least partly, different from
those in which the person who is searching for answers here
and now finds himself? It is a matter of course that he who is
confronted with existing norms brings along his own interests
and his personal questions and, obviously, the self-awareness
that is imparted by them. These norms are then challenged:
What is their meaning from the viewpoint of the enquiring
subject? Do they offer him help in understanding and, also, can
they somehow be modified by the interested subject according
to his response to them? Thus a process of mutual questioning
and understanding begins, and this can definitely yield a valuable and concrete answer to the question on moral behavior.
Need it be emphatically stated by the theologian that the described hermeneutic problems are also existent in respect of
biblical formulations and of those from the Church?

3.4 *Compromise and the Conscience*

The group of problems connected with 'norm and conscience' is
closely related to that of 'compromise and the conscience'. As it
is, the word 'compromise' does not have only one meaning.
Here it is not used in its actual meaning of a moral compromise.
It would concern this meaning should one be convinced of the
rightness of a judgment made by the object-orientated
conscience and, consequently, know oneself to be absolutely
bound by the subject-orientated conscience; however, and

perhaps in order to avoid a possibly significant difficulty, one believes one should decide contrarily to the judgment made by the conscience. That this is morally not right is supported by both the Protestant and the Catholic theology. Nevertheless, there is a difference in that Protestant theologians very often rely on the incompatibility of divine commandments with the actual world; whoever decides to follow one prescription as opposed to another in a situation where the commandments are incompatible should know that God will not approve of this, but, however, offers forgiveness in view of this predicament. In this respect, Catholic theologians think differently. Many of them would not refer so easily to divine commandments as unconditional (universal) norms, but would rather consider such norms as being interpretations about the reality of Creation formulated by human beings and, therefore, as possibly very inadequate, if not altogether false. Apparently incompatible norms may possibly be in reality not incompatible at all. In a situation which may appear impossible, one might be reminded of the possibility of a limited moral norm, even if the validity of the one or other norm is not formulated as being limited. This sort of recall does not only come to pass in the course of reflection on difficult situations in life which precedes the concrete situations themselves, but also in the conscience in individual cases *in situatione*. It would then accordingly be not a case of a real but only of an apparent moral compromise.

Closer examination of the problems to be solved would, according to some moralists (the author included), show that norms regarding right conduct within the world always reflect the earthly, and therefore, the limited goods/values possessed by human beings. Such limited goods/values can, of course, prove themselves to be incompatible in a concrete and confined situation. The question is then which of the goods/values that are under consideration in a situation of incompatibility are to be given precedence by reason of their hierarchical order or their concrete urgency. A solution to a problematic situation arrived at in such a way, perhaps in the conscience alone, would at any rate be a compromise, but not a moral compromise in respect of a demand which is considered to be absolutely binding; it would be a compromise made within the limited sphere of human beings' goods/values that are *not necessarily* demanding.

4. CONCLUSION

The fact that the conscience exists as a phenomenon is doubted by nobody; as to whether it is an ethical phenomenon in the true sense is doubted by some. Even where there is no doubt about this, there are, nevertheless, great differences regarding the explanation and the interpretation of the ethical phenomenon. And even in Christian ethics, where there is largely a consensus of opinion, there have been some problems and these are still under discussion. I believe that within the sphere of Christian ethics the focus should be placed, above all, on the primacy of moral goodness as opposed to moral rightness in the world, and that proportionate focus should be placed on the primacy of the conscience's subject-orientation as compared with its object-orientation.

Pontificia Università Gregoriana, Rome

NOTES

1 F. Böckle, *Fundamentalmoral*, Munich 1977, 12.
2 A. Molinaro, 'Coscienza e norma etica', in T. Goffi and G. Piana (eds.), *Corso di Morale, I,* Brescia 1983, 449 and especially 453.
3 Cf. also: K. Golser, *Gewissen und objektive Sittenordnung. Zum Begriff des Gewissens in der neueren katholischen Moraltheologie,* Vienna 1975.
4 Cf. H. Preuschoft, 'Angeborene Verhaltensmuster, Konflikt, Norm, Gewissen: Wie frei sind Entschlüsse?', in J. Fuchs (ed.), *Das Gewissen. Vorgegebene Norm verantwortlichen Handelns oder Produkt gesellschaftlicher Zwänge?* Düsseldorf 1979, 9-18.
5 Cf. J. Fuchs, *Das Gewissen, op. cit.,* Foreword.
6 J. W. Glaser, 'Conscience and Super-Ego: A Key Distinction', in *Theological Studies* 32 (1971), 30-47.

7 Thomas Aquinas, *In Eth. Nic.*, 1. VI, 1.1., n. 1131. Cf. also the essay by D. Capone, *Intorno alla verità morale* (Excerpta ex dissert. Pont. Univ. Greg.), Naples 1951.

8 Cf. also the essay by K. Golser quoted above.

9 Cf. J. Fuchs, 'Moral Truths - Truth of Salvation?', in J. Fuchs, *Christian Ethics in a Secular Arena*, Washington, D. C. 1984, 48-67.

10 This is how I believe D. Capone's interpretation of *Persona humana* (1975) with regard to homosexuality (in: *L'Osservatore Romano* of 28. Jan. 1976) and also his interpretation of *Humanae vitae* (in: *Lateranum* 44 (1978), 195-227) should be understood.

11 Cf. Vat. II, *Gaudium et spes*, n. 16.

12 Cf. J. Fuchs, 'The Question Addressed to Conscience', in J. Fuchs, *Personal Responsibility and Christian Morality*, Washington, D. C. 1983, 216-228.

13 Cf. also J. Fuchs, 'Moral Truth - between Objectivism and Subjectivism', in J. Fuchs, *Christian Ethics in a Secular Arena*, op. cit., 29-41; and: 'Hermeneutics in Ethics and Law: Points of Comparison', ib. 41-47 (German version in M. W. Fischer, E. Mock, H. Schreiner (eds.), *Hermeneutik und Strukturtheorie des Rechts* (ARSP, Beiheft Nr. 20), Wiesbaden 1984, 9-12). Cf. especially: K. Demmer, *Sittlich handeln aus Verstehen. Strukturen hermeneutisch orientierter Fundamentalmoral*, Düsseldorf 1980.

DISCUSSION

Josef Fuchs SJ, Ann Higgins, Georg Lind, Hans Strotzka, Paul Weingartner, Thomas E. Wren, Gerhard Zecha

WREN: You have spoken of a subjective and an objective orientation, but I would like to propose now the idea of an intersubjective orientation. I think that this is what is really needed in order to deal with the kinds of issues that Kohlberg's work is dealing with, and that it would also keep a place for something more or less like this "spark of the soul". Now the intersubjective orientation, I gather, is intimately connected to the possibility of having moral norms. These moral norms will be constituted most obviously by verbalized intersubjective projects, whose general form is speech. But what other interpersonal projects are there that would be constitutive of norms, moral or otherwise, within which the rightness and wrongness of behavior might be assessed? Here I think of various things like games, both nonverbal games and wordplay such as jokes. Perhaps the most vivid examples of this kind of interpersonal but nonverbal exchange are found in love, especially its sexual mode in which the thrill of the desire is constituted in a large part by the knowledge that the other person is responding, is thrilling, is pleasuring, is appreciating, and so on. What I'm driving at with these examples of what I've called "nonverbal interchanges" is the same thing that Kohlberg drives at with his more elegant examples of verbal interchanges; and that is the idea that the meaning that a person has, which objective relationships have, or Fuchs' objective orientation and subjective orientation have, all these meanings are constituted by their roots in an interpersonal action. What is primary is this field of action, not the spark of the soul nor the vision of a well-ordered state of affairs in the world. To sum it up: between the integrity of oneself and the concern for the product of our wordly projects is an intermediate intersubjective concern for the process, the very activity of being together, which is primary because that activity constitutes a meaning for both the subjective and the objective.

FUCHS: First of all, if I speak of "person", I suppose everybody knows that persons are interpersonal. A person is by its humanness, by its own nature interpersonal. In order to come to moral insights, evaluations in this world, we interchange with societies, but it is not a society as a person but a society is a lot of persons in interrelationship. Therefore in formulating moral norms I am never alone but always under the influence of traditions, communities, etc. And only by this am I also to find out whether I can accept a certain norm, or not. This is intersubjective searching. Nevertheless, everybody has to come to accept something as his norm. In an interchange then, when I seek, "What is the right thing to do?", I find this human world, which means, first of all, human beings, myself included. I, with others, have to come to a judgment about "How will we behave now?", not only as single persons alone, but in relation to one another.

WREN: I'm relieved to know that you have this primary conception of the person as interpersonal, but I don't see that conception as really functioning in what you're doing in this paper. Contrary to you I regard the very idea of a moral norm as something that is intersubjective. It's not that the intersubjective person has his own moral norms. He must have moral norms that are, in some rudimentary sense, private. I would say, following Wittgenstein, that there is no such thing as a purely private language: furthermore, that there is no such thing as a purely private joke and that there is no such thing as a purely private moral norm. All of these things are inherently referential to the real or potential presence and cooperation of another person.

FUCHS: Yes, I thank you. Moral norms are interpersonal, they have to do with the moral rightness of the realization of this world. I agree. But sometimes a group has norms I can't accept. Think, for instance, of a church society with declared moral norms. I find out: in this concrete situation according to what I have heard, I have to do this. But there is something new in my situation, therefore I cannot simply use this norm. This is an object-oriented, society-oriented norm. Now I have to find out, and in the last moment I have to decide what I should do. So, I accept your formulation on moral norms. Moral norms are a real help, but only a help. Still in conscience if I have to decide, I have to have a light within me. This cannot be the outside norm of society alone.

HIGGINS: The question that bothers me is this notion that the conscience is in a participated freedom somehow with an absolute, you said, and that there could be different ideas of conscience, when you gave the example of the Marxists sitting down with the Catholics. On the other hand it seems as if you're talking about conscience in a very non-relativistic fashion. It's not that your conscience thinks something is good that my conscience would disagree with. Well, it's my question about whether or how the origin or understanding the origin of conscience really handles this notion of relativity.

FUCHS: Relativistic or non-relativistic: different people will find different solutions how to realize, for instance, piety to elderly people. It is relative, not relativistic, to different consciences. But this has to do with the moral rightness, yet you say this has to do with moral goodness. Moral goodness is the same in all people. I gave you this example of Poland, where three quite different groups agree on this point.

HIGGINS: Even though they don't agree on the origin of moral goodness.

FUCHS: No. There are differences. But there is a first experience not reducible to anything else: moral goodness. How to explain it is another question. There are several things. This is a first experience to find out that A and not-A cannot be the same under the same aspect. It's a contradiction. It is a first experience. I think you cannot reduce it to anything else. Similarly on the practical level, this understanding of human beings as moral beings, is a first experience not reducible to anything behind it. So your question was rather on rightness than on goodness. On goodness, I think there is no question. Finally, almost all people would accept this. Maybe not in reflection but in effort, otherwise they could not speak on morality. And they do.

STROTZKA: You mentioned compromises in conscience. For us psychoanalysts compromises are of extreme importance, because intrapersonal or intra-individual we are forced to make permanent compromises between our drives, instincts, needs, and the prohibitions and pressures coming from the Super-Ego, which is perhaps the same, perhaps different from the conscience in your sense. But my concern is a different one: interpersonally we have to make permanent compromises between good and bad, allowed and forbidden and so on. Interpersonal democracy is more or less a compromise, living in compromises between persons and groups. But if we allow stepping into the boundaries of compromise, please allow me to touch the most important point that we must make in practical life: that's overpopulation and family planning. For my feeling, this whole scene is a moral problem of high priority from the responsibility point of view, from the social justice point of view. We all know that there are enormous tensions, theoretical and practical ones, in this respect and I understand that the Christian churches can make no compromise with regard to interruption of pregnancy, for instance. But I think you should see an obligation to make a compromise with regard to family planning. And here I must say most of my friends and my reference-group are deeply disappointed by the practical attitude of the Catholic church which is not helping their believers in this respect. It is a question of compromise.

FUCHS: My purpose was not to talk on this. But you think in our society interpersonal compromises are needed, otherwise we cannot live. I would make a few distinctions: First we are in a world of goods and values. But our world is a very limited one. Therefore, we cannot always realize all the values and goods we want to realize. We have to find out the predominant right, then we can say, "This is the only right existing in this moment. The other right doesn't exist". This in a certain sense is a type of compromise between different values, rights, etc.

But there is something else. If I know in my conscience, this is really what I have to do and I decide against it in order to avoid difficulty - this would be in the strict sense a moral compromise. I think this is against moral goodness, therefore I will explain this in the example you have given, and I accept the example.

You said for family planning and overpopulation we have to compromise, because there is a certain norm, etc. And we have to compromise this moral norm. If this is a moral norm, a right moral norm, we have not to compromise it. There is something else. It is not the question of compromising morally, it is the question of the norm itself. We sometimes have similar norms proposed from the outside: they function only as a Super-Ego. Am I bound by the Super-Ego? You say, "No"; I say, "No". But it should be a help to form my conscience. So I would say, "Maybe this norm has been formulated, but it is not formulated too well". So we have to reformulate it. There are many people of the Catholic church who say this explicitly and do it. This is a pity, however, because many of them are not able to reflect sufficiently on this norm. I think in a society, also in the church society, we have not only one opinion. There are competent

people with real personal responsibility who say, "Maybe
something in the formulation of the norm is wrong".

WEINGARTNER: My first point is this: As far as I understood
it you think that human beings are the only one to reflect on
themselves. I'm not so sure if this is an essential statement for
your theory. I think one would have to distinguish different
categories of reflection and then find out what is really essential for humans.

The second point deals with the erroneous conscience. You
gave two formulations. The one was, "The person who follows
his or her conscience is morally good". And the other was, "He
who follows his even erroneous conscience does not sin". I
mean the second was the formulation by St. Thomas Aquinas
and you said he did not allow himself to conclude from "follows
the erroneous conscience" that the action is morally good. I
thought always he had some good reason for not making such a
conclusion. Somebody who follows his conscience does not
sin. This is what Aquinas says. It also holds for him: If he does
not follow his conscience, then he sins. But from "not sinning"
he does not allow himself to derive "good", because of the following reason: He wants to have a neutral space between good
and bad, or consequently between sinning and being good. In
general, "not-bad" does not imply "good", and "not good" does
not imply "bad" according to him. Whereas "bad" always
implies "not-good" and "good" always implies "not bad". So
the one who follows an erroneous conscience would be excused
in the sense that he would not sin but from this one must not
derive - according to Thomas -. that his action is good in an
objective sense.

FUCHS: I said earlier, animals do not reflect on themselves "as
far as we know". The point lies in reflection: do they go to
themselves as a whole, as can a "person"? This was the main
point, but it is another question.

The question on Aquinas, this neutrality: I am not so convinced
of this. I remember that Aquinas says explicitly, "Human acts
are always moral acts, therefore good or wrong". If he says
here he does not sin, I would say, "Aquinas, Thomas, you have
not yet realized that the man who follows his conscience of

necessity makes himself positively good, because by following his conscience he shows coherence with himself". This is moral obligation. Thomas was not yet able to see this. This is my interpretation now.

ZECHA: I have three questions and a remark on the animals: Dogs for instance are said to have a bad conscience. That's nothing uncommon; there must be something about it, but how much they can reflect upon their behavior is another question. My three questions are the following: One of the traditional concepts of conscience is the application of a standard to a concrete situation. Now you have chosen a different, perhaps more narrow definition: it is something that allows us to judge what is good and what is bad in a certain situation. Your justification for saying this is the common experience that man as a person has a fundamental first experience that he is a moral being. My question is: What does normatively or evaluatively follow from that experience? That is by no means clear. From the feeling, "I am obliged to a certain norm", we cannot know what is good or bad in this situation. Secondly, you talk about the lonely conscience in your paper: "The conscience is not an isolated island", and also later you say, "There is no lonely conscience". But then you maintain, "The judgment of our conscience is left to itself". How can you explain that?

Thirdly: Why do you put emphasis on the distinction of values and norms as functional for the conscience? Because we can say "Well, if I know what is good and what is right, then I automatically know also what I have to do" according to what has often been called "basic conscience": what is good ought to be done and what is bad, should be shunned.

FUCHS: If among animals the mother has a child, the mother behaves like a human mother. Is it morality? By analogy you can call it so, by transferring moral concepts to a material behavior. Practically very often many of our activities come partially from non-moral orientations, from psychological and biological ones. At the same time also by a moral orientation. Who can divide these? So, I think we use these moral terminologies and project them into animals. Nothing more.

Norms have to do with moral rightness. How do I realize myself in this situation? If I have to come to a decision in conscience, this is an object-oriented decision, "What should I do?"
But your question was, "What is the content of moral goodness?" Precisely, moral goodness has not to do with the world,
but only with the subject. What is moral goodness? For
instance, you are a human being, a person, not an absolute. You
enjoy freedom, but still not absolute freedom. Therefore you
have to be yourself. Find it out; it's an experience.

ZECHA: Let me just use your own example. If I understood
you correctly you said, "Honor the elderly", that's just a morally good thing. How we honor them, that's a matter of rightness. But "Honor the elderly" is exactly the same inner norm as
"Love your neighbor as yourself" which you say is a norm.
What is the difference?

FUCHS: Moral goodness means: Be yourself, interpersonally,
be good to others, respecting others who are the same as you.
The word "good" in this context can have a double meaning:
"Realize the 'goods' within this world". But you can never be
obliged to do all the good things within this world. You cannot.
So, you have to be good. Certainly! You have to realize all the
goods and values in this world. Impossible! The goodness of
the person will tell me: If you are good, you have to find the
right way to realize justice, sex, marriage, etc. How to do it
does not belong to goodness. It's the question of rightness.

ZECHA: May I apply it to the elderly people? I have to find the
right behavior to these. But that does not mean I have to honor
them, there may be other ways of right behavior.

FUCHS: You have to honor them! This is the question of
goodness. But there is the other question, the question of
rightness: "How do we have to 'honor' them?" Goodness does
not say, by what action I have to concretice my goodness; but
goodness makes me ready to try to find out what is the right
thing to do, and to be ready to do it once I have found out. This
is marvellous. Then I realize myself as a person: not as an absolute, but as a given person.

Then the question of "lonely, not-lonely". We are never alone.
We come from society's customs, from biological sources etc.

That is one thing. On the other hand, when we're talking about our conscience in a given situation, I have to make a decision for acting and how to act. There I am alone. For this decision I need a light *within* me. Norms could help me to form this light, but when preparing this light within me, I am not alone. Values and norms are not the same. You cannot realize all values in this world. For instance, you cannot at the same time realize the value of celibacy and of being married. You have to make a choice. Norms are something else; they express what sort of values under certain conditions you have to realize and what eventually you do not have to realize.

ZECHA: Does not each norm have an underlying value?

FUCHS: Oh yes. Norms protect values, but moral norms for acting within this world have to be found out by human beings. Because they are human, they can bear errors, they can be formulated in a very inadequate way. We have to find them and we have to clarify the underlying values.

LIND: In your paper I find some reinforcement for the idea that psychologists should also make a distinction between what you called "the right behavior" and "the good behavior". What I have difficulties with is to fit it in a psychological scheme: On the one side there is this absolute good and on the other there is a relativistic right. That's a very tolerant theory. But don't you need something between the two? You say you can come to a solution of moral problems, you did not say "to a better solution". You say, if somebody tries to be morally good, that's an absolute good. It cannot be qualified. But in psychological theory, or even more in every day action, you do have a qualification according to better or worse. Isn't there any criteria by which you can say some norm is better than the other in the case of population or politics or norms protecting life? Can you rank?

FUCHS: Well, psychologists should also consider rightness and goodness. I remember your paper yesterday precisely: these school children try to find out what should be done; this is not only academic. In a certain way at least, this affects them; they have the experience of moral goodness. Therefore they insist, "This is what has to be done".

Then the better and the right: Oh sure, there are many things you can distinguish as better. But nevertheless if you say, "This is better than that" you still suppose, "This is a right solution and that is also a right solution". It's very often possible. It's a free choice and you can often give a reason why this one is better. There is nothing else that human beings have to try to understand but human reality. In understanding this reality, I find a suitable "right solution" which can be concretized. And if I find two or three solutions possible, I could figure out that maybe this one is more corresponding to reality than that one. There is not, however, a special method for finding the better "right solution" - what we can do here and now. It is the method of practical reason which has been able to understand through the centuries this changing human reality and moral norms. I cannot give you another answer because there is none.

End of discussion.

PART 2

CONSCIENCE: SOCIAL AND EDUCATIONAL ASPECTS

GERHARD ZECHA

VALUE-NEUTRALITY, CONSCIENCE, AND THE SOCIAL SCIENCES

It is common-place that the main virtue of the scientist is object-ivity. Objectivity, however, is necessarily connected with value-neutrality (or value-freedom) according to many philosophers and social scientists. Actually, these value-neutralists claim that if there is any such thing as a scientific conscience, then it should force the scientist to faithfully observe the method-ological rules of the social sciences including the postulate of value-neutrality. Opponents of this view, on the contrary, point to the moral responsibility of the scientist: as the learned, knowledgeable expert he is expected to work to the best of his abilities, convictions and moral beliefs. On this basis he has to clearly state what he thinks to be the goals and basic values in his field of research. Conversely, he also has to protest against everything that he thinks to be dangerous, perverted or evil according to his knowledge of the subject. Thus, by his very conscience the social scientist must not be value-neutral.

In this contribution, I shall show that the problems of val-ue-neutrality and the scientist's responsibility are not that simple. In the first section I shall try to clarify the notion of val-ue-neutrality. Then I will distinguish various types of respons-ibility in section II and point out the crucial role of moral rules in those types. In the search for moral rules for the responsibility of the scientist I shall in the third section discuss two proposals to overcome value-neutrality in the social sciences. Finally, I shall argue that the responsibility of the social scientist must be seen in connection with his conscience. But if the expression 'conscience' is to have any meaning beyond crude relativism or scepticism, then it must be linked with a set of definite values to be acknowledged and accepted by the whole scientific com-munity.

G. Zecha and P. Weingartner (eds.), Conscience: An Interdisciplinary View, 59–89.

1. VALUE-NEUTRALITY

1.1 *Two Concepts of Science*

Let me, first of all, remind us that it is useful to distinguish between two meanings of 'science'. 'Science' can be understood as an activity. In this sense a number of activities fall under the concept of science: posing problems, observing, describing and explaining relevant facts in order to solve these problems. Usually such activities are called scientific if and only if they correspond to a series of methodological rules that make them, roughly speaking, systematic, rational and testable activities with the aim to find a true or valid answer to a certain problem.

Since activities are necessarily aim- or value-oriented, it would be paradoxical to speak of a value-neutral or value-free science in this sense. Hence, science as an activity cannot be value-neutral. The values for which such activities are performed are truth, knowledge, information, explanation etc. They determine the whole scientific process; without them there can be no science.

There is a second meaning of 'science' which refers to a class or a system of sentences that satisfies several conditions. Among these conditions are the following:
- the sentences must be logically correct (i.e., they must correspond to certain syntactical and semantical rules)
- the sentences must contain at least some empirical concepts
- some of the sentencers must be universal, some must be singular
- there must be a logico-deductive relationship among some of these sentences
- the sentences must be testable: at least in principle they should be either confirmable or falsifiable.

When I speak of a value-neutral social science then I have this latter concept in mind: a system of sentences about a particular aspect of man's social life that satisfies the methodological rules mentioned above.

1.2 *The Postulate of Value-Neutrality*

The so-called Postulate of Value-Neutrality [PVN] (sometimes also called the Principle of Value-Freedom) is one of the most controversial methodological issues in the philosophy of social science. The discussion for and against it goes back to Max Weber (1904/1968), but an agreement has not been reached as exactly what this PVN amounts to.

Hans Albert (1985, p. 80ff.) who has elaborated Weber's doctrine of value-neutrality distinguishes three levels: (1) the objects of the social sciences, i. e., the social facts that are described by scientific statements; (2) the object-language in which these scientific statements are expressed; (3) the metalanguage in which all necessary methodological sentences are formulated. Value-neutrality is concerned neither with (1), because the social scientist can describe and explain the valuations of individuals and groups without himself being committed to these valuations; nor with (3), because there can be no scientific activity without methodological valuations and rules. The problem of value-neutrality has to do with the object-language used by social scientists for the description, explanation and prediction of social facts, events or states of affairs: "The real point at issue in the controversy over value-judgments is, therefore, the necessity or possibility of value-judgments in the context of object-language statements of the social science that formulates value-judgments about its field of objects, the social facts." (Albert 1985, p. 82/83).

According to Weber's and Albert's conviction, the solution of this problem depends on the aims of the scientific activity. If these consist in knowledge of - and consequently in truths about - reality, its structures and relationships, then neither value-judgments nor norms are necessary within the object-language of the social scientist to reach these aims. The reason lies in the non-cognitivistic meta-ethical interpretation of value-judgments and norms that both Weber and Albert defend. Since these kinds of sentences are non-cognitivistic, i. e., do not convey information about reality, its structures and relationships, they are useless if not disturbing in the social sciences with regard to their aims. They have to be excluded, therefore, from the system of scientific statements.

This is roughly what has often been called (especially by Hans Albert) *Max Weber's Postulate of Value-Neutrality* or *Max Weber's Principle of Value-Freedom*. But I have written elsewhere (Zecha 1976), neither Max Weber nor Hans Albert have ever formulated such a principle or postulate. Therefore I suggest according to their intentions the following version:

PVN: A social science is value-neutral if and only if value-judgments and/or norms do not occur in descriptions, explanations or predictions formulated in the object-language of that science.

PVN is a relatively strict and fairly precise principle. It reduces value-neutrality to descriptions, explanations and predictions in the object-language. Scientific critique of value-judgments and norms, however, does not fall under the verdict of value-neutrality, since already Max Weber and even more the so-called Critical Rationalists (like Popper 1970a and Albert 1985) consider all-encompassing criticism as the central task of science.

PVN has been defended by many analytic philosophers (e. g., Nagel 1971) as well as by numerous social scientists (e. g., Brecht 1959). It is usually this type of value-neutrality[1] that the *responsible* social scientist is asked to pursue (Albert 1971). Yet other thinkers believe that the responsible scientist has to reject value-neutrality altogether (Picht 1969; Scriven 1974). In order to clarify these controversial views, I have to discuss the notion of responsibility.

2. RESPONSIBILITY

The expressions 'responsibility', 'responsible' and 'responsible for' are used in many different ways. The most detailed analysis of these expressions I came across is the one by H. L. A. Hart (1975). He distinguishes role-responsibility, causal responsibility, liability-responsibility and capacity responsibility. Following this division, I will briefly describe each kind and then find out which kind of responsibility is relevant for the problem of value-neutrality.

2.1 *Role-Responsibility*

Role-responsibility refers to the fulfilment of the duties or obligations that are connected with a certain position or title. The sea-captain is responsible for the safety of his ship, parents for the upbringing of their children, and the scientist is responsible for the truth of his claims. Hart (1975, 330) generalizes from such examples that

"Whenever a person occupies a distinctive place or office in a social organization to which specific duties are attached to provide for the welfare of others or to advance in some specific way the aims or purposes of the organization, he is properly said to be responsible for the performance of these duties, or for doing what is necessary to fulfil them. Such duties are a person's responsibility".

Which expectations and duties are connected with the position of a social scientist? That depends on the institution for which he works, but it also depends on the particular philosophy of science he adheres to. When we want to determine his role-responsibility, we have to take into account the values and norms of these two factors that establish his duties.

2.2 *Causal Responsibility*

Causing or producing a certain effect, result or event is what is meant by "causal responsibility". According to Hart, it is possible in many contexts "to substitute for the expression 'was responsible for' the words 'caused' or 'produced'" (p. 330). For instance, "The drought is responsible for the disastrous economic situation in many African countries", "His failure to clarify the matter was responsible for the misunderstanding", and "Max Weber's postulating a value-neutral social science was responsible for a long-lasting debate on the foundations and goals of the social sciences". In such examples we can replace 'was responsible for' by 'caused' without change of meaning, but the reverse is not always true. It is interesting that in this causal sense of the phrase 'to be responsible for' mainly the past tense is used. This is not true in the case of a living person who is said to have caused something, who is responsible for an undesired event or harm (here another kind of responsibility comes in which Hart calls liability-responsibility).

In the causal sense, not only human beings or their actions, but also things and events of all sorts can be said to be responsible for certain results.

With respect to value-neutrality I can only say that, for example, Max Weber was responsible for the constant value-debate in the social sciences. Or I discovered that Arnold Brecht in his book *Political Theory* (1959) is responsible for a faulty argument, since in his defense of the is-ought distinction he derives from the fact that there is no proof for our value-beliefs the norm that these beliefs must be excluded from science. But the notion of causal responsibility does not help to solve the problem of whether or not the responsible scientist should accept value-neutrality.

2.3 *Liability-Responsibility*

When someone breaks a law he is usually liable to punishment or enforced compensation. In this sense, the expression "He is liable to be punished for his actions" is in many contexts identical with "He is responsible for his actions". And yet, Hart tries to make clear that the statement 'A man is responsible for his actions' is directed to a narrower and more specific issue (p. 332). To him, such issues are connected with three criteria of responsibility:

(i) Mental or psychological criteria of responsibility: The accused person that is liable to be punished should at the time of his action have satisfied certain mental and psychological conditions:

"When a person is said to be not responsible for a particular act or crime, or when ... he is said not to be responsible for his 'acts and omissions in doing' some action on a particular occasion, the reason for saying this is usually some mental abnormality or disorder". (p. 333)

(ii) Causal or other forms of connection with harm: Liability-responsibility is not confined to psychological conditions. In legal contexts there is the question, for instance, "whether some form of connection between a person's act and some harmful outcome is sufficient according to law to make him liable" (p. 333). Even if the accused person did not act at all, but the harm was caused by a dangerous thing or animal that escaped from his possession (one can think here also of a piece of knowledge or speculation that may escape from the mind of the scientist and prove dangerous to other people as well as to himself), this connection is a condition for legal responsibility for harm (that can also be expressed in terms of liability).

(iii) Relationship with the agent: The normal condition for a person to become liable for punishment is that that person himself broke the law. But there are also other cases where a master or employer is liable to pay compensation for the harm done by his servant or employee (which Hart calls 'vicarious responsibility').

To sum up: Liability responsibility means 'being held liable, accountable for what was done or not done according to or contrary to certain laws'. Legal liability refers to a legal system, moral liability to a moral code.

With respect to value-neutrality it does make sense to use these three criteria for the description of the scientist's responsibility: He must meet certain mental and psychological conditions. Also, it should be clear what kind of harm could be caused by his action if he chooses PVN or an alternative postulate or if he rejects value-neutrality altogether. The concept of harm, however, is a value-concept and we cannot state any harm without explicit reference to a value-hierarchy or value-system. Hart's liability concept does not contain such a value-element.

2.4 *Capacity-Responsibility*

Very often the expression 'He is responsible for his actions' is used to point out that a person possesses certain necessary qualities or capacities:

"The capacities in question are those of understanding, reasoning, and control of conduct: the ability to understand what conduct legal rules or morality require, to deliberate and reach decisions concerning these requirements, and to conform to decisions when made." (p. 337)

In other words: that a person can be said to be responsible for an act he must have understood the underlying legal or moral rules relevant for that act, he must have reached a definite decision concerning these rules and he must have acted correspondingly. Again, mainly psychological conditions must be fulfilled in relation to certain rules - but which rules these are is left open by Hart.

2.5 *The Common Denominator*

It is not possible now to confront each of Hart's notions of responsibility with PVN. Instead I want to point to a very important common characteristic of these types of responsibility (except perhaps causal responsibility) which Hart himself does not mention: That they all refer to specific rules, standards or norms. Role-responsibility refers to rules connected with the duties of the social scientist, liability-responsibility refers to a legal or moral code, whereas capacity-responsibility is the ability to understand certain rules and act accordingly. In short: 'to be responsible' means 'to be responsible *for* someone or something *to* some rule, standard or code' (Kaufman 1967, Zecha 1981).

In view of this analysis the main question is now: Which rules make the social scientist responsible for value-neutrality? The rules of the society in which he lives? The rules of the institution for which he works? His own conviction or world view? Or are there values and rules that enable the responsible social scientist to dismiss value-neutrality? In the relevant literature one can find a wide spectrum of answers to these questions. In the following section, I shall briefly describe and discuss two of them which I shall call the objectivist and the subjectivist point of view.

3. VALUE-JUDGMENTS AND NORMS IN THE SOCIAL SCIENCES: OBJECTIVE OR SUBJECTIVE JUSTIFICATION?

3.1 *The Objectivistic View*

According to value-neutralists, the responsible scientist strictly observes the methodological values and prescriptions of science. And exactly these imply value-neutrality in the sense of PVN. Against this opinion Paul F. Schmidt argues in a well-known article (1959) "that scientific method can provide fundamental ethical norms" (p. 645).

In other words: When a scientist accepts the rules of the scientific method and acts accordingly, he will find himself necessarily bound to moral rules that can both serve as a universally acceptable moral code as well as a value-foundation for the social sciences. If this is true then there will be neither a necessity nor even the possibility to promote value-neutrality in the sense of PVN.

First of all, Schmidt rejects what he calls the "false dichotomy of science and values" (p. 645). His starting point is then the practice of science. Science, he says, is transcultural: "The one thing that East, North and South have in common is the practice of science" (p. 646). But the practice of science is not taken as an ultimate or unquestionable value; it is just a fact about man: "The acquisition of reliable knowledge about matters of fact through observation, hypothesis, and experimentation" (p. 646). It is "reliable" knowledge because of a lack of certainty. The same is true about values: It is neither necessary nor possible to get certainty about values.

Within this framework, Schmidt wants to obtain ethical norms from the method of science that provides reliable knowledge. What he is aiming at are ethical norms "that are not affected by the changing content of science ... (but) are sufficient for social and individual conduct" (p. 647).

Concerning these norms, Schmidt distinguishes three perspectives:

(a) Norms to be found in the scientific method:

1. The norm of tolerance: is the prescription to investigate knowledge claims. Since no hypothesis can be established or refuted with absolute certainty, any alternative hypothesis must be tolerated for further control.

Tolerance is the basis for free speech, free press, freedom of thought and religion. All these are "concrete manifestations of tolerance" (p. 649). Hence, tolerance is a necessary means to reliable knowledge.

2. The norm of testability or evidence which prescribes that evidence must be offered for knowledge claims: "A test is objective when any trained observer can perform it, and evidence is objective when its reference is open to public scrutiny" (p. 650).

3. The norm of objectivity is involved which requires us to make tests and evidence public. The opposite is secrecy, withholding of information, hiding of evidence, censorship which is incompatible with the free advance of science.

(b) Norms relevant to people who use the scientific method:

Since the scientific method cannot work by itself, the following norms are part of it:

4. Honesty, which is necessary for reliable knowledge and leads to trust in the reports of other scientists.

5. "Humility is readiness to sacrifice a pet theory" (p. 651). It is possible that our own ideas would fail severe tests: if the evidence is convincing, we have to accept it.

6. Respect for other persons, because they are as likely as we to discover reliable theories.

(c) Norms connected with the forms of the social organization of the practice of science:

There is individual research, scientific societies, research teams of private industry etc. They all have some goals in common:

reliable knowledge for the explanation, control or prediction of natural or social events.

To sum up: These are some ethical norms to be found in the scientific method. They are a sufficient supply for an internationally acceptable set of ethical norms.

This means for value-neutrality: PVN can certainly no longer be upheld, because these ethical norms follow directly from the methodological rules. And if Schmidt's suggestion is really correct then the social scientist can introduce value-judgments and norms that are universally acceptable and correspond exactly to the ultimate values of science (truth and validity).

I do not intend to discuss each of the above mentioned ethical norms, but I do want to indicate that Schmidt's final conclusion is not what actually follows from his assumptions.

Basically Schmidt offers the following two arguments:
I. (1) Reliable knowledge is transcultural important.
(2) The scientific method is a necessary means for the attainment of reliable knowledge.
Concl. I: The scientific method (and its implied ethical norms, respectively) is (are) transculturally important.
II. (3) If M is a scientific method (or a part of it), then M is transculturally important.
(4) "The scientist must be tolerant, objective, honest etc." is part of the scientific method.
Concl. II: "The scientist must be tolerant, objective, honest etc." is transculturally important.

These simplified arguments are logically correct. Conclusion II, however, does not imply what Schmidt has in mind, namely, that each human being of this world should be tolerant, objective and honest. Conclusion II is a value-judgment about a specific norm (or set of norms) for the behavior of the scientist. Taking into account the is-ought gap, there is no logical possibility to derive from this value-judgment a universal ethical norm. Therefore, Schmidt's attempt to show that there are ethical norms in the scientific method may be interesting but it proves nothing to the effect that methodological prescriptions lead us to accept certain moral rules as universally reliable norms. Thus,

Schmidt's device does not force the responsible scientist to reject PVN, it simply does not work.

3.2 *The Subjectivistic View*

A very prominent social scientist who holds this view is Gunnar
Myrdal (1968). Myrdal distinguishes between theoretical and
practical research. Theoretical research is concerned with describing facts and determining causal connections among them.
Practical research has to do with purposive relationships. Value-
judgments in relation to factual situations and actual trends serve
as a basis for scientifically grounded procedures in solving
practical problems ("social-engineering"). For this purpose, value-premises have to be used according to the following conditions (1968, pp. 157/158, Myrdal's italics):

"(a) They must be *explicitly stated* and not hidden as tacit assumptions.
(b) They must be as *specific* and *concrete* as the valuation of reality in
terms of factual knowledge requires.
(c) They cannot be derived directly from factual research but they will have
to be *purposively selected*.
(d) They cannot be *a priori,* self-evident, or generally valid; they can have
only a *hypothetical* character.
(e) Since incompatible valuations are held in society, the value premises
should ideally be given as a number of sets of *alternative* hypotheses. ...
(f) In a scientific treatment of the practical aspects of social problems, the
alternative sets of hypothetical value-premises should not be chosen arbitrarily. The principle of selection should be their *relevance.* Relevance is
determined by the interests and ideals of actual persons and groups of
persons. ...
(g) Within the circle of relevance so determined a still more narrow circle of
significance may be taken to denote valuations which are held by substantial groups of people or by small groups with substantial social power. ...
(h) The goals set by the value-premises must also be *feasible.* ...
Valuations bent upon premises but be theoretically criticized as infeasible.
This theoretical criticism in terms of feasibility of people's actual valuations is, indeed, one of the most important tasks of social science.

(i) The set of value-premises selected must not include mutually incomp-atible ones but must be *consistent*. ..."

Finally, Myrdal emphasizes the goal of practical research that consists in a clear-cut list of possibilities how practical decis-ions can be made from various value-perspectives with respect to factual knowledge that is available at present.

I want to add a few comments on Myrdal's proposal to introduce and use value-judgments in the social sciences. I call this view subjectivistic because the social scientist when facing a practical problem is asked to explicitly introduce his subjective value-judgments. This is quite important because the scientist should become aware of his evaluative and normative assump-tions.

On the other hand, one can ask if he will ever realize all of his value-beliefs and why these should be regarded more scient-ific or better than any other person's value-beliefs. Of course, Myrdal does not want a merely arbitrary choice of value-pre-mises, but what can he offer against such a choice? The interests and ideals of society, of influential people or groups within society, he says. But again: Are the goals, values and purposes of them any better? And if yes: How can we show that they are better?

Here we are left again with our original problem: What are the moral rules that help us to determine the responsibility of the social scientist?

Do Myrdal's conditions help us to support or to reject the Postulate of Value-Neutrality via liability-responsibility? Yes, they do help. PVN must be rejected because of (i). But ques-tions remain: What happens when a scientist chooses values contrary to the goal-values of science (truth and validity)? When he values utility over truth or when he prefers practicality to val-idity? It should be noted that there are *discipline-oriented values* like health in the medical sciences, the common welfare in econ-omics or peace in political science. These values are beyond subjective beliefs and enable, therefore, the scientist to justify value-judgments (Scriven 1974, p. 241). But even in the case of

using discipline-oriented values, problems with ethical standards may arise. Here is an example:

In a recent article on the responsible psychotherapist, the
authors point out that the U.S. therapist has to be APA-ethical
(i.e., ethical according to the *Ethical Standards of Psychologists*
(1979) and according to the *Standards for Providers of Psychological Services* (1977) of the American Psychological Association, Washington, D.C.), "but at times being ethical may be
anti-therapeutic. What is ethical may not be effective, and what
is effective may not be ethical" (Widiger & Rorer 1984, p. 507).
What if the medical researcher does not accept health as leading
value, but painlessness instead? Or if the educationist does not
promote the growth of the child's personality as a supreme
value but rather self-determination of the child?

Such examples of value-selections in practical research follow Myrdal's suggestions. It is clear, however, that value-de-
cisions are necessary for such selections. Does the scientist's
conscience provide a basis or criterion for such decisions?

4. THE CONSCIENCE OF THE SOCIAL SCIENTIST

So far I have stated a postulate for value-neutrality. Then I used
Hart's fourfold division of responsibility to ask which kind of
responsibility would allow to accept or reject this PVN. The
most relevant type of responsibility in this case, the liability-responsibility, formally refers to a set of rules that an acting person has to pursue if he/she is to be liability-responsible. But
which rules can be said to be relevant if not obligatory for the
social scientist? I discussed two suggestions in the previous
section: firstly rules that are claimed to follow directly from the
scientific method and are claimed to be universally reliable. A
closer inspection reveals, however, that this claim is not correct.
Secondly, Gunnar Myrdal's proposal to introduce value-judgments and norms explicitly into science according to certain conditions. But here basically "anything goes" (as Paul Feyerabend
would say), i.e., almost every value-judgment may be chosen -
no reliable directive for the selection of values is being pro-

posed, thus any moral rule could be adopted to back up the scientist's responsibility.

But from where do we get a set of values or rules that marks off the scientist's responsibility from any other type of responsible behavior? My suggestion is: from the conscience of the scientist.

I understand "conscience" in its traditional meaning of *conscientia* (which is "being conscious of" as well as "knowledge with respect to ...", Hörmann 1969, p. 547) as the rational ability to produce according to a known standard or rule an immediate value-judgment about the moral character of one of our beliefs, decisions and actions (cf. St. Thomas Aquinas, *Summa Theologiae* I, II, p. 19, a.5: *"Conscientia nihil aliud est quam applicatio scientiae ad aliquem actum"*).

In other words: In order to be able to use one's conscience one has to be aware of or to know a rule or set of rules plus the determining factors of a specific situation and has to derive the consequence for the action in that situation. Hence, knowledge of rules and knowledge of the relevant facts in a particular situation or area are the two elements with which we get through a logically correct inference a statement of conscience.[2]

Very often just one of these two elements is being considered which yields a one-sided and misleading conception of conscience. Many people believe, for instance, conscience is nothing but a bundle of the traditional dos and don'ts (without taking into account any particular factual knowledge). On the other hand, there are scientists that believe just in factual or empirical knowledge without paying much attention to values or moral rules (cf. for example Andrè Mercier who claimed for the scientist "sagesse oblige" rather than "noblesse oblige", 1970, p. 342).

Both views are incomplete. Moral standards without the data of a particular, concrete situation are not sufficient. In the same way, pure knowledge of facts, even the most sophisticated expert knowledge does not lead the scientist to any particular moral or value-conclusion. "Sagesse oblige" seems correct only in connection with certain value-judgments and norms.

Conscientia means literally "knowing together": particular empirical knowledge plus certain moral rules (Hörmann 1969, p. 547). I am stressing the role of the moral rules because in many of the social sciences they have been neglected altogether: It has been a misconceived imperative to eliminate moral considerations from the scientific perspective. But my emphasis would be pointless unless I listed certain values that are beyond the subjective interests and arbitrary wants of the individual scientist. This would amount just to a descriptive notion of conscience. And if "conscience" would reflect only personal views, then it would be of little use or even "a complete ruin of ethics itself" (Laun 1984, p. 88). Therefore I am suggesting a *normative concept of conscience* in connection with a number of basic values that are grounded in man's nature (Messner 1965; Finnis 1980):
- the value of human life in its perfection[3]
Values that are necessary means for the protection and propagation of human life:
- knowledge and information
- peaceful social life
- labor and study
- protection and cultivation of the world with its wealth of animals, plants, and natural resources
- culture in all forms that aim at beauty and relieve man's daily hardships and sorrows
- faith in God, worshipping and loving Him as the aim of all human activities

I think that this or a similar list of values is basic to a set of universal moral rules that can be taken as reliable standards for the scientist's conscience, in fact, for everybody's conscience. There is nothing new about this list, but it should be made clear when uncertainty and unclarity about these primary values are commonly experienced. When, for instance, Karl Popper (1970b, p. 335) writes: "Everybody has a special responsibility in the field in which he has either special power or special knowledge", then this is just half of the truth. I now can complete and modify this quotation with the above mentioned list of values: "Every social scientist has a special responsibility *for* his special knowledge *to* his conscience, i. e.: to the pursuit of the value of human life and the values that are necessary means for its protection and propagation."

Maybe every scientist and even every human being has such a responsibility[4], but the enumeration of concrete values has definite consequences for the social scientist and his research work. His capacity of understanding these values, of reasoning about them and reaching decisions accordingly by taking his expert knowledge into account is what can meaningfully be called "scientific conscience". This comes very close to what H. L. A. Hart terms 'capacity-responsibility' for which he sketched but a formal framework.

At the end I conclude that a scientific conscience of this sort does not support the kind of value-neutrality as suggested by PVN. The values that make up the general capacity responsibility or the conscience of the social scientist set the general value-framework for practical but nevertheless scientific valuations and norms. The details of this program are still to be elaborated.

Institut für Wissenschaftstheorie
International Research Center Salzburg
and
University of Salzburg

NOTES

1 There are many different conceptions and interpretations of value-freedom. Contrary to what PVN above says, Talcott Parsons (1977, p. 60), for instance, writes: "Value freedom I thus interpret as freedom to pursue the values of science within the relevant limits ...".

2 Cf. P. Weingartner's contribution in this volume, especially his *Thesis 5* in 3.1.

3 It is interesting that this value is also reflected in Kohlberg's principle of respect for human personality where each person is conceived as an end in himself (cf. L. Kohlberg's contribution in this volume, especially section 3). Similarly, J. Fuchs' fundamental imperative made by the conscience al-

ludes to the supreme value of the personal subject (cf. 2.2 of his article in this volume).
4 Cf. the valuable collection of studies on knowledge and conscience ed. by O. Neumaier (1986).

BIBLIOGRAPHY

Albert, H.: 1971, 'Wissenschaft und Verantwortung' in H. Albert (ed.): *Plädoyer für kritischen Rationalismus*, Piper, München, pp. 76-105.

Albert, H.: 1985, *Treatise on Critical Reason*, Princeton Univ. Press, Princeton, N. J.

Brecht, A.: 1959, *Political Theory. The Foundations of Twentieth-Century Political Thought*, Princeton Univ. Press, Princeton, N. J. (German edition: *Politische Theorie. Die Grundlagen politischen Denkens im 20. Jahrhundert*, J. C. B. Mohr, Tübingen, ^{2} 1976).

Finnis, J.: 1980, *Natural Law and Natural Rights*, Clarendon Press, Oxford.

Hart, H. L. A.: 1975, 'Responsibility' in J. Feinberg and H. Gross (eds.): *Philosophy of Law*, Dickenson, Encino, California.

Hörmann, K.: 1969, 'Gewissen' in K. Hörmann: *Lexikon der christlichen Moral*, Tyrolia, Innsbruck, pp. 543-569.

Kaufman, A.: 1967, 'Responsibility, Moral and Legal' in P. Edwards (ed.): *The Encyclopedia of Philosophy*, Vol. 7, MacMillan, New York, pp. 183-188.

Laun, A.: 1984, *Das Gewissen: Oberste Norm sittlichen Handelns. Eine kritische Analyse*, Tyrolia, Innsbruck-Wien.

Mercier, A.: 1970, 'Science and Responsibility' in P. Weingartner and G. Zecha: *op. cit.*, pp. 337-342.

Messner, J.: 1965, *Social Ethics. Natural Law in the Western World* , Herder, St. Louis-London.

Myrdal, G.: 1968, *Value in Social Theory*, ed. by P. Streeten, Routledge & Kegan Paul, London (German edition: *Das Wertproblem in der Sozialwissenschaft*, Verlag Neue Gesellschaft, Bonn-Bad Godesberg, 1975).

Nagel, E.: 1971, *The Structure of Science*, Routledge & Kegan Paul, London.

Neumaier, O. (ed.): 1986, *Wissen und Gewissen. Arbeiten zur Verantwortungsproblematik*, Verband der wissenschaftlichen Gesellschaften Österreichs, Wien.

Parsons, T.: 1977, 'Value-Freedom and Objectivity' in F. Dallmayr and Th. MacCarthy (eds.): *Understanding and Social Inquiry*, University of Notre Dame Press, Notre Dame, Indiana, pp. 56-65.

Picht, G.: 1969, *Wahrheit, Vernunft, Verantwortung*, Klett, Stuttgart.

Popper, K.: 1970a, 'Die Logik der Sozialwissenschaften' in Th. Adorno et al. (eds.): *Der Positivismusstreit in der deutschen Soziologie*, Luchterhand, Neuwied-Berlin, pp. 103-123.

Popper, K.: 1970b, 'The Moral Responsibility of the Scientist' in P. Weingartner and G. Zecha: *op. cit.*, pp. 329-336.

Schmidt, P. F.: 1959, 'Ethical Norms in Scientific Method' in *The Journal of Philosophy* , Vol. 56, pp. 644-652.

Scriven, M.: 1974, 'The Exact Role of Value-Judgments in Science' in K. F. Schaffner and R. S. Cohen (eds.): *PSA 1972. Proceedings of the 1972 Biennal Meeting, Philosophy of Science Association*, D. Reidel, Dordrecht-Boston, pp. 219-247.

Thomas Aquinas: 1966, *Summa Theologiae* , Vol. 18: *Principles of Morality* (ed. by Th. Gilby OP), Blackfriars, London.

Weber, M.: 1904, 'Die 'Objektivität' sozialwissenschaftlicher und sozialpolitischer Erkenntnis' in M. Weber (1968): *Methodologische Schriften*, S. Fischer, Frankfurt/Main, pp. 1-64.

Weingartner, P. and G. Zecha (eds.): 1970, *Induction, Physics, and Ethics. Proceedings and Discussions of the 1968 Salzburg Colloquium in the Philosophy of Science*, D. Reidel, Dordrecht.

Widiger, Th. A. and L. G. Rorer: 1984, 'The Responsible Psychotherapist' in *American Psychologist*, Vol. 39, pp. 503-515.

Zecha, G.: 1976, 'Wie lautet das "Prinzip der Wertfreiheit"?' in *Kölner Zeitschrift für Soziologie und Sozialpsychologie*, Vol. 28, pp. 609-648.

Zecha, G.: 1981, 'Über Wertfreiheit und Verantwortung in den Sozialwissenschaften' in M. Heitger (ed.): *Verantwortung, Wissenschaft, Fortschritt*, Herder, Wien-Freiburg, pp. 59-65.

DISCUSSION

*Ann Higgins, Lawrence Kohlberg, Georg Lind,
Heinrich Scholler, Hans Strotzka, Günter Virt,
Paul Weingartner, Thomas E. Wren,
Gerhard Zecha*

LIND: I understand that Max Weber's postulate of value-free-dom is in some way a projective test which one can read into different things. I have read his statement quite different from you: We must indicate that we are not misusing our competency or our authority as scientists for value-statements for which we cannot have a higher authority than any other human being. The second remark is somehow questioning your premises. You say, 'science' has two meanings: one is the process-meaning, and the other is a statement-meaning. I think a very important meaning of value-freedom refers to the first meaning and we cannot exclude it from the discussion. I read Weber's statement also, "Do not let value-judgments distort the logical deductions or the process of data-gathering, or the process of reporting, documenting and recording data". In this respect I especially think of famous cases like that of Cyril Burt who has certainly let value-judgments or a belief which was outside the scientific empirical knowledge, namely that intelligence is inborn, distort his process of data-gathering and so making and faking empirical evidence. I think this interpretation of value-freedom is also included when one talks about value-freedom of scientific statements, so I would like to question your decision to take this out.

There is a third objection against your decision of just dealing with statements: a scientist can easily omit any value- or value-like statement or mixed statement from his utterance and still make a value-action. The very timing of making a factual statement or the very selection of certain factual statements can be motivated by a value-judgment, that can be very influential in a valuing process.

So, by only concentrating on statements and on the logical form of a statement, one can miss the actual value-process behind and

can by this promote what I would call a 'spurious value-neutrality' where the value-judgment comes in from the back-door.
I can find something similar in the last pages of your paper where you cite norms which should protect against this, "You should always be explicit about your value-statements", but easily the person addressed by this norm can misunderstand you by formally complying with your norm, but in his action, in the context of his statement not complying with it and not revealing the motivation for the value-judgments behind.
ZECHA: Most of what you said can be accepted as far as I understand it, because Max Weber said many things about value-freedom. I think I had to choose for this paper just one relevant example of value-neutrality that has been adopted by the majority of social scientists. At the same time it is the most provocative in relation to conscience and responsibility. The last point you indicated that formally we have statements of fact, but actually they work like value-judgments or norms is well-known and was well-known already to Max Weber. I think precisely this was the reason why he did not even try to give a clear-cut definition of either "norm" or "value-judgment". He himself confessed, "I know that it is very hard to identify norms as norms and value-judgments as value-judgments". That's all he said and he left the problem to us. In fact, we in Salzburg are working on these problems, Prof. Weingartner for instance, has published a series of proposals to identify and define value-judgments and to take into account this pragmatic dimension that is around the mere verbal clothing that actually has a big influence on the understanding of value-judgments. I am aware of this also, but I must confine myself to references (Weingartner 1985).
STROTZKA: I would like to tell a story and ask you how you feel about it. During the Vietnam war, I discussed with the director of the National Institute of Mental Health in Washington/Bethesda, from which all research money comes in my field, if it is possible that NIMH would finance a project on mental health of migrants and refugees in Austria, and he said to me (in a private conversation), "We are now in a war and all research which is being financed by us should help to strengthen

the country in this situation and therefore there is not the slightest chance that money could go out for other projects". What happens to the responsibility and the moral judgment of the scientists who know that they should work under these premises? That's a question of reality of research.

WREN: This is to add to the same question: And what would happen if there were certain areas of research that were forbidden? For instance in the fifties a study had been done which analyzed what the sociological and economic situation would be if America did have a defeat. When this was made known, the United States Congress passed a law against public money being used for any research that would have to do with the prospect of an American defeat.

ZECHA: Well, it is exactly in this respect that we do need such basic values otherwise I cannot imagine how we can justify such a law, a prohibition of certain scientific projects. We can do that, of course, with respect to a national interest for a certain period of time, but national boundaries are becoming less and less important - at least for the scientists. Therefore for the scientists more interesting are internationally applicable rules. Such rules must deal with interests that go beyond national needs and are concerned with the basic values of human life and its dignity.

KOHLBERG: These questions just show how difficult it is to use your criterion. I have a question of clarification. To what extent are your conclusions limited to social science as opposed to natural science? Within social science there is a morality in some sense. Do you see a different kind of value-neutrality possible in the natural science, in mathematics and the physical sciences than in the social sciences?

ZECHA: I do not see a different kind of value-neutrality but I think the sciences as such are different, because the objects differ. As far as the natural sciences are concerned, I must say I do not see what kind of moral judgment or norm we can derive from the study of minerals or animals. But we do see a connection, I believe, between value-judgments and the study of children or the study of political circumstances, the study of man's health and so on.

KOHLBERG: Let me push a little further, because one set of issues deals with the relationship between what is usually called theoretical knowledge and practice and the responsibility. Clearly the atomic scientist is a natural scientist, but his scientific activity has profound consequences for human life. But yet it still seems to be different from what is to be called a moral science or a social science. At least it seems to me in the moral sciences that you have to make moral assumptions at the beginning of the inquiry. The moral conclusions come then out as a result in scientific inquiry: The only thing that has to be neutral is the relationship between the inferential process, that is, a scientist can state his moral premises at the beginning, he can state the moral conclusions, but where he gets from the premises to the conclusions there needs to be in some sense value-neutrality. This seems to me to be the critical point of scientific activity.

ZECHA: The inference from the premises to the conclusion is a logical process and that's certainly a value-neutral process. So here you are quite right. But the problem is that in empirical inquiries quite often value-judgments or at least value-loaden premises are used (mostly unconsciously) that distort the initial value-assumptions (if there are any) as well as the empirical findings. This is the reason why criticism, including self-criticism, is one of the most important methodological postulates in science.

WEINGARTNER: In my view - but here we go beyond social science - values come into scientific discourse on four occasions: First, as an aim or as a task: every science is in the same boat here, even mathematics has aims, truth for instance. Second, methodological rules in the different scientific disciplines: these rules are norms, but they are very much aim-dependent. The third and fourth case: the values occur in the premises or in both premises and conclusion. This is very formal. What I mean is this: I think there is a group of sciences perhaps beginning with biology, that use what I call 'teleological explanation'. This is my third case. It means: values are used in the premises. History, too, is a case in point, a very interesting one. So, a famous historian tried to explain why

Queen Elizabeth I on a certain occasion has used an ambiguous formulation in the proclamation of her title. The explanation was very simple: Elizabeth was confronted with the alternatives either of acknowledging the ecclesiastical supremacy of the Pope or voiding the Marian Statutes and breaking with Rome as her father had done. Both alternatives were unacceptable to her. In order not to offend any of the two parties, she proclaimed her title in an ambiguous way. In other words, we have a teleological explanation of the following sort: For Elizabeth it was a positive value not to offend somebody important. This is the value-judgment. Then we have a law-like statement of the sort: "Always if a politician is in the situation to have only two alternatives in proclaiming something publicly and both alternatives when stated unambiguously lead to an offence ..., then he speaks ambiguously" (perhaps this is statistically true). And with these two premises we can explain (and derive from them) that Elizabeth spoke ambiguously. What is at stake here is that facts are explained with the help of values (for details see my paper on Teleological Arguments).

The fourth case is that we have value-judgments or norms in both, in premises and conclusion. In this case we have an evaluative or normative explanation. Examples of disciplines which use this type are of course ethics but also the theory of literature, political science as well as pedagogics: their task is to justify or to explain value-judgments and norms.

[Note added after the discussion: Some further questions and critical remarks of Prof. Weingartner and Prof. Kohlberg led to a lengthy discussion to the effect that part 1.2 of my paper was completely re-written afterwards. Hence it would be pointless to present these parts of the discussion: they have been omitted. G.Z.]

SCHOLLER: I would like to start with another story. I recently met an East-German scientist, who worked in East Germany years ago on chemical weapons. And the only way to act by conscience against this was to give this information to the West, so he was imprisoned for lifetime. After seven years he was allowed to go to the West, now he is doing research on chemical weapons in the West. So, it's amazing, but it's a fact.

Second point, the scientist may have a special knowledge and a special conscience, but he is completely incompetent or he will be made completely incompetent, when there is no possibility especially in a totalitarian system to act according to his conscience: he has less power, less possibilities than any other citizen; he is controlled and so on. It's obviously a discrepancy between his knowledge, his scientific responsibility and his possibility to act in society. I don't know how we can bridge this problem.

ZECHA: In the last case we have to consider the possibility to say that such a man has no responsibility. The notion of responsibility implies freedom of decision. So, if in a totalitarian system a scientist has less or no possibilities to act according to his conscience, then I would say he has less or no responsibility. But in my paper I emphasized the following: If a scientist has a certain responsibility then we must fill up this notion with a few material values or rules. Without them all talk about responsibility is empty. That's my main point.

And whether we say 'responsibility' or 'conscience' is finally one and the same thing in a certain respect. If we cannot guarantee that the scientist is in the position to meet the basic rules or values, then it makes no sense at all to require him to be scientifically responsible. And in the first case, what should I say?

SCHOLLER: Yes, the first case would mean that naturally we in the West where we have freedom, we have very subtle means to make somebody quiet and to offer him chances; maybe his conscience wouldn't speak at all. There are different means by which to achieve this aim.

ZECHA: Yes, I agree.

STROTZKA: You say that there are discipline-oriented values like health for the medical sciences, the common welfare for economy, peace for political science. In my understanding I must confess that I have always thought that profit is the discipline-oriented value in economy and power for the political science. Isn't that a little too idealistic?

ZECHA: Yes, it's just an example. It's not always clear what the dominant values of a certain discipline are. I only think that there are such values in these disciplines. Take, for example, education (or pedagogics), I believe we have to take the child as something that has to be valued and the physical, psychical and intellectual growth of the child is a value in itself. If we forget that or exclude it from the inquiries then I don't know whether we can do justice to the subject. The same is true in medicine, where health is taken as a value without further questioning. Also in psychotherapy, of course, values are implied without further questions. One of the difficulties there seems to be: which values are to be preferred? The one of the analyst or the one of the patient? That's open to me, but anyway - values are involved.

STROTZKA: There is one word to this: what are the values of the patient? What are the values of the therapist? And, finally, what are the values of the institution? They are quite different! See my book for further information (Strotzka 1983).

HIGGINS: I hope this is not unfair I start with that, but for the social or moral sciences I want to ask the following question: You positively stated a list of values that would fill up this idea of responsibility; and then you said they could be criticized. I'm now asking: is the scientific method an adequate way for this criticism? Do we need more?

ZECHA: This question is a bit too general. Can I have a more concrete example?

HIGGINS: I guess a concrete example, as far as I understand would be - I guess that Dr. Kohlberg tries to do by bringing in philosophy and saying, "There really has to be an endpoint of development. And that has to rest not only on the basis of scientific investigation, but also some philosophical basis!"

ZECHA: Yeah, right here - that's exactly the place where such deliberations come up. But they must be kept open to further discussion.

HIGGINS: But then philosophy can stand outside this?

ZECHA: I am not quite sure about "stand outside" because these assumptions must be open to further investigation and criticism, otherwise we'll end up with dogmatism, and this is what we do not want.

WEINGARTNER: You say that no value-judgment or normative sentence can be derived from a set of purely descriptive sentences. I agree. But I want to point out something which seems to me important. There are important principles which are invariant against all legal systems. For instance, the ought-can principle: If an action is obligatory, it must be possible that it can be carried out. This is a basic principle which is incorporated in all the legal systems. But it is not a principle, valid for all individual decisions as it is clear in the case of strong intentions to reach difficult goals (competitors in Olympic Games, aiming at high moral values). Though it is not, therefore, a most general law, the following view of some philosophers is not correct: If the connection between ought and (possible) facts is not a logical one (and certainly it is not), then there is no justifiable or true connection at all. Though not a law of logic it may be an underlying basic law for legal systems.

ZECHA: It is not quite clear to me what is the connection between the ought-can principle and ...

WEINGARTNER: Of course the ought-can principle is not a principle of logic. But this does not say that it is not a very interesting lawful connection because it's not nothing if it is an invariance principle of all legal systems.

ZECHA: Certainly, such invariance principles play a crucial role in many sciences. But is this ought-can principle really invariant to all systems? Because we do have moral rules, moral ideals, virtues and so on of which it is quite clear that they cannot be reached by any human being.

VIRT: In the Catholic theological perspective I would say, 'Ought implies Can'. But on the other side - in the Lutherian tradition - there is otherwise a principle to the effect "Können setzt Sollen voraus", i. e., you can do it, because you ought to do it.

LIND: Let me come back to the Burt case which I find very interesting to, maybe, tell a little more. Of course, the scientist's conscience and many of your norms - as I feel it - obliges any human being, not only scientists.

The Burt case, the case of the faking of data has all the ingredients of a conscience drama. I have had a chance to read the biography of Sir Cyril Burt by Hearnshaw where he tries to show or to explain the behavior of breaking moral norms of a scientist which made me feel very sympathetic with Burt after I had the feeling of disgust. Somebody who is so highly respected committed such a bad thing. Hearnshaw says, one way of understanding his doing is that he was in a conflict of conscience. He has felt very responsible for a theory, namely for the theory of intelligence inheritance. He was a little boy when he heard of the theory of inherited intelligence and was very impressed by this.

So we can understand his lifelong commitment to empirically prove that theory (that's a hypothesis of Hearnshaw). And this responsibility for the theory conflicted with the responsibility for being truthful about facts. What interests me most here in connection with your paper is: If you put up a list of values or rules, how could these rules prevent a case like this where immanent in a science a scientist is directly breaking a central norm of his profession and is not discovered of having done that for a long time, because nobody would have suspected him to do that.

ZECHA: Conscience - as I have chosen the concept - is not only the knowledge of certain values, rules and particular situations or circumstances, but also the acting according to this knowledge. And the only thing that is required, simple as it sounds, is: One should act according to this. So, we know the problem that perhaps many people know more or less exactly what they should do or what they are expected to do. They feel it somehow, but to do that is another question. Prof. Kohlberg has written on the underlying psychological connection between moral judgment and moral action (Kohlberg/Candee 1984).

KOHLBERG: The questions that this paper raises are very deep and, I think, the usual people that defend value-neutrality make a distinction between the producers of knowledge and the consumers of knowledge, so to speak, and they assume that the job of the producer of knowledge is to produce the kind of knowledge that is up to the consumer to decide how to use. If you take a different point of view, then you really have to take the point of view of the consumer of knowledge. This is perhaps why I get involved in moral education as a practitioner, because I have to see what it looks like from being a teacher as well as from the research scientist's point of view in order to produce responsible knowledge. I know since I used to do pure social science research about morality. I think this is a question that really raises the issue of what you are saying about the responsibility of the social scientist. It means that the social scientist is required to be a moral practitioner of the knowledge he is attempting to create as well as having some moral postulates in the production of knowledge.

ZECHA: Yes, thank you. I think this point of view is very helpful: That the scientist as producer should take also the perspective of the consumer. That's certainly a strong recommendation that makes good sense to me. But this other argument which you pointed out that the scientist just produces knowledge and information and doesn't care how it is used by the consumer seems quite plausible, because all the other examples that are given to support this seem plausible. For instance, a car is produced and the producer is not responsible for what is being done with the car afterwards, the same with the knife and so on. But now we have reached, as far as science is concerned such a stage where we cannot accept any longer this type of argument, because I would say, not every type of knowledge should be produced that can be produced. Therefore it is very much to the point, when you say we should look at the consumer; and I would just add: We have to take into account a certain consumer morality, otherwise we do not know what exactly the consumer's point of view is.

VIRT: There is a little problem not only in connection with this paper. When we are in the process of making value-judgments, then I find always three classes:

- actions, for instance, worshipping God; that's an action according to the own conscience, a right action according to a right conscience;
- habits, for instance, humility or faith in God;
- human life, knowledge, information, peaceful social life, labor and so on: These are not immediate moral values. Life, for instance, is a pre-moral value, but very important for morality.

I think I can solve a problem if there is, for instance, a conflict between life and property. These are not moral values, these are goods, I can solve this problem. But how can I solve value-problems and what is a value?

WEINGARTNER: This is, of course, a very complicated problem. To what 'things' can we attach values? We say, for instance, an earthquake is a catastrophe. This is an evaluation. Almost every predicate, can be in some kind of context, value-loaden. That's the difficulty. Now, to find out whether a certain predicate is value-loaden in some context, I would propose a criterion which is not so difficult: Try to replace the word or predicate in question occurring in a sentence by 'good' or 'bad'. If this makes sense, if you can say, the sentence still remains true or false or it does not turn into a meaningless sentence, then you could say, "It must be a value-predicate in some sense". But this is only a first step. You have to investigate further what kind of value it is.

ZECHA: Thank you, Paul, for this answer. We are all aware of the great complex of problems that is connected with this question.

End of discussion.

BIBLIOGRAPHY

Hearnshaw, L. S.: 1981, *Cyril Burt. Psychologist*, Vintage Books, New York.

Kohlberg, L. and D. Candee: 1984, 'The Relationship of Moral Judgment to Moral Action' in W. Kurtines and J. Gewirtz (eds.): *Morality, Moral Behavior, and Moral Development*, John Wiley & Sons, New York, pp. 52-73.

Strotzka, H.: 1983, *Fairness, Verantwortung, Fantasie. Eine psycho-analytische Alltagsethik*, Deuticke, Wien.

Weingartner, P.: 1985, 'Vorschlag für eine Definition von Werturteil' in R. Born and J. Marschner (eds.): *Philosophie, Wissenschaft, Politik*. Springer, Wien-New York.

Weingartner, P.: 1984, 'On the Introduction of Teleological Arguments into Scientific Discourse' in: *Archives de l'Institut International des Sciences Theoretiques* 26, Bruxelles.

GEORG LIND

MORAL COMPETENCE AND EDUCATION
IN DEMOCRATIC SOCIETY

1. INTRODUCTION

This paper views 'conscience' in the context of society and education. Modern states, in particular democratic ones which rely on the rule of law and popular voting, require an adequate stage of moral-cognitive development in their citizens. Schooling is widely thought to be a necessary and indispensable means for achieving this, although it may not be a sufficient one and other social institutions may be equally necessary. Our main question is: Do institutions of education in our societies foster moral judgment competence? After reviewing a large body of research findings related to this questions, the answer is that yes, by and large education does facilitate cognitive-moral development. This seems to hold true at least for secondary and university education. Before beginning this review, I would like to comment briefly on the salience of moral-cognitive development and education for the survival and development of a democratic society, and on problems of definition and measurement.

2. EDUCATION AND MORAL COMPETENCE IN DEMOCRACY

In his recent essay on the cognitive prerequisites of "Political Observers and Market Participants", the political scientist Robert Lane (1983) observes a most interesting difference in learning mechanisms. According to Lane, the abilities needed in economic market interaction are developed by participation in the market itself, that is, through "punishments and rewards." The competence for coping with the tasks facing a democratic society does not have a comparably powerful reinforcement. One might object and point out the catastrophic punishments that "low political performance" has inflicted upon soci-

91

G. Zecha and P. Weingartner (eds.), Conscience: An Interdisciplinary View, 91–122.
© *1987 by D. Reidel Publishing Company.*

eties throughout the course of history. However, as Lane rightly asserts, politics is less concrete, personal, and quantifiable than are economic markets, and involves abstract and remote ideas about justice and human needs and rights which might be difficult to promote through rewards and punishments. Hence other means of teaching, even if less effective than the immediate rewards and punishments of the market, must be considered when attempts are made to promulgate democratic culture.

More than 150 years ago, Alexis de Tocqueville, one of the first commentators of politics in a democratic society, asserted that general education in schools and universities is among the most important prerequisites for the political behavior of the *citoyen*. He believed that only education can make the individual discover the advantages of political competence. Tocqueville foretold "a time when freedom, public peace, and even the social order will not be able to endure without education". For this reason he emphatically demanded: "People should be educated whatever the cost" (Tocqueville, 1976, p. 613, my transl.).

Both times after the catastrophes of World War I and II, this advice seems to have been recalled. Politicians endeavored to reconstruct the educational system in such a way as to provide a better education for a broader class of people. This was not only to make up for the high unemployment rates among young veterans or to provide a good starting base for individual professional careers, but above all to instill a higher moral and democratic competence in the citizenry as a whole. After the Second World War, the importance of democratic education and the development of democratic personality was recognized once again. As Ralph Barton Perry wrote, "Education is not only a boon conferred to democracy, but a condition of its survival and of its becoming that which it undertakes to be. Democracy is that form of social organization which most depends on the personal character and moral autonomy. ... Democratic education is therefore a peculiarly ambitious education." (1954, p. 425).

In Germany, after the terror of the Nazi-regime, which today is perceived less as the deed of a single man than as the failure of society as a whole, the reconstruction of schools and universities was guided by similar beliefs. In 1947 the "Committee on the Reform of West German Higher Education" began to turn out a series of influential papers (the *Blaue Gutachten*). The committee states, "The conviction that each citizen should have a full share in the political responsibility must never again be lost. The practical realization of this insight in Germany is particularly important, though also particularly difficult" (cited in Neuhaus, 1961, p. 293, my transl.).

Unfortunately, the lessons taught by the man-made catastrophes of the two wars were in both cases soon in danger of fading away. In the first time, in the Weimar Republic, the striving for better and broader education could not endure long enough to produce democratic and moral competence in a sufficient number of people. The problems involved in the reorganization of postwar Germany and resulting from worldwide economic turmoil at the time were beyond the coping capabilities of society, and produced anti-democratic and anti-intellectual sentiments. The second time, after World War II, a similar development appeared to take place. Postwar difficulties as well as fear of communism and the cold war fostered the enlargement of the educational system. However, there was soon a shift from democratic and moral aims to economic and military emphasis. As Hersh and his colleagues wrote, "The 1950's were an inhospitable time for moral education, or for any form of study that smacked of 'progressivism' ... Moral education took a back seat to technical and academic training ... Democracy seemed to hinge less on the moral autonomy of the individual than on the size of the gross national product and the quantity of nuclear warheads." (Hersh, Miller and Fielding, 1980, p. 23).

In any event, education was for many individuals considerably increased. Within eighty years, in (West) Germany university attendance rose from less than one to more than twenty percent. There was a temporary decrease during the Third Reich when university education faced suspicion. But after the Second War, many new universities have been built and the attendance rate rose strongly (cf. Peisert and Framhein, 1980). And in the sixties it was the university students who revived such ideas as morality, democracy and education, amongst others in the United States (Haan et al., 1968; Yankelovich, 1974) and in

West Germany (Nitsch et al., 1965). While one cannot overlook the negative role that the "new mandarins" or the "back door boys", as Chomsky has called the intellectuals, can play in modern society, one may speculate that without the moral and critical competence of the highly educated, complex societies like ours would uphold freedom and justice to an even lesser degree than they do now. With the new movements, politics and morality are seen to be closely related again. As early as the 1920's, it had been suggested that moral and democratic competence be viewed not as separate, but as overlapping domains of personality (cf. Piaget, 1932; Allport, 1929). Recently, Christian Bay restated this by saying that "political activity is almost synonymous with moral activity and each citizen ... is a political and moral being" (1971, p. 168). Empirical research has supported this view by showing that the correlations between moral judgment competence and various aspects of political attitude and action are substantial and largely consistent with each other (cf. Haan et al., 1968; Alker and Poppen, 1973; Rest, 1979; Lind, Sandberger, and Bargel, 1981-82; Schenk and Bohm, 1983; Heidbrink, 1983; Weinreich-Haste, in press). In his research, Kohlberg has found "that reasoning and decision making about political decisions are directly derivative of broader patterns of moral reasoning and decision making. We have interviewed high school and college students about concrete political situations involving laws to govern open housing, civil disobedience for peace in Vietnam, free press rights to publish what might disturb national order, and distribution of income through taxation. We find that reasoning on these political decisions can be classified according to moral stages and that individual's stage on political dilemmas is the same level as on nonpolitical dilemmas (euthanasia, violating authority to maintain trust in a family, stealing a drug to save one's dying wife)" (Kohlberg, 1978, p. 43-44).

Consequently, there has been a return to the idea of 'moral education'. However, this type of 'moral education' is not to be understood as the teaching of conformist behavior or the indoctrination of values, but as "education for the analytic understanding, value principles, and motivation necessary for a ci-

tizen in a democracy if democracy is to be an effective process" (Kohlberg, 1978, p. 43). It is notable that in discussing
new educational policies, the notion of general education has
been partly de-emphasized in favor of specialized programs in
civic and moral education (cf. the papers in Purpel and Ryan,
1976; Scharf, 1978; Mosher, 1980). This may have been
because there was little trust in the overall democratizing effect
of school education. Individual impressions nourished the suspicion that the organization and "hidden curriculum" of our
schools may be inadequate for, or even adverse to, fostering democratic competence and behavior. However, with regard to
moral and democratic competence, there had been little or insufficient empirical data to evaluate such an educational aim.
Only now, with the new concepts and methods that cognitive-
developmental theory has provided, the evaluation of the democratizing effects of schooling can be based on a broader and
more adequate set of empirical data.

3. ISSUES OF DEFINITION AND OPERATIONALIZATION

According to Kant, human behavior is to be called "moral behavior" only if it is motivated by moral concerns or principles.
Hence, labelling a behavior as "moral" always requires psychological properties, motives and judgments to be taken into account when assessing it. A person's behavior or judgment that
is not related to his or her own moral motive cannot be rightly
called a moral behavior, even if it were objectively in accordance
with external, that is, socially defined norms. Roughly
speaking, only those rules can be called "moral" which are universally valid. Hence "moral behavior" is defined as behavior
that obeys internalized and universally valid moral maxims.
Therefore, we may distinguish three forms or meanings of moral behavior:
1. Behavior which is merely objectively in accordance with
social norms, enforced by the "law of effect", that is, by punishments and rewards. The question of moral goodness does
not arise because the behavior is pre-moral.

2. Behavior which subjectively (through internalization) complies with conventions and laws. This type of behavior is enforced by feelings of shame and social insulation.

3. Behavior which does not obey social norms blindly, but on the basis of a critical evaluation regarding their consistency and universality. Only in this case can conscience be said to have developed into moral autonomy or autonomous moral judgment competence.

"Moral competence" means both the willingness to base one's behavior on universalizable moral maxims (= the affective aspect), and the ability to apply these principles in one's behavior consistently, i.e., for example to evaluate an action consistently with regard to moral principles even if this is contrary to one's prior habits and opinions (= the cognitive aspect). We may call this the ability to decenter (Piaget) or to take the perspective of the generalized other (G.H. Mead, Kohlberg). Cognitive-developmental theory is to be credited withdrawing our attention to this cognitive or structural aspect of moral conscience and behavior. Nevertheless, we must be aware of the fact that the affective aspect, i.e., the affective binding of behavior to social norms and moral principles is not secondary or less important. There is no cognition without affect.

This conceptual differentiation between the affective and the cognitive aspect of moral judgment behavior, as obvious as it may seem, was not easily translated into the language of research. Early assessments of moral attitudes and moral behavior have mostly been confined to the individual's affective tendency toward social or moral norms, but have seldom addressed the structural properties of moral judgment, i.e., the question of logical consistency and universal validity. How and how well is a person's moral conscience organized? How well is his or her moral judgment competence developed?

The strength and weakness of a purely affective approach are best exemplified in the much quoted "Studies in Deceit" by Hartshorne and May (1928). The goal of this study was to determine whether children's behavior was objectively in accordance with socially defined norms. The authors failed to assess the degree of subjective internalization of those norms, and completely left out the issue of reflective and critical judgment. Although these and other researchers were aware of the cognitive aspect of moral behavior, they nevertheless employed measurement instruments that were not able to assess this aspect (for an excellent review, see Pittel and Mendelsohn, 1966).

Among the first authors who attempted to overcome this gap between theory and research were Levy-Stuhl, Moers, Hetzer, and Piaget who did most interesting research on moral behavior in the nineteen-twenties. However, manageable research instruments for assessing the effects of education or of an educational system as a whole were only developed later, foremost by Kohlberg. He created a standardized, yet very flexible interviewing and coding system which allowed him to assess both the affective and cognitive aspects of moral judgment (cf. Kohlberg, 1958; Colby and Kohlberg, 1984). On the basis of Kohlberg's method, James Rest (1979a; 1979b) and others have developed questionnaires similar to classical attitude tests or based on a mixture of interview and test (cf. Kuhmerker et al., 1980). Building more on Kohlberg's theory than on his method, we have created the "Moralisches-Urteil-Test" which is based on the new methodology of "Experimental Questionnaire" (Lind, 1982). The major aim of the MUT, in addition to assessing the affective aspect, is to measure the cognitive aspect of an individual's moral judgment behavior (i. e., its universality) in an analytically differentiated way without desintegrating it from the affective aspect. We assume that both aspects can be distinguished from one another but cannot be ontologically devided and, therefore, cannot be assessed through sampling different sets of behavior (cf. Lind and Wakenhut, 1983; Lind, in press).

4. HYPOTHESES ABOUT THE IMPACT OF EDUCATION ON MORAL DEVELOPMENT

Although many of us would regard it as highly desirable that schools foster moral and democratic competencies, there is great scepticism whether our school system is actually able to do this. Modgil and Modgil (1976) quote research which found that "educational attainment does not appear to be an effective factor in moral judgments in adults and the elderly" (p. 98). Some see the aims and the structure of formal education as being directly opposed to such a development. Education for citizenship and moral development implies goals which are at least in part "incompatible" with one another within the school framework (cf. Nelson, 1980, p. 257). Other institutions of education indeed seem to add little to the progress of moral-cognitive development. A study of apprentices showed that vocational training without general education has a significant effect on the moral development of apprentices, however, this effect is still small when compared to the differential impact of the level of previous schooling (Lind, 1983b; Oser and Schläfli, in press). Socialization in the military seems to have no or even a slightly negative effect on the development of moral judgment competence (Wakenhut, 1984; Räder and Wakenhut, 1984). Surprisingly, even higher education is said to have no (enduring) effect on the acquisition of democratic attitudes (Newcomb, 1974; Cloetta, 1975).

From cognitive-developmental theory, on the other hand, one can derive an opposing hypothesis, namely that the multiple opportunities of participation and interaction which institutions of education provide, together with the moral ideas on which they are based, will eventually foster moral growth (cf. Kohlberg, 1969; Lind, 1983a). In particular, the experiences of responsibility and freedom provided by higher education are considered by Kohlberg as both necessary and sufficient for promoting democratic competence beyond the level of conventional, obeisant morality (Kohlberg, 1973, p. 196). Although the rates and absolute degrees of development may vary considerably, in most cases this development should be empirically evident, invariant, and enduring.

5. REVIEW OF EMPIRICAL FINDINGS

A number of research projects have in the meantime tried to validate the cognitive-developmental hypothesis. The hypothesis that education affects moral development has been examined in three ways, (a) through analyses of the correlation between the level of moral development and the level of education, (b) through longitudinal studies of effects of socialization and selection produced by institutions of education, and finally (c) through educational experiments in which special pedagogical programs in schools, like the Just Community approach, were introduced to foster cognitive-moral development of students. To provide a common basis of comparison, I have throughout transformed the figures reported into the Pearson coefficient of correlation r between two variables.[1]

5.1 Correlational Studies

A corroboration of the positive role of schooling in moral-cognitive development can already be found in correlational studies. Although a high correlation does not positively prove the alleged relationship, it can, if calculated from findings of thoughtfully designed studies, rule out a number of objections. A negative or consistently low correlation would of course call into question the notion of a cognitive-developmental basis of moral judgment.

As a matter of fact, all studies reviewed showed very high correlations between the level of education and moral judgment competence.[2] Kohlberg's (1958) original cross-sectional study of modes of moral thinking in adolescence showed an educational effect between the ages of 10 and 16 of more than one stage of reasoning (from Stage 1.3 to 2.6). The correlation between both variables accounts for about 44 % of the total variance in judgment (which is equivalent to a r of +0.66).[3] However, because of the design of the study the effects of education cannot be distinguished from effects of other age-related variables.

Candee, Graham and Kohlberg (1978) provided correlational evidence from subjects of their longitudinal study which indicated that the level of education attainment was very closely associated with adult moral reasoning ($r = 0.71$). This association was higher than any of the correlations with job status, IQ, father's job, and even with the level of moral reasoning in the subject's adolescence.

Rest (1979a), using the Defining-Issues-Test, has produced findings very similar to these. In his first study on students from high school, college, and Ph. D. courses in philosophy and political science, Rest found a correlation as high as $r = +0.69$; in a second sample as $r = +0.67$; in a combined analysis of data from 136 different studies on 5,714 subjects, the correlation was $r = +0.62$ (computed from the omega-square statistic reported by Rest, 1979a, p. 110). There were moral score differences (P-score) due to education of more than 35 percentage points of a total of hundred points (pp. 108-111). In this study, education and age could also not be differentiated, but studies with adults indicate that, after the completion of education, judgment competence decreases rather than increases with age (pp. 111-112).

Kitchener and King (1981, p. 107), drawing upon the similar concept of reflective judgment found that from high school to graduate students there was an increase of more than three stages (on their 7-stage development scale). The correlation between educational level and development, as computed from the F-statistic, was $r = +0.77$. This correlation "could not be statistically accounted for by other theoretically or potentially confounding factors related to intellectual development: verbal ability, formal operations, socio-economic status, and verbal fluency" (p. 112).

In a study on Swiss vocational school (Berufsschule) students, there was a small but noticeable effect of three years of education ($r = +0.09$, p .05). The effect may be so small because this education provides only one-day-a-week general education at school while the other days are devoted to on-the-job training. The quality of previous general education (as based on the tripartite system of secondary education in Switzerland) is more strongly correlated to moral-cognitive development (r = +0.29) than is vocational training. In this study, the "Moralisches-Urteil-Test" was used (cf. Lind and Wakenhut, 1983).

A cross-sectional comparison of high school graduates, university graduates, and scientists in the Federal Republic of Germany which used the same instrument showed that there are considerable differences in moral judgment competence and that they are attributable to different degrees of general education (Lind, 1983a).

5.2 *Longitudinal Studies*

The evidence for a decisive impact of formal education on moral and democratic development is of course more convincing when obtained from longitudinal studies.

With their 20-year longitudinal study, Kohlberg and his colleagues could show that the correlation of education and moral development is indeed independent of age, as it remains high within all age periods studied (Colby et al., 1983, pp. 50-51). They were also able to once more demonstrate that the correlations between moral judgment competence and level of education are higher than the correlations between moral judgment and either social class or IQ, and that these correlations remained substantial even after socio-economic status and IQ were taken into consideration (pp. 55-56). The most important finding was that the attainment of "consolidated stage 4" of moral judgment (which was formerly partly scored as stage 5) was closely correlated to college attendance (p. 56). This finding conforms well with the theoretical expectation, stated by Kohlberg in 1973, that college experience is very important for the development of a principled moral reasoning.

In a very thorough and encompassing comparison of longitudinal development of students with college education and without, Jim Rest (1979b) also found strong support for the hypothesis that higher education fosters development in moral judgment: "While both college and non-college groups show increases immediately after leaving high school, by the time that four years have passed, the college students are still showing gains while the non-college subjects are not." (p. 33). These gains could not be attributed to other variables studied.

In our own, still ongoing, longitudinal study on university socialization in five European countries[4], we have some preliminary findings that are consistent with the findings of Kohlberg, Rest and others. In the interval between high school graduation and entrance of university, and in the time between the first and fifth semester of study, we found consistent progress in the cognitive-moral development of German students (Lind, 1983c). Regressions, which Kohlberg and Kramer (1969) have discussed, occurred only superficially. There are good reasons to believe that the regression phenomenon is mainly caused by inadequacies of the assessment method used (Colby et al., 1983; Lind, 1983c).

This latter study also gives some insight into the interrelation of the development of the affective and cognitive aspect of moral judgment competence, which may be of importance for educational practice. Both aspects seem to develop in parallel fashion, as Kohlberg has suggested, but also in a predictable time order. It is astonishing how systematically the direction and strength of students' attitudes toward the different stages of moral justification (= affective aspect) correlated with the degree of moral judgment consistency (= cognitive aspect). This finding has been replicated without exception in several studies on university students and other subject groups (Lind, in press). However, in developmental terms the high esteem for high-stage moral reasoning (and the rejection of low-stage reasoning) seems to take place prior to the development of the competence of integrated and differentiated judgment in concrete situations of moral conflict. Even in their first semester of study, almost all students prefer stages of moral reasoning which have been ascribed a higher ethical value, and hardly change this preference order during study, whereas the competence aspect, i. e., the consistency of students' moral preference judgments, seems to be not fully developed yet and still increases while attending university (Lind, 1983c).

One educational implication of this finding seems especially worthy of mention. We have seen that many young students are morally very sensible even though they still lack full capability to apply their moral principles consistently. This sensibility seems to be extremely important for the growth of students' personality, though it may also be a major source of an individual's frustration and discontent. Obviously, in most instances the environment is supportive and understanding, and discontent ultimately leads to the enhancement of moral judgment competence. But moral development may take another path when there are no opportunities for discussion, participation and role-taking. Then moral sensibility may turn into either moral rigorism or moral cynism and resignation.

5.3 *Experimental Studies: Educational Intervention*

A number of studies provide us with information on the effectiveness of educational interventions on the level of individual school classes and schools. While in the beginning these interventions where designed as a specialized curriculum in a classroom, there are now also interventions which comprise a whole educational institution, like a school. Their aim is not only to stimulate moral development but also related psychological processes, and to enhance the moral atmosphere of the supportive social environment (Kohlberg, in press; Lempert, in press; Oser and Schläfli, in press).

In sum, these studies show that special moral curricula can succeed in fostering cognitive-moral development. There have been promising theoretical and practical attempts in this regard (for reviews see Althof, 1984; Mosher, 1980; Oser, 1981; Rest, 1979a). Preliminary but most impressive effects have been reported from experiments involving a whole educational institution and which succeeded in changing its moral climate (Higgins, 1980; Kohlberg, in press).

Some limitations of these pedagogical experiments should also be mentioned: (a) Rarely could any of the educational interventions proceed like an experiment in physics in which all relevant variables are held constant; therefore, we cannot be sure whether the effects are really attributable to these interventions. (b) Typically, these interventions are rather complex. Most researchers have designed their own specific configuration of educational treatments for achieving a measurable growth in moral maturity. Therefore, it is difficult to say which single treatment or which constellation of treatments is the most effective. Finally, (c) the range of educational means that could be used was more or less constrained by the institution in which the experiment took place (Oser and Schläfli, in press).

These objections apply to almost any educational intervention and certainly do not invalidate moral education. The process of identifying effective educational means for moral-democratic development is a very arduous one, and new insights will have to be gained by evaluating both present and planned educational programs in this field. Neither in physics nor in education are isolated experiments sufficient to validate a theory. We will achieve a better understanding only through a process of simultaneous improvement of the theory of moral development and of educational practice (Kohlberg called this process "bootstrapping"). As the basis of our experiences widens we will be more able to determine which educational means must be held constant and which variable in order to adjust moral education to the particular circumstance. This will be especially true when moral-cognitive interventions are adapted to other institutions of socialization and other countries. New programs and studies will have to be designed which attend to the special needs of students, parents, teachers, the school system and the political environments of these countries. Moreover, most of the moral education programs whose effects have been studied so far were new and exceptional. Their effects can be, for the better or for the worse, considerably different when moral education becomes a common curriculum in a state's educational system.

6. CONCLUSION

Most of us would probably agree with Tocqueville that democracy should be interested in the formation of the individual personality not only for the sake of the individuals' vocational career, but also for the sake of democracy itself. As the cognitive-moral research of two decades shows, our educational systems seem to have by and large fulfilled this objective. All findings have shown with surprising consistency that general education actually does foster cognitive-moral development and hence democratic competence. For example, the impact of education cannot be reduced to effects of socio-economic status, IQ, verbal abilities, or age. The effects remain substantial even after competing variables have been considered. This fostering effect of the educational system has been shown in the United States through a series of well-designed cross-sectional, longitudinal, and experimental studies. For the Federal Republic of Germany and other European countries only scarce evidence is available yet.

This achievement of general education applies in particular to the cognitive aspect of moral judgment, i. e., a person's ability to deal with moral dilemmas and to make consistent and differentiated moral judgments in the face of conflicting needs and principles. Whereas the affective binding to moral principles seems to have been largely established before schooling, i. e., in childhood or even in infancy, schooling apparently helps the individual to develop competencies in organizing and applying these moral principles to concrete action in complex social situations. We have noted that moral competence is not equivalent with rigid adherence to general principles but with the ability to eliminate inconsistencies in one's judgments and to regard differentially the situation to which they apply (cf. Döbert and Nunner-Winkler, in press).

Feelings of guilt and shame are certainly an important prerequisite that the child becomes conscious of moral issues. They make one also aware of conflicting values and principles. But feelings and emotions do not suffice to solve those conflicts. The individual must in addition develop moral-cognitive capacities. For this, education is without doubt of great importance.

However, though schools and universities foster cognitive-moral development, the degree to which they do so may not suffice in view of the number and difficulties of the problems before us. Extraordinary problems call for the development of extraordinary moral competency. For this, it may be necessary to provide not only parts of society but all its members with a higher level of education. Apart from this, education on all levels may need improvement with regard to its capability to foster moral-cognitive development. This may be achieved by implementing special moral education curricula and perhaps better yet by improving the moral atmosphere of schools, colleges, universities. Moreover, moral education must be brought into balance with *general* education, that is, with the teaching of such other subjects as physics, history, chemistry, languages, mathematics, economics and so on, because the individual also needs those subjects to develop comprehensive judgment competency in a complex environment.

University of Konstanz

NOTES

1 The correlation coefficient r ranges from $+1$, indicating a perfect linear relationship between moral development and level of education, over 0, no relation, and to -1, a perfect negative relation. The formula for computing r from the F- statistic is:

$$r = (\frac{F}{F + N - 2})^{-2} \qquad \text{(cf. Bredenkamp, 1970)}$$

2 A linear correlation of r greater than $+0.60$ (not corrected for attenuation) can be called "very high". It is rare when two psychologically distinct variables are involved.

3 The formula for computing r from percentage of variance (PV) is simply

$$r = (PV : 100)^{-2}, \qquad \text{with } PV = 100 * r^2.$$

4 The countries participating in this international panel study into the conditions and effects of higher education (FORM) are Austria, Fed. Rep. of Germany, the Netherlands, Poland and Yugoslavia. The study is coordinated by the Vienna Center for Social Sciences, Grünangergasse 2, P. O. Box 974, A-1011 Vienna, Austria. In charge of the German part is the project

group *Hochschulsozialisation* at the University of Konstanz: Tino Bargel, Barbara Dippelhofer-Stiem, Gerhild Framhein, Georg Lind, Hansgert Peisert (director), Johann-Ulrich Sandberger and Hans Gerhard Walter.

BIBLIOGRAPHY

Alker, H. A. and Poppen, P. J.: 1973, 'Personality and ideology in university students' in *Journal of Personality* 41, pp. 653-671.

Allport, G. W.: 1929-30, 'The composition of political attitudes' in *American Journal of Sociology* 35, pp. 220-238.

Althof, W.: 1984, 'Moralerziehung in der Schule: Theorie und Praxis. Ein Literaturbericht' in A. Regenbogen (ed.): *Moral und Politik. Soziales Bewußtsein als Lernprozeß* , Pahl-Rugenstein, Köln, pp. 148-212.

Bay, C.: 1971, 'Human development and political orientations: Notes towards a science of political education' in G. Abcarian and J.W. Soule (eds.): *Social psychology and political behavior*, Merill, Columbus, Ohio, pp. 148-182.

Bredenkamp, J.: 1970, 'Über Maße der praktischen Signifikanz' in *Zeitschrift für Psychologie* 177, pp. 310-318.

Candee, D., Graham, R. and Kohlberg, L.: 1978, *Moral development and life outcomes.* Paper submitted to the National Institute of Education.

Cloetta,B.: 1975 ,*Einstellungsänderung durch die Hochschule. Konservatismus-Machiavellismus-Demokratisierung. Eine empirische Untersuchung über angehende Lehrer*, Klett, Stuttgart.

Colby, A., Kohlberg, L. et al.: 1983: 'Moral development' in *Child Development Monographs*, University of Chicago Press, Chicago.

Colby, A. and Kohlberg, L.: 1984, *The measurement of moral judgment*, Cambridge University Press, New York.

Döbert, R. and Nunner-Winkler, G.: 'Morals and changing values', in press.*

Feldman, R.E.: 1980, 'The promotion of moral development in prisons and schools' in R.W. Wilson and G.J. Schochet (eds.): *Moral development and politics*, Praeger, New York, pp. 286-328.

Haan, N., Smith, M.B. and Block, J.H.: 1968, 'Moral reasoning of young adults: Political-social behavior, family background, and personality correlates' in *Journal of Personality and Social Psychology* 10, pp. 183-201.

Hartshorne, N. and May, M.A.: 1928-30, *Studies in the nature of character*, Vol. I: *Studies in deceit*, Vol. II: *Studies in service and self-con-*

108   GEORG LIND

trol, Vol. III: *Studies in organization of character* , Macmillan, New
York.
Heidbrink, H.: 1983, 'Moralische Urteilskompetenz und politisches Lernen'
in G. Lind, H. Hartmann and R. Wakenhut (eds.): *Moralisches Urteilen
und soziale Umwelt*, Beltz, Weinheim, pp. 238-248.*
Hersh, R.H., Miller, J.P. and Fielding, G.D.: 1980, *Models of moral education*, Longman, New York.
Higgins, A.: 1980, 'Research and measurement issues in moral education
interventions' in R. Mosher (ed.): *Moral education. A first generation of
research and development*, Praeger Press, New York, pp. 92-107.
Kitchener, K.S. and King, P.M.: 1981, 'Reflective judgment: Concepts of
justification and their relation to age and education' in *Journal of Applied Developmental Psychology* 2, pp. 89-116.
Kohlberg, L.: 1958, *The development of modes of moral thinking and
choice in the years from ten to sixteen*. Doctoral dissertation, University of Chicago.
Kohlberg, L. and Kramer, R.: 1969, 'Continuities and discontinuities in
children and adult moral development' in *Human Development* 12, pp.
93-120.
Kohlberg, L.: 1969, 'Stage and sequence. The cognitive-developmental approach to socialization' in D. Goslin (ed.): *Handbook of socialization
theory and research*, Rand McNally, Chicago, pp. 347-580.
Kohlberg, L.: 1973, 'Continuities in childhood and adult moral development revisited' in P. Baltes and W. Schaie (eds.): *Live-span developmental psychology, research and theory*, Academic Press, New York,
pp. 179-204.
Kohlberg, L.: 1978, 'The cognitive-developmental approach to moral education' in P. Scharf (ed.): *Readings in moral education*, Winston Press,
Minneapolis, MI, pp. 36-51.
Kohlberg, L.: 'The just community approach to moral education in theory
and in practice', in press, in M. Berkowitz and F. Oser (eds.): *Moral
education: international perspectives*, Erlbaum Associates, Hillside, NJ.
Kuhmerker, L., Mentkowski, M. and Erickson, L.: 1981, *Evaluating moral
development*, Character Research Press, New York.
Lane, R.: 1983, 'Political obvservers and market participants: The effect on
cognition' in *Political Psychology* 4, pp. 445-482.
Lempert, W.: 'Moralische Entwicklung und berufliche Ausbildung', in
press, in H. Bertram (ed.): *Gesellschaftlicher Zwang und moralische
Autonomie*, Suhrkamp, Frankfurt.
Lind, G.: 1982, 'Experimental questionnaires: A new approach to personality research' in A. Kossakowski and K. Obuchowski (eds.): *Progress
in psychology of personality*, North-Holland, Amsterdam, pp. 132-144.

Lind, G.: 1983a, 'Sozialisation in der Universität. Einstellungsänderung oder kognitiv-moralische Entwicklung' in G. Lind, H. Hartmann and R. Wakenhut (eds.): *Moralisches Urteilen und soziale Umwelt*, Beltz, Weinheim, pp. 153-170.*

Lind, G.: 1983b, *Moralische Urteilskompetenz und berufliche Ausbildung*, Bericht 2/1983 des Forschungsprojekts Humanisierung der Arbeitswelt durch Förderung der sozial-moralischen Entwicklung (HASMU), Pädagogisches Institut, Universität Fribourg, Switzerland.

Lind, G.: 1983c, *Growth or regression in cognitive-moral development? A follow-up study of young university students*, Paper presented at the Sixth Annual Scientific Meeting of the International Society of Political Psychology (ISPP), July 1983, Oxford.

Lind, G.: 'Affect and cognition: the hypothesis of parallelism and the problem of its testing', in press, in C. Harding (ed.): *Moral Development Colloquia*, Precedent, Chicago.

Lind, G., Sandberger, J.-U. and Bargel, T.: 1981-82, 'Moral judgment, ego-strength and democratic orientations - some theoretical contiguities and empirical findings' in *Political Psychology* 3/4, pp. 70-110.

Lind, G. and Wakenhut, R.: 1983, 'Tests zur Erfassung der moralischen Urteilskompetenz' in G. Lind, H. Hartmann and R. Wakenhut (eds.): *Moralisches Urteilen und soziale Umwelt*, Beltz, Weinheim, pp. 59-80.*

Lind, G., Hartmann, H. and Wakenhut, R. (eds.): 1983, *Moralisches Urteilen und soziale Umwelt*, Beltz, Weinheim.*

Modgil, S. and Modgil, C.: 1976, *Piagetian research. Compilation and commentary*, NFER, Windsor, Berks.

Mosher, R.L. (ed.): 1980, *Moral education. A first generation of research and development*, Praeger, New York.

Nelson, J.L.: 1980, 'The uncomfortable relationship between moral education and citizenship instruction' in R.W. Wilson and G.J. Schochet (eds.): *Moral development and politics*, Praeger, New York, pp. 256-285.

Neuhaus, R. (ed.): 1969, *Dokumente zur Hochschulreform 1945-1959*, Franz Steiner, Wiesbaden.

Newcomb, Th.: 1974, 'What does college do for a person? Frankly very little' in *Psychology today*, September 1974.

Nitsch, W., Gerhard, U., Offe, C. and Preuss, U.K.: 1965, *Hochschule in der Demokratie*, Luchterhand, Neuwied.

Oser, F.: 1981, 'Moralische Erziehung als Intervention' in *Unterrichtswissenschaft* 9, pp. 207-224.

Oser, F. and Schläfli, A.: 'The thin line phenomenon - helping bank trainees form a social and moral identity in their workplace'*, in press.

Peisert, H. and Framheim, G.: 1980, *Das Hochschulsystem in der Bundesrepublik Deutschland* (second enlarged edition), Klett-Cotta, Stuttgart.

Perry, R.B.: 1954, *Realms of value*, Harvard University Press, Cambridge.

Piaget, J.: 1973, *Das moralische Urteil beim Kind* (original: 1932), Suhrkamp, Frankfurt.

Pittel, S.M. and Mendelsohn, G.A.: 1966, 'Measurement of moral values: A review and critique' in *Psychological Bulletin* 66, pp. 22-35.

Purpel, D. and Ryan, K. (eds.): 1976, *Moral education ... It comes with the territory*, McCutchan, Berkeley, CA.

Räder, G. and Wakenhut, R.: 1984, *Morality and military organization*, Paper presented at the seventh Scientific Meeting of ISPP, Toronto, June 24-27, 1984, Sozialwissenschaftliches Institut der Bundeswehr, München.

Rest, J.R.: 1979a, *Development in judging moral issues*, University of Minnesota, Minneapolis, MI.

Rest, J.R.: 1979b, *The impact of higher education on moral judgment development* (Technical Report), Minnesota Moral Research Project, University of Minnesota.

Scharf, P. (ed.): 1978, *Readings in moral education*, Winston, Minneapolis, MI.

Schenk, M. and Bohm, G.: 1983, 'Bürgerinitiativen: Politisches Engagement und Moralisches Urteilen' in G. Lind, H. Hartmann and R. Wakenhut (eds.): *Moralisches Urteilen und soziale Umwelt*, Beltz, Weinheim, pp. 223-235.*

Tocqueville, A.: 1976, *Über die Demokratie in Amerika*. Deutscher Taschenbuch Verlag, München.

Wakenhut, R.: 1984, 'Moral und Militär' in *Vierteljahresschrift für Sicherheit und Frieden* 1, pp. 31-38.

Weinreich-Haste, H.: 'Kohlberg's contribution to political psychology: a positive view', in press, in S. Modgil and C. Modgil (eds.): *Kohlberg: Consensus and controversy*, Falmer, Brighton.

Yankelovich, D.: 1974, *The new morality. A profile of American youth in the seventies*, McGraw-Hill, New York.

NOTE

The asterisked papers (*) have been published in English in: Lind, G., H. A. Hartmann and R. Wakenhut (eds.): 1985, *Moral Development and the Social Environment. Studies in the Philosophy and Psychology of Moral Judgment and Education*. Precedent Publ. Inc., Chicago, Ill.

DISCUSSION

Josef Fuchs SJ, Ann Higgins, Lawrence Kohlberg,
Georg Lind, Heinrich Scholler, Hans Strotzka, Günter Virt,
Paul Weingartner, Thomas E. Wren, Gerhard Zecha

STROTZKA: I am the only psychoanalyst in this group and my experience comes from a very different field than yours. I would like to put my contribution into a question: We know from many studies that children in pre-school age are still developing what we would call later on ethnocentricity, xenophobia, chauvinism or some such thing by early identification and imitation and by some imprint-mechanism what we would probably call "object-introjections". And I think this attitude which is developed in children before they start going to school is to some extent a background to later moral development. Now it's very interesting in your report and in all the other literature I have seen that there is so much optimism that later education can change this early imprint. I'm not quite sure if all researchers have taken into account these early influences. I have certain doubts with regard to this optimism.

LIND: There are studies which are directly related to the problem of xenophobia and ethnocentrism by Adorno and others, which you of course know, which also indicate that in later age this kind of ethnocentricity is very strongly correlated with the level of education. This finding is matched by the more recent moral judgment research. But still I did not want to depict an optimistic picture. Schools could and should do more to foster the individual's moral judgment competency.

VIRT: In your paper you say: "The attempt to localize any particular life experience as being responsible for cognitive moral development was not successful yet". How has this life experience been measured?

LIND: The studies I was thinking of are studies conducted by Jim Rest and some of his students who were asking students to name different experiences in their life which they felt were critical and made them think about their life. They tried to correlate these experiences with measures of moral maturity. But these attempts were not yet very successful. It was not possible to identify any type of critical experience for the differences in moral development.

WEINGARTNER: I want to make two remarks. The first remark is this: I agree that in any ethics there have to be some law-statements or some law-like norms. Without that no ethics is possible. But the question is whether the kind of universalization Kant would require is the correct one, because it has already been pointed out by Schopenhauer and then by Scheler and some others that important individual moral decisions cannot be solved at all with the Categorical Imperative.

The second point: This seems to me to be a mistake in Kant's ethics: Virtue must always be difficult and every inclination to facilitate it must be excluded from virtue. The old theory, by 'old' I mean Aristotle and the Scholastics, was that virtue is produced by repeatedly doing good acts that a good habit is developed which facilitates and makes inclined towards good action. But Kant's ethics is such that the action is only good and is even better if there is no inclination involved, so, if it is difficult. Contrary to the old theory, the difficulty in satisfying the *Pflicht* is the essential, and this, I think, is a mistake.

LIND: Well, I am a psychologist and an amateur-philosopher, since researching in the field of moral psychology obviously necessitates to deal with problems of moral philosophy. Kant's ethics in that sense has informed our research of cognitive developmental theory such as Kohlberg and Piaget, yet it is really not sufficient as Kant himself has stated that he has not put up a psychological theory, but this was something what he called 'practical philosophy'. So, only in this sense I use the Categorical Imperative for thinking about and for doing research in moral psychology. (Postscriptum: I disagree with the notion that the Categorical Imperative is an instrument for solving particular moral problems. I like to think of it as a standard against which any solution needs to be measured.)

SCHOLLER: Your findings are very interesting that college students have a higher standard in moral education than noncollege students. I think it is a very important and maybe a cruel statement that this is due to the downbreaking of our family system. Did you research on moral education with regard to numbers of students in classes at college? As far as I am concerned the number is very important and there might be a very great danger to believe we can have better and broader education in morality with just increasing numbers. Next question: How can we transform our findings about curricula in morality from scientific findings into state-laws concerning curricula? And can we really by law enforce moral education?

LIND: I think laws cannot enforce moral development; that would be partly a contradiction in itself, but the proper laws can smooth the path for cognitive development. You are certainly right if you have a mass population in college then there are a lot of difficulties. We have done studies in Konstanz in the *Zentrum für Bildungsforschung* which show that the number of students in a faculty is very decisive, but not in a university. The size of universities does not matter, but the number of students in a department is a problem and surely has to be addressed.

SCHOLLER: I suppose there must exist more research on the interrelationship between a number of students and cognitive morality. I just would like to mention a statement by Freud. He said: 'The only two institutions that were able to handle big masses of population are the Church - the Catholic Church - and the Army'. So, if we have masses then we have the choice to change the school into an army or into a church.

LIND: I think schools and universities have also demonstrated to be able to handle a large number of individuals in an effective way. The special problem of the educational system seems to be that its task is more multifold and diverse and in need of the active participation of all involved. We are currently undertaking a longitudinal study in six German universities. We have just finished the empirical research and we have 2.000 students collected according to sex, to subject, but also to the number of students in a faculty. Our findings are to show what effect is actually there. Within the next one or two years we'll certainly have report on this.

FUCHS: Education and moral competency in democratic society:

Why do you relate the question of moral competency to democratic society? Second: You describe moral competency with
cognitive moral development. 'Cognitive' has to do with contents. But afterwards you said also, we have to foster judg-
ment-competency, ability. Do you insist more on contents of
moral education, or do you insist more on preparing people to
have a competency in making moral judgments?

LIND: I conceive this to be a crucial question of clarification.
Indeed, I'm considering cognitive not as content, but as a process, as an organization of thought.

Your first question: Why is it that I put such a heavy emphasis
on the relation between individual moral competency and democratic society? Well, in a democratic society I feel it's more
obvious, since the power should be derived from the individual. The individual's competency to make judgments is crucial for the well-being, for the functioning of a democratic society. Of course, you could say this would be more important
and more decisive in non-democratic societies.

WREN: I'm wondering if there is any easy distinction that
Dr. Lind has between moral education and moral indoctrination,
where by 'moral education' I mean something good and by
'moral indoctrination' I mean something bad.

A second question which I have concerns the following apparent paradox: It would seem that Dr. Lind has discovered a
linear relationship between cognitive sophistication as developed through the education process and competency for living
in a democratic society. But it occurs to me that there is an
optimal mix of individualism and conformism as far as having a
well-integrated, well-functioning, happy, humane society is
concerned. The optimum mix of individualism and conformism
may not be a particularly high level of moral functioning. In
Kohlberg's terms: It may very well be that the best societies are
dominated by Stage-3- and Stage-4-conventional-moral-judg-
ment-kinds of people. Now, if it proved to be the case that
society is best furthered by people who are at only a relatively
high stage of moral development, then we would not want them
to be too well developed. But with this we have the paradox that
this close, almost linear relationship between cognitive sophist-

ication and competency for living in a democratic society breaks down at the higher levels of moral autonomy. This question may include my first question on the difference between moral education and moral indoctrination. I am sorry these are such horrible questions!!

LIND: It's not only a horrible question, it's also a question I ever liked to ask Prof. Kohlberg. I may skip it after I have answered your first question. The difference between moral indoctrination and moral education in the cognitive developmental sense: I think everybody is aware of the difference and it is intuitively appealing and one can give examples. But it is indeed very difficult to conceptualize the difference precisely and even make it operationalizable in a sense of telling pedagogues what to do and telling researchers how to assess the differences and the different outcomes. Maybe the best indication for non-indoctrinating education is the degree to which students are respected as individuals and take part in non-trivial decision making in school.

KOHLBERG: I might mention in this connection that these cognitive moral stages don't have to be considered specifically from a Kantian endpoint. That becomes only problematic about a definition of Stage 6 which I take to be a Kantian view but that's very problematic. For the earlier stages you could use a utilitarian reality as well as a Kantian reality or even a neo-aristotelian justification for the progression: that's with regard to Professor Weingartner's question. With regard to Professor Wren's question let me say that his first comment about society in the Stages 3 or 4 reminds me that Professor Wren is Plato's philosopher king. We think that's appropriate for the mass of society could be the lower guardian class for social harmony and to restrict Stage 5 or 6 to himself and a few of us (that's only a joke).

On indoctrination I'd like to elaborate a little bit because that's so central to the approach to moral education. I would discriminate indoctrination:
- first in terms of intention,
- second in terms of method,
- third in terms of content.

The first point is *intention* which is respect for the autonomy of the child. The *method* is some appeal to reason. This is done through argumentation among children. The third issue about indoctrination is the *content*. That is, whether in some sense the content can be justified as well without appeal to a special authority.

This takes me to the question of why tie this to democratic society. In America Thomas Jefferson - the author of the *Declaration of Independence* and so on - was the first promulgator of public education in the United States. His main ground for having public education was not so much to teach either literary skills or vocational skills but what he considered to be the necessary characteristics for a citizen of a free and democratic society. This argument that if this was to be a democratic society then all members of this society must be able to be citizens of this democratic society. And that meant for him and for me certainly that a citizen must have a well-developed sense of justice which is what these stages focus upon. That is: A sense of individual rights and the rights of others, the rights which a democratic society is defined to protect and to further; that's the American view.

STROTZKA: I have a general awkward feeling to the whole methodology. A well-developed sense of justice verbally expressed in tests like yours may not always correspond with the real behavior in this sense. There is no doubt a big gap between verbal statements of people and real behavior. Because people, both adolescents and children, are very well aware of what answers we expect them to give and behaving in that way. It's the easiest way to come out and if they are intelligent and highly sophisticated then the answers are coming out much better and easier. They are wonderful moral persons and then they go out and steal the next moped or whatever. I think, research on moral behavior should be based on behavior and not so much on tests, because there is the danger that we are getting an absolutely wrong picture. That's my basic objection against much of the research I have read and heard of.

LIND: I'm reluctant to answer at length because Dr. Higgins is, I think, in her paper alluding on this. As a matter of fact, every

time you do empirical research, you approach a person and you
have all problems that go with that interaction whether you do it
by a questionnaire, by a psycho-analytical interviews, by observation - always you have some problems which are caused
by the very fact that you are doing research. But this is not a
sole objection to research, it's a general problem involved.
HIGGINS: One comment to Tom Wren about individualism and
conformism. At least in democratic societies the people are also
to make the laws and to create the norms and the rules of that
society which seems to me to go beyond conformism. I personally would be happy if everybody would be postconventional. I
don't think it would create a chaotic or unhappy society particularly. To Dr. Strotzka: I hope I will be able to address some
of your doubts in my paper. To Georg: I was interested in your
comment which I agree with that the level of education (college
education) is necessary for consolidated Stage 4-judgment. We
know when we look at the relation of Piagetian formal operation
it also has a necessary but not sufficient relationship to moral
judgment.
WREN: I wonder if you can tell us a little about some other
research that I know you have done on the consistency of moral
judgments and how this consistency is related to other factors of
psycho-social development.
LIND: At the outset of the research at the University of Konstanz actually not Larry Kohlberg's stage-theory but the studies
into the authoritarian personality and also the Frankfurt-study by
Habermas on student politics had motivated us to investigate
into the problem of democratic competency. One of the requirements of living in a democracy should be that you should be
able to carry on a democratic discourse; and you should be able
to revise your opinion in the light of opposing principles. This
ability then was operationalized as consistency of judgment with
regard to moral type principles. That was the point to take in
Larry Kohlberg's stage model and typologize answers and the
judgment-behavior of students. Now, this consistency of judgment with regard to these stage types plays a major role in our
research. So far as our data show this is very much related to

the level of education and seems to be very close to what is
called the cognitive structural aspect of judgment behavior.

FUCHS: I like this observation of Mr. Strotzka. We have not
only to see what people know and how they are able to make
judgments. It is much more important that people be moral! I
distinguish between 'morality' as 'personal morality' and as
'cognitive morality': The person is moral, the attitudes and the
decisions of the person are moral. Distinct from this is the cognitive morality. In my paper I will insist on this distinction. I
will say this second one is only a morality by analogy. Morality in the strict sense is only personal morality. But there is a
relationship between these two, especially in moral education.
The question is whether moral education will give only this
judgment attention or whether education will also give motivation. These are two quite different things, which are,
however, related to one another.

LIND: I'm grateful for your question. I have a straightforward
view on this.

When people fill in our questionnaire where we have presented
a so-called hypothetical dilemma, there is nothing what the person himself is being involved as an actor; but we always observe that people become involved. They read the dilemma of
euthanasia or the Heinz-dilemma; they get excited and become
involved, although they are not an acting person in it. They
defend their opinion and that asset would be their own decision.
So, I have difficulties in drawing a clear distinction between
hypothetical behavior and real behavior; where you observe
their filling in you can hardly tell the difference.

I view this testing behavior as behavior; I get people involved
by telling them a dilemma. Then I ask them to take part in a
discussion where I have some arguments which are favoring the
opinion he has just given me and those which are opposing the
opinion. Now, the opposing arguments are the decisive ones.
Younger kids often refuse to even look at these opposing
principles. They are so upset by the idea that you could want
them to talk about opposing arguments that they reject even
commenting on them. Therefore, the crucial question is: Would
they also accept moral arguments if they were opposing their

action, their decision? This question is what our tests are based on. They probe into the ability of the person to really apply this principle to the decision and not just merely superficially mentioning it.

ZECHA: I'm going back to the essential notions of your paper. Your are talking about general education, formal education and moral education. I would like to ask whether or not 'moral education' is already implied or somehow contained in the notion of general education. If 'general education' implies 'moral education', then that would on a definitional basis support your empirical findings.

LIND: Not so much, I think. What it supports is my claim that general education should foster moral cognitive development as it is implied by the word "general education" : I agree with that. But I would not think that it also implies that moral development actually happens. It implies only that this is an aim of general education. Whether these aims are finally fulfilled or realized is a different question. So, I still think that research that I have reviewed in my paper has given us enormous information.

ZECHA: Do you have a definite idea of these or some aims of general education?

LIND: The general aims of education - I can speak mainly for the university level because I am more acquainted with this - would find still all those aims enumerated which already Wilhelm Humboldt, the founder of the modern German university, has enumerated: promoting critical ability of students, promoting judgment ability and promoting social responsibility of academics, of scientists when applying their knowledge in their profession and in everyday life. These are the three most important and always requested aims which in my view are clearly related to aims of moral education in a cognitive developmental sense.

ZECHA: Thank you very much for this answer. - I now come back to another question that was first asked by Prof. Strotzka that early moral experience has a certain influence on the moral behavior and also moral judgment abilities of children. In your paper you said it is so complex to find out the causing factors of the moral development through such empirical studies. My question is: If that is difficult already, how can you find out the degree to which such early experiences are responsible for the moral development or is school education responsible for the moral development?

LIND: I think there is no way of accounting for the causes in making proportions like 10% cause here and 10% there. Most of these instances which you named are necessary causes that is: You must not leave out any of these. Authors like Bill Damon, Martin Hofmann and Jean Piaget have clearly shown that there is a lot of moral development going on already in childhood, and that parents and peers have a great impact; but the tasks set before an individual in our modern societies are too large that moral competency which is being developed in family would suffice to cope with it. The education in schools and colleges is equally necessary.

KOHLBERG: Just one word about the school point of view. There is a line of educational thought that goes back to Durkheim, John Dewey and so on, which would point to the school as a necessary transition between the family and a large society; this you might call "early conscience". It may be normal in the family that the morality of a large social organization is rather overwhelming to the eighteens or older whoever is now supposed to be a member of a larger social moral order and that the school is an organization which is intermediate between the family which is a primary moral community with close affective bonds and an impersonal societal order with societal goals. This is a particular reason why schools and institutions of higher education have a critical role to play in "democratic education".

VIRT: I have a question about studies in totalitarian regimes, e.g., in Communist states in Eastern Europe. Can you point out an influence of the society and of the institutions of Communist societies, for instance, at the university on students and their moral competency? Could it be that in a society certain values get another weight during the time?

LIND: We have data on moral judgment of students in Poland and Yugoslavia. The problem is interpreting these data. You can characterize these countries in different ways by the governmental system, but also, for example, by the status of development of their higher education system like in Poland. In Western Europe, almost all students of the first generation of higher education have parents who have already had a higher educational training. In Poland and Yugoslavia we have a quite different situation; these people have mostly rural or working class background. Then there is a difference with regard to the impact of the Church in Poland which is incomparable to most Western countries. In Poland the Church is in a way more political than in Western European countries. So, all that comes together. We will have to consider this when interpreting the data.

VIRT: But it seems that Poland and Yugoslavia are exceptions among Communist states.

LIND: In a way, yes; but Poland would clearly consider itself a true and faithful member of the Communist states. Yet each state is in a way particular.

VIRT: The second question: Isn't there a change in the realization of values in a society when people make their decision for one value rather than for another value in conflict situations?

LIND: Yes, I have personal experience. I have friends in East Germany. It's interesting to see people of my age who have been raised in East Germany and never lived in another kind of system, how they cope with the social norms and I think there is a transformation taking place: These people have a high knowledge of the present system and they can use this knowledge to argue within their units. In regard to their value system, they have also developed a high judgment competency. Eventually this will lead to some transformations of the system.

SCHOLLER: I have a comment on our ideal of democracy as a condition of education. We are not questioning our system. We say it is not the best form of government but it's the only one we can live in. But if we go to Third-World-countries (you just mentioned Eastern Europe) and if you have a chance to work there - I was working for three years in Africa - then we suddenly realize our principle is Euro-centric or America-centric. If I refer to Stage 6 of Kohlberg's theory, it's Lockean and

Rousseauan, isn't it? I'm just saying that the individual conscience is formulating values and that we have to educate a person to be able to have this insight and this voice to follow his
own principle. But if you go to Asia, to Africa, we are in quite
different societies where the group is important. If we try educating them to listen to their own conscience, the whole social
system will be endangered and come to a downfall. So, we have
to be careful, we have to accommodate our educational system
to the development of our society, but we cannot say, "It's a
universal rule or principle which can be applied at any time in
any society".

End of discussion.

ANN HIGGINS

THE IDEA OF CONSCIENCE IN HIGH SCHOOL STUDENTS. DEVELOPMENT OF JUDGMENTS OF RESPONSIBILITY IN DEMOCRATIC JUST COMMUNITY PROGRAMS*

Today I want to discuss the idea of judgments of responsibility for moral action as one manifestation of the idea of conscience and to show the influence of certain social environments of institutions on the development of the ability to make judgments of responsibility.

1. CONSCIENCE AS JUDGMENTS OF RESPONSIBILITY

Before I do this, I first want to put the ideas of conscience and guilt into a cognitive developmental perspective in contrast to a Freudian or neopsychoanalytic perspective. The psychoanalytic perspective points to the childs' identification with the parents as central to conscience formation. For them identification has meant the general tendency to take the role of the punishing or criticizing other. This means that in order to criticize or punish themselves after a transgression, children must take the role of the parent toward themselves. Otherwise they would continue to see themselves and the situation as they did when they performed the act. For this self-criticism to be *guilt,* the child must take the role of the parent in a deep internalized sense, regardless of whether the parent knows of the transgression.

This deep, fixed role-taking of identification has been hypothesized as resulting from the need to substitute for an absent or rejecting love object for Freud, and from the need to defend against fear of aggression for Anna Freud.

It is evident that identification is seen as a special or particular form of role-taking. Identification theories have assumed: a) that the child's role-taking of her parents represents a unique and necessary basis for conscience formation rather than one of a number of role-taking relationships; b) that the basic moral ro-

123

G. Zecha and P. Weingartner (eds.), Conscience: An Interdisciplinary View, 123–162.
© *1987 by D. Reidel Publishing Company.*

le-taking tendencies leading to conscience formation are created in early childhood when the child's weakness can create overwhelmingly strong tendencies to love, fear and respect and lead to introjecting the parents and their prescriptions; and c) that basic role-taking of parents leads to direct introjection and copying of fixed parental standards rather than being a step in the development of general role-taking capacities.

In contrast developmental theory holds that participation in all social groups, including certainly the family, and the experiences of role-taking others in social groups is necessary for moral judgment development and conscience formation. We would say that parents are important in the moral development of children because positive and affectional relations to others are generally conducive to ego-development and to role-taking and acceptance of social standards rather than that parental identification provides a unique and direct basis for conscience formation.

Projective measures of internal guilt show the same general age trends and social correlates as measures of moral judgment in the school years. I will give an example of a study illustrating one aspect of this relationship. Generally delinquents tend to reason at moral Stage 2, the preconventional level. Ruma and Mosher (1967) compared delinquents reasoning at moral Stage 2 with delinquents reasoning at moral Stage 3, the conventional level. The delinquents were asked how they felt and thought about their own crimes or misbehavior. They were also given a projective (picture stories) measure of guilt. Only the delinquents reasoning at Stage 3 expressed guilt and remorse about their crimes and showed guilt on the projective measure. The delinquents reasoning at Stage 2 showed no evidence of guilt.

This and other studies show that the idea and expression of guilt comes with conventional thinking, that is, when one sees himself as having social roles and accepting social norms and laws. However, feelings and expressions of guilt are only a part of what we mean when we speak of conscience. Another aspect of conscience seems to be the commitment to act morally.

Our idea of judgments of responsibility captures both of these aspects. Judgments of responsibility are backward-looking, that is, they are judgments in which the person holds herself accountable for past actions or failures to act and assigns guilt, blame or praise to the self.

Judgments of responsibility are forward-looking as well; they are judgments about the person's commitment to action, that is, that the person *will* act in ways she has decided are morally right.

In our work we operationalize this idea of a responsibility judgment as having at least one of the following characteristics:

1. a consideration of meeting the other's need or enhancing her welfare, whether or not it rests on a deontic claim;
2. a consideration of the involvement or implication of the self in the action or in the consequences to the other;
3. a consideration of personal moral worth of the self and also of others as the basis for performing a moral action or for having failed to do so (making aretaic judgments);

lastly,

4. a consideration of the intrinsic value of social relationships and community or recognition of the bond of humanity as the basis for performing a moral action.

Thus judgments of responsibility are one manifestation of the idea of conscience. Our work in the schools has shown that direct participation in the governance of the school with the role-taking that such a participation demands leads to the development and use of responsibility judgments as well as to moral judgment development generally.

Direct participation in the governance of the school not only aids individual development, at the same time student discussions, creating their own rules, and handling the misbehavior of each other leads to the creation of a strong feeling or sense of community - to what we term a positive moral atmosphere.

It is this positive moral atmosphere that results from the active participation in the life of the school that seems to be a context or environment in which students can exercise their conscience, that is, to feel responsible and to be responsible for doing what they have agreed to or think is morally right or good.

2. A DESCRIPTION OF THE DEMOCRATIC SCHOOL INTERVENTION

Before going into more detail, I will now describe the schools in this project. Three alternative democratic high schools using the just community idea of education and their companion traditional high schools in each town were studied. The schools varied in their representation of upper middle, middle, working and lower class populations. Two pairs of schools were racially and ethnically mixed and one pair was white, both Jewish and Christian. The traditional high schools are typical, large American high schools.

The three democratic schools covered the grades 9 or 10 to 12 and each was comprised of about 70-100 students and 5 to 7 teachers. One program is self-contained while students in the other two democratic programs take some of their courses in the regular high school from teachers not affiliated with the democratic program.

The core of any just community program is its system of governance and participation which occur in a weekly one and a half to two-hour community meeting. Each person, both teacher and student, has one vote. Prior to this meeting small groups of 10 students and a teacher meet to decide upon proposals for rules or for solving issues through moral discussion. In both community meetings and small groups the teachers ideally act as advocates or speak for the growth and welfare of the democratic school as a whole as well as giving their own opinions and helping students to formulate theirs.

The third primary institution is a fairness of discipline committee, a group of several students and two or three teachers that hears cases of rule violations or misbehaviors and decides, again through moral discussion, upon fair punishments or restitutions which often include finding some way to offer increased support to the students in trouble.

3. HYPOTHESES ABOUT THE INFLUENCE OF THE DEMOCRATIC SCHOOL AND ITS MORAL ATMOSPHERE UPON THE DEVELOPMENT OF JUDGMENTS OF RESPONSIBILITY

We hypothesized that the democratic school students would both make more responsibility judgments and make them at a higher stage than the regular school comparison group of students. There were two reasons we expected this. First participatory democracy puts socio-moral decisions in the hands of the students giving them a greater sense of responsibility for school related actions. Second participatory democracy, we believed, helps to create a sense of the school as a caring community. Students would develop shared or collective norms of helping, of trust, and of active participation on behalf of the group, norms supported by a sense of community or of a valued sense of group solidarity and cohesion. Students' judgments of responsibility, we believed, would derive from their perception of the moral atmosphere of the school, that is, by their perception of the school norms and its valuing of community.

One theoretical interest lay in developing concepts and measures which would bridge moral psychology and sociology. According to Durkheim's *Moral Education,* the classroom or school group creates collective norms and attachments to the group which are group phenomena *sui generis.* We agree with him. We thought a Stage 3 collective norm is not the same thing as an average of individual stage judgments at Stage 3. In a schoolpromoting moral development, collective norms would be formulated at a stage which was a leading edge for the group and adapting to these norms would stimulate those students whose individual stage was lower to grow. (Kohlberg, 1980, 1981, Power, 1979).

Still more basically we thought by building collective norms and ideas of community at a higher stage we would promote morally better student action. Moral action usually takes place in a social or group context and that context usually has a profound influence on the moral decision making of individuals. Individual moral decisions in real life are almost always made in the context of group norms of group decision-making processes.

Moreover, individual moral action is often a function of these norms or processes. For example, in the massacre at My Lai, individual American soldiers murdered noncombatant women and children. They did so not primarily because, as individuals, their moral judgment that the action was morally right was immature nor because, as individuals, they were "sick" in some sense, but because they participated in what was essentially a group action taken on the basis of group norms. The moral choice made by each individual soldier who pulled the trigger was embedded in the larger institutional context of the army and its decision-making procedures. Their decisions were dependent in large part upon a collectively shared definition of the situation and of what should be done about it. In short, the My Lai massacre was more a function of the group "moral atmosphere" that prevailed in the place at that time than of the stage of moral development of the individuals present. The realization of the important role that moral atmosphere or group norms play in individual moral action has led us to hypothesize that in many cases the best approach to moral education is one that attempts to reform the moral atmosphere in which individual decisions are made. This is the hypothesis that has guided our interventions and research in the schools and prisons.

With this background in mind, I will describe our methods and results by quoting from four prototypical members of four of the six schools. These students classical moral judgment scores are the same as the averages for their groups. Jay is a student in the regular Brookline High School; Sarah in a democratic alternative school in Brookline called the School-Within-A-School (SWS); Rob is a student in the regular Cambridge High School, and Betsy is a student in the democratic alternative school called the Cluster School in the Cambridge High School.

4. ANALYZING RESPONSIBILITY JUDGMENTS OF DEMOCRATIC ALTERNATIVE SCHOOL STUDENTS AS COMPARED TO THOSE OF TRADITIONAL HIGH SCHOOL STUDENTS

4.1 *Jay: Judgments of Responsibility with an Individual Focus*

The first case, Jay is a tenth grader in the regular Brookline High School, a school composed primarily of adolescents from the middle and professional classes. Most of the students in this school are white and most are either Jewish or Irish-Catholic ethnically. Of the 10% minority, most of the Blacks are bused to the high school.

On the classical hypothetical moral dilemmas Jay was Stage 3/4. This transitional stage was the median stage for the regular Brookline High School control sample.

An example of Jay's Stage 3/4 reasoning is his response to the standard dilemma which asks whether a girl should reveal a confidence about her sister's disobedience to the mother. The interviewer asks:

Should Louise, the older sister, tell their mother that Judy had lied about the money or should she keep quiet?

Jay says, "Keep quiet. Lying is involved but a promise should be kept, the promise should be honored more."

Why should a promise be kept?

"Because you expect a person will keep their word and you respect them for that. Relationships won't happen without trust and respect."

Is it important to keep a promise to someone you don't know well and probably won't see again?

"Yes, because I would want them to do the same for me." In this and the other classical dilemmas it is clear that Jay has a sense of justice obligating him to keep contract and trusts even to unrelated strangers based on Golden Rule reciprocity. His sense of obligation to an unrelated stranger is very different in our Practical School Dilemma 1, the Caring Dilemma (see Table 1). In answering this dilemma, Jay equates obligation with responsibility and concludes that he is not responsible to or for the stranger.

TABLE 1

The Practical School Dilemmas

1. CARING DILEMMA

The college Harry applied to had scheduled an interview with him for the coming Saturday morning at 9:00 a.m. Since the college was 40 miles away from Harry's town and Harry had no way of getting there, his guidance counselor agreed to drive him. The Friday before the interview the guidance counselor told Harry that his car had broken down and was in the repair shop until Monday. He said he felt badly but there was no way he could drive him to his interview. He still wanted to help him out so he went to Harry's homeroom and he asked the students if there was anyone who could drive Harry to the college. No one volunteered to drive him. A lot of students in the class think Harry shows off and talks too much and don't like him. The homeroom teacher says he has to take his children to the dentist at that time. Some students say they can't use the family car, others work, some don't have their licenses. One student, Billy, knows he can use his family car but he wonders whether he should do something for Harry when the few students in class who know him best say they are busy or just can't do it. Besides, he would have to get up really early on a Saturday morning which is the only morning during the week he can sleep late.

1. *Should Billy volunteer to drive Harry to the college?*

2. *Why or why not?*

Should Billy volunteer to drive Harry to college?
"I don't think he has any obligation. If I was in his place, and I didn't know the kids too well, if I wanted to sleep late, I don't feel that it is my responsibility to go drive somebody to their interview, it is up to them, they are responsible. If I were going there, if I had an interview there at the same time, sure I would. But if I had the opportunity to sleep late and didn't know the kid at all, I wouldn't."

Why is it not a responsibility?
"It's not really that you are obligated to a person because you are more responsible to yourself and your actions. I know I have been through this year, a whole mess of garbage with my friends about driving around, since I got my license. People seem to think as long as you have a car they have a ride, and in my opinion it doesn't operate that way. If I wanted to give him a ride, I will give him a ride, if I am going there and they want to go there. It is my car and I am the one who is driving and I don't see why I should give him a ride."

You think you shouldn't give them a ride?
"It doesn't mean I shouldn't give them a ride, but if I don't know them well enough, I think just out of protection for myself and my property, I wouldn't. I think people may say that being responsible to yourself is more important than other people. I think there is an extent where you put yourself first. And when you believe in putting yourself first, like I do, or try to, at least I don't feel I should be obligated to do somebody else's work, especially if I don't know them, I don't think I should give them a ride."

Jay helps us to understand that there are two kinds of judgments, deontic judgments of duty and judgments of responsibility can be individual or group focussed. Jay's introduction of *his* idea of responsibility into the Caring Dilemma helps us make sense of the discrepancy between the moral stage or level of his response to that dilemma and his response to the classical moral dilemmas.

In the Caring Dilemma Jay understands well the Stage 3 niceness of helping Harry. But he makes a "Stage 2/3" judgment of individualistic responsibility in making his decision. A judgment of responsibility as Carol Gilligan has also pointed out depends upon the positing of a particular social bond or relationship as necessary. Jay posits a relationship of friendship, but defines it in "Stage 2/3 reciprocity" terms. He says, "I think it really depends on the relationship of a person to the person who needs a ride. If they are good friends I don't think he has an obligation. I think it would be nice and I know if it was my friend, if it was

TABLE 2

Criteria for Judgments of Responsibility and Stages of Responsibility Judgments

A. Judgments of responsibility go beyond deontic judgments in one of four ways:

1. Judgments which consider the needs and welfare of the other as an individual where the other's welfare seems to be a matter of a right or claim the other has or where it is a matter of not harming the other's welfare is a deontic concern. Judgments which consider filling the other's need when it is not based on a right or claim or where it is a matter of enhancing his welfare not only preventing harm is a responsibility concern.

2. Judgments of responsibility consciously consider the involvement and implication of the self in the action or in the welfare consequences to the other.

3. Judgments of personal moral worth (aretaic) of the kind of self the actor wants to be (perfecting character) or would be if he failed to perform the action (judgments of blame, guilt, loss of integrity) are judgments of responsibility when explicitly used as a basis for action rather than rights and/or obligations.

4. Judgments that use an intrinsic valuing of social relationships such as friendship or relationships of community as justification for performing a moral action are judgments of responsibility.

B. Stages of Responsibility Judgments:

Stage 1 -   Responsibility and obligation are seen as being the same. The person feels compelled to fulfil the commands of superiors, authority figures or the rules given by them.

Stage 2 -   Responsibility is differentiated from obligation from this stage onward. The person is responsible only to and for himself, his welfare, property, and goals.

Stage 2/3 - There is a recognition that everyone is responsible to and for themselves, their welfare, property, and goals. Persons who are irresponsible or careless lose some of the right to have themselves and their welfare, etc., respected. For example, being careless mitigates the right to have one's property respected as well as justifying a lessended concern for the person's welfare.

Stage 3 -   Responsibility for the self is to do the "good" thing, to live up to generally known and accepted standards of a "good person". Responsibility to others is limited to those with whom one has a personal relationship and is defined as meeting their needs or promoting their welfare.

Stage 3/4 - Responsibility is seen more as a process for maintaining and enhancing feelings of closeness and affection in personal relationships. Being irresponsible is defined as "hurting the other's feelings" within a relationship and is considered a valid basis for a lessened concern of the other's welfare.

Stage 4 -   Responsibility is seen as a mutually binding set of feelings and agreements among people in relationship, groups or communities. Being responsible for the self means one must act out of dependability, trustworthiness and loyalty regardless of fluctuating feelings among people. Irresponsibility on the part of those people within the same group does not mitigate concern for their welfare or rights by other group members.

an important interview he would do the same for me, then I would do it."

A brief summary of our definitions of stages in judgments of responsibility is given in Table 2.

We may note that responsibility judgments are a species of practical judgment, they are not readily elicited by our classical moral dilemmas which more often elicit deontic judgments. Jay speedily falls into psychological or "would" language in explaining his idea of responsibility in the Caring Dilemma. We see responsibility language as at the intersection between prescriptive moral structures and the descriptive language of an acting self.

Having said this, the question remains as to whether Jay's Stage 2|3 response to the Caring Dilemma is due to his practical or real life moral judgment being lower than his classical moral judgment or whether it is because his reponsibility judgments are lower than his deontic judgments. In our opinion it is the latter case. We hypothesized that the stage development of judgments of responsibility lags behind deontic judgment if there is a discrepancy between the two. In the Caring Dilemma Jay makes only a judgment of responsibility. We find Jay is consistently lower stage in his judgments of responsibility than in the deontic judgments he makes - which we see as we move from a caring situation to a justice situation, stealing (See Table 3 for the Stealing Dilemma) in which he makes both types of judgment.

In responding to the practical school dilemma of stealing, Jay says, "I would leave the money there because I respect people's property because I expect them to do that to my property. I know it is a big temptation but it's her money, she earned it however way she did. Besides its being against the law, it's also respect of a person's property and you don't have any right to take it just because you want it. Otherwise we would have a pretty sick society with no laws and with chaos."

Jay's use of deontic justice reasoning in this response is indicated by his use of rights, of the Golden Rule and of the need to maintain social order. We score this as deontic Stage 3/4 consistent with his classical moral judgment stage.

Jay's Stage 2/3 responsibility reasoning comes out in astealing situation in his response to the dilemma in Table 4 about responsibility for restitution to Mary, the victim of the theft. In reply to the idea of the whole class chipping in to help Mary because the thief is unknown, he says, "No, because there

TABLE 3

2. STEALING DILEMMA

When Mary arrived at her history class, she notices that although the students were all there the teacher had not arrived. She sat down for a few seconds but decided to chat with a few of her friends in the hall until her teacher came. She opened her pocketbook, pulled out a letter she wanted to show her friends and ran out of the classroom, leaving her pocketbook unsnapped and lying on her desk. Tom, a student in the class looks into Mary's pocketbook and sees a twenty dollar bill. He thinks about taking the twenty dollar bill from her pocketbook.

1. *What do you think a student like Tom would do in a situation like this? Why?*

2. *Should Mary have been trusting like that in this situation or should she have been more careful?*

TABLE 4

3. RESTITUTION DILEMMA

Tom took the money. When Mary returns to the classroom she looks into her pocketbook and notices the twenty dollar bill is missing. She goes to the teacher and tells what happened. The teacher asks the person to return the money but no one does. Zeke, a friend of Tom's, saw him take the money.

1. *Should Zeke persuade Tom to return the money? Why?*

2. *If Zeke tries to persuade Tom to restitute and Tom will not, should Zeke report Tom to the teacher?*

3. *If no one in the class admits to taking the money or knowing who did it, what should the teacher do? Why?*

4. *Would there be a general feeling or an expectation in your school that everyone should chip in? Are people supposed to chip in?*

5. *Would you expect all members of your school to chip in? Would you feel that any member of your school, because s/he is a member of your school should chip in? Why?*

are two reasons. One because it was Mary's fault or lack of responsibility by leaving her purse out. She was too trusting. The second thing is why should I pay for what somebody else did? Why should I get involved?" Jay also feels other students would not want to chip in. He says, "The same thing, why should they pay for what other people are doing, or other people's lack of responsibility that it got stolen."

Jay's low Stage 2/3 judgments of responsibility compared to his higher Stage 3/4 judgments of justice is closely connected to his perception of the moral atmosphere of the high school. According to Jay the high school lacks collective norms for caring and responsibility and lacks a sense of community. He is asked on Dilemma 1, "Should the school have some kind of agreement or understanding that someone should help out someone else?". In response he says, "I think this school really lacks that. It lacks in togetherness, I think. Nobody really takes pride in the school except a few who are good students or very good athletes. Where people don't take pride in something, go out of their way to help each other, the community doesn't really benefit. It doesn't benefit. It doesn't promote the welfare of the school. Kids go vandalize a lot. There is no sense of caring, helping each other."

Jay thus tells us that there are no collective norms of helping and little sense of community in his school. He responds in a similar way on the dilemma about stealing. When asked, *"Would you express your disapproval and try to find out who took*

Mary's money?" , Jay says, "It depends. I wouldn't go much out of my way, again it's her responsibility... In school people care too much for themselves and they wouldn't really go out of their way to do something. We have a lot of things stolen from lockers. Nothing seems to get done about it. In that sense I guess nobody really cares. There is a lack of trust or caring about other people's property in this school."

4.2 *The Case of Sarah: Judgments of Responsibility with a Collective Focus*

In contrast to Jay let us take another tenth grader from the Brookline High School, in this case a democratic alternative school member from School-Within-A-School, Sarah. Sarah was scored Stage 3/4 on the classical moral dilemmas as was Jay. In contrast to him, she also scored Stage 3/4 on the responsibility reasoning. On the practical school dilemmas, her responses to the Caring Dilemma are quite different than Jay's.
What do you think Harry should do?
She says: "I think he should drive him. [*Why* ?] Even if he doesn't like him, he is a classmate of his and he is the only one who is able to help him."
But Billy wants to sleep late.
"Right, but he is not losing anything by it, he is losing sleep by it, but that is only one day of the week. But it is for the benefit of his classmate, it is sort of his responsibility somehow."
What would you do in this situation?
"I would feel that I had a moral obligation to him, but I don't know that I actually would. I would think of myself first. I might be selfish, but I would realize that I would feel guilty if I didn't do it. I can't say for sure that I would. But I would feel that I had an obligation to do it."

Sarah feels that there is a responsibility to help in a case like Harry's. Her judgment of responsibility considers filling Harry's need in a way that doesn't rest on the idea that he has a claim or right which Billy has an obligation or duty to respond to. She makes it clear that the moral obligation to help Harry arises out of his need alone and the bond of being classmates and should be responded to by the person who can help in the situation. Second, in considering what she would do in the situation, she says if she wouldn't help then she would feel guilty. This personal judgment of her moral worth tells us that for Sarah action is a necessary part of her definition of moral responsibilities. Sarah's judgments of responsibility are Stage 3/4.

On the dilemma about stealing (Table 3), Sarah focusses her concern on the relational norms of trust.

Should your school have an agreement or understanding about trust?

She says: "Yah, I think we do have an agreement about trust. It should be an agreement that people respect everyone else's property."

Why is that important?

"Because if you can't leave things around and trust people, then you can't really get to know them. You can't get to know a person you don't trust or relate to them and care about them, if you don't trust them and they don't trust you."

On the Stealing Dilemma, Jay talks about property rights and the need to respect property rights to prevent chaos in society and for the justice of keeping what one has earned. He feels that trust as a value is separate from upholding property rights. Sarah, on the other hand, is primarily concerned about trust and considers trust as a valid basis of upholding or respecting other people's property rights. Sarah relates the idea of respect or others' property to the larger issue of maintaining trust in a community. In these terms Sarah's response is primarily a responsibility judgment at Stage 3/4 rather than a deontic judgment.

Sarah's responsibility reasoning is based on a conception of her school as a community. Sarah says about caring for others in school:

Why should people help out?

"Because they care about other people, but you can't say to someone, care about this person, but they should do it out of reasons of caring for other people and in that, I really think it should be because they care about other people, but also because they care about the community."

So you think your school should have an agreement that members of the community should help out other people?
"Not a written agreement, you can't have a written law of respect. It comes out of the atmosphere of the community. I think in SWS there is a lot more caring atmosphere and people really care about each other a lot more than in a bigger, unpersonal school."

Speaking as a member of the democratic school Sarah prescribes a strongly held collective norm of caring based on intrinsically valuing the community, that is, she supports the norm of caring out of concern for the community itself.

We see that Sarah has a Stage 3/4 conception of community. She tells us that the collective norm of caring arises out of the "atmosphere of the community and the idea that members should care about the community as well as each other." We understand this to be a transitional idea to a Stage 4 conception of community as a whole greater than the sum of its parts.

On the Stealing Dilemma Sarah also refers to a collective norm, that there is an agreement about trust. She again grounds this in a strong sense of community. She says that "in a community you should be able to trust people and they should be able to trust you and you should be able to have faith in other people in your community. I have faith in people in SWS. People are afraid of stealing by people in the regular school, but here I have pretty much a feeling of faithfulness in people of not taking things. Because I know them and because I trust them."

The differences between the democratic alternative school and the regular high school are more magnified in the Cambridge High School than in the Brookline High School. To illustrate the differences between the two groups in Cambridge I will contrast Betsy, a tenth grade student in the Cluster School, the democratic just community school, and Rob, a tenth grader in the regular high school. Both Betsy and Rob were also scored Stage 3/4 on the hypothetical classical moral dilemmas. These students are onehalf stage higher on individual moral judgment than the median of their groups which were Stage 3. Both Betsy and Rob are middle class white students in schools where at least half of the students are working class. Ethnically Cambridge High School was 25% Black and 10% Hispanic and other minorities; Cluster School was half Black and half White in 1978.

4.3 The Cases of Betsy and Rob: The Influence of the Moral Atmosphere on Judgments of Responsibility

In answer to why people in her school should help out on the Caring Dilemma, Betsy says: "Yes, they should because Cluster is a community. Because you have a responsibility to the kids in this school, even if you don't like them all that much, you are in school and you're with them every day, you know, you are supposed to think of them as part of the school and part of the community, so you should do it."

Betsy clearly expresses the idea of intrinsically valuing the community in her idea that the school is a community which expects members to help each other because they are all members of the same group. This implies an awareness and valuing of community which creates moral obligation and norms. The interviewer asks:

What does it mean? It sounds like a cliche when you say it, we are a community so we are supposed to help each other?

Betsy responds: "Because everyone is supposed to be one, it is our school, it is not a school that all these separate people go to that don't care about each other."

Betsy's response indicates three aspects of a high level of community valuing. First is the idea that a community implies a strong degree of unity, a oneness, or solidarity. Second, it expresses the idea of personal identification with one group and its objectives, "it's our school". Third is the feature that membership in the group means mutual caring about one another as group members. She also clearly indicates the existence of a shared or collective norm of helping. She says, "Anyone who is in Cluster knows they should help out... there is the general feeling and everyone knows that."

Should someone help out?

"Yes, they should because Cluster School is a community. Because you have a responsibility to the kids in this school. You are supposed to think of them as part of the school and part of the community, so you should do it."

Betsy's response depicts a group with a highly collective norm. Her statement exemplifies the three aspects of a high level on collectiveness for the helping norm. When Betsy says "you are supposed to", she is speaking as one member of a collective to other members of the collective and she is representing the point of view of the group as a whole. This aspect of her response we call the *speaker's perspective,* a perspective ranging from speaking from the standpoint of oneself as an individual to speaking from the standpoint of we - the other members of the group. Betsy's command, "You have a responsibility to the kids in this school", doesn't come from her as an individual, but there is a statement from the perspective of the group and representative of the collective norm. The speaker perspective defines the group *for* whom the subject is speaking or representing. The second aspect, the *group constituency,* defines the group membership of the persons *to* whom the person is speaking or prescribing a rule or action. In this example it is clear to whom Betsy is speaking; she is prescribing *to* the members of the Cluster School.

The third aspect is that a collective *norm is stated prescriptively* in terms of an obligation. We distinguish norms which are prescriptive from norms which are aggregate or stated as descriptive of the behavior of individuals or groups. Aggregate norms reflect a "statistical tendency" rather than a clearly shared idea of obligation.

In contrast to Betsy, Rob, a student of the regular Cambridge High School, does not see a shared valuing of a community, and it is not even clear whether he sees the school as a valued organization serving learning and other goals. He individually values the school but others do not. "I don't consider this school a community. Too many people hold grudges against each other, because maybe they look different or act different. Or some kids come to school to be with their friends or to be stoned, (some marijuana) and some kids come to do

work. Like the kids who smoke marijuana might stand around
and see someone with a lot of books walk by and laugh. But
they won't laugh when graduation comes. No, most people
think of themselves, really."

*How do you think thinking about the community would affect
that?*

"If they did think about it, I don't really know, because I don't
know if they ever did, like I said only people in committees and
stuff would think about it and talk about it, and those would be
a small minority."

*In handling issues about respecting other people's property and
trusting other people, do you think Cambridge High School is
really a community?*

"Well, not really, because in a way like we own this school and
a lot of kids mess it up. Like write on the walls, there is no need
for that, there is paper to write on. I don't know, some people
do and some people don't. I don't really know the percentage."

These comments indicate that Rob as an individual attaches
some value to the school as an organization and says, "In a way
like we own this school and a lot of kids mess it up." He feels
some ownership of the school and finds vandalism or injury to
it offensive. He also values its major function, academic
learning, even though he sees many other students do not.
Thus, there is a contrast between his individual valuing of the
school as an organization and his perception of the attitudes of
most of the students in this regard. Moreover, Rob does not
perceive any shared norm of helping. He believes that it would
be a good thing to have a shared norm to help but he doesn't
believe it exists. When asked if his school should have a shared
agreement to help out, he says: "Yah, right. Like it is not a law,
but everybody knows that it is good to help someone out. But
people just don't care about anybody else."

Going on the theme of a lack of a sense of community and
caring at the high school he comments that: "Seventy-five
percent of them wouldn't care."

Why?

"They are worried about their own problems probably."

Rob himself as an individual holds a norm of helping but he is conspicuously aware of the discrepancy between his individual norm of helping and the absence of any collective norm of helping.

What should the agreement be and why should it be such an agreement?

"It's really - it should be an agreement with yourself, you know. It is like, I have strong feelings toward other people. I don't like to think bad things and I never say anything bad about anybody, and it is more of an agreement with yourself than with anybody, you couldn't make an agreement with somebody about something like this."

Not only is Rob aware of the discrepancy between his individual norm of helping and the lack of any collective norm, but also his response indicates that he thinks it is impossible to develop shared moral norms on issues such as helping.

The statements by Rob that "I just believe in helping people" and "it should be an agreement with yourself" demonstrate clearly that he is speaking only for himself rather than from a "we perspective" as is involved when students speak about a collective norm. His responses indicate that his idea that one should help is not defined in terms of a specific group, like members of the school, who should follow the norm and be the persons toward whom help is directed. He sees that any "good person" would hold this norm for him or herself. His norm does not define a group constituency, a bounded group of people where responsibilities are felt toward one another. For Rob the idea of helping is not obligatory or prescriptive but is a positive value that is based on a concern or caring of others. When this concern is absent, he sees no possibility for expecting someone to help out another person. Accordingly, Rob's conception of the norm of helping is non-prescriptive.

While Rob does not see a positive collective norm of helping, he does perceive a counter-norm (a norm going against helping) in this situation which makes helping an unpopular student disapproved of by the peer group.

What would you do?

"I would wait till after class, I would keep it quiet so nobody might know about it, and then I could help the kid. Then nobody would say anything to me, because they would not know about it."

Rob's feeling that he would help but in a way so that others didn't know about it indicates he is concerned about disapproval for helping presumably because of the existence of a peer group norm which makes it "uncool" to associate with or aid an unpopular student.

For example, when Rob says he would be secretive about helping he is responding to his daily observation that students do not help their unpopular classmates. The consistency of his observation shows both Rob and ourselves that there exists an *aggregate* descriptive counter-norm. This aggregate norm of not helping influences Rob's articulation of the norm for helping. Explicit shared agreements in a group have obligatory force whereas the power of statistical or "average" behaviors do not. Aggregate norms arise out of a concern to fit into the average behavioral pattern of one's peers.

Another dimension in the perception of school norms is the phase of commitment to upholding the norm. The phase of the norm came to be defined when we were observing Cluster School's community meetings in terms of the development of its norms over time.

In our observations of the development of collective norms from meeting to meeting and from year to year in the Cluster School, we identified this dimension of phase of commitment to an institutionalization of the norm which could be distinguished from whether the norm is held collectively. The evolution of collective norms seems to go through distinct phases from the time they are first proposed to the time people are expected to act consistently with them to the time when sanctions are expected to be given for any violations.

On the Caring Dilemma Betsy says that the Cluster School is committed to its collective norms of helping at a strong phase. She says, "They would disapprove ... I think the kids would be very mad at him if he didn't do it. They would have said something (to Billy)... because of why it's important to do it (that is, to help) and why they would complain at him for not doing it."

On the same idea of caring and helping, Rob says, "You couldn't make an agreement with somebody about something like that." When he was asked, *Should there be an agreement?*, he said, "It wouldn't get followed anyway". These statements tell us three things; that there is no existing agreement in the Cambridge High School to help, there is not even a shared ideal of helping, and that Rob feels it would be unrealistic to propose such an ideal or an agreement to others.

The remaining concepts in analyzing "moral atmosphere" using individual interview material are the stage of the representation of the collective norm and the stage of the representation of community valuing.

We define the stage of representation of the collective norm as the stage the individual uses to explain how most people in the school understand the meaning of the particular norm. Betsy represents the stage of Cluster School's collective norm of caring as being 3/4. She says, "This school is supposed to be a community. Because you have a responsibility to the kids in this school, even if you don't like them all that much, you are in school and you are with them everyday, you know, you are supposed to think of them as part of the school and part of the community, so you should do it." Furthermore, Betsy understands the school community in a transitional 3/4 sense, as being an entity separate from the individuals that make it up. Betsy's response illustrates that both the norms of caring and the value of community can be stage scored.

While we distinguish for analytical purposes an individual's stage of the collective norm and the stage of the community value, on any particular school dilemma these are almost always the same.

As we discussed earlier, speaker perspective is important in defining how collective a group norm is. It is equally important in determining what responses in an interview are stageable representations of the collective norm rather than simply the individual's own stage of reasoning. The speaker's perspective defines *for* whom the subject is speaking or who is being representing. Thus the speaker's perspective helps to identify the interview material that is representative of the collective norm. When a student, like Betsy, speaks *to* the group on *behalf* of the group and does so prescriptively, we identify and use that material as indicative of the collective norm. Material isolated in this way, furthermore, generally has clear stageable characteristics. In other words, the way we assess the structure or stage of the collective reasoning is parallel to the way we assess the structure or stage of an individual's reasoning.

After Betsy prescribed that Cluster School members should uphold their own norm of caring, she then states an exception when she as an individual would not uphold this norm. She says, "The only way I would say he shouldn't help him is if he was a creep and he really did something rotten to him in the past, if he showed he didn't care about Billy or anyone else, then I wouldn't help him out." In this statement Betsy is prescribing only for herself; she is specifying for herself the conditions and reasons for which she would not uphold the norm under certain circumstances. Her individual reasoning in this case is Stage 3. She feels no obligation to help someone who has in the past violated the group's shared expectations of caring.

Contrasting Rob's interview with Betsy's, we know that on the Caring Dilemma, there is no collective stage of a norm of helping in the Cambridge High School. However, remembering that Rob did report an aggregate counter-norm in his school, one that said it's "uncool" to be seen helping an "unpopular" student, he represents it as being known and accepted by most students and at a strong phase; he believes other students would actually say he shouldn't help if they saw him doing it. Although assigning a stage to counter-norms is ambiguous since they are descriptions of behavior often times given without any justification, we feel we can assign guess stage scores. In this case Rob is representing a counter-norm of not helping that seems to be Stage 2 or 2/3. The important point is that we and Rob agree that it is clearly a lower stage than his own individual norm of care, which is Stage 3. Rob's representation of the Stage of community valuing is also 2 or 2/3. He describes the school as an institution which is legitimately used by some for their own academic ends and abused by others for arbitrary and personal reasons.

5. SUMMARY OF RESEARCH RESULTS

The differences between Sarah and Jay, and Betsy and Rob are prototypical of the differences between the democratic alternative school students and the comparison groups of students attending the traditional high schools in terms of making judgments of responsibility and in their prescriptions of the moral atmospheres of their schools. The proportion of students in the democratic schools who chose the prosocial action for themselves on the dilemmas was 78 - 85%. The proportion of students in the comparison groups who chose for themselves the prosocial action was exactly the same, 75 - 88%. However, when the students were asked to predict what choices their peers would make, 56 to 59% of the democratic school students thought their peers would perform the prosocial action (e.g., driving Harry to his interview on a Saturday morning) in contrast to only 27 to 35% of the students predicting the same for their peers in the traditional high schools.

The disparity between answering for themselves and for their peers is interesting. While the majority of regular high school students make the prosocial choice for themselves, about one-fourth to one-third feel their peers would make the prosocial choice. This phenomenon seems to be an example of "pluralistic ignorance", that is, the belief each has that s/he would help combined with the stereotype that few students believe in being helpful. We think this is primarily a result of the traditional school environment which has few opportunities for discussing and creating explicitly shared norms.

In contrast, the data for the democratic schools show closer agreement between the prosocial action choice for the self and for others. The greater accuracy of the democratic alternative school students' perceptions of their peers' choice is evidence that pluralistic ignorance can be overcome through the democratic process of discussion and creation of group norms and group solidarity.

There are sharp differences between the democratic school students and the regular high school students in terms of the frequency of using judgments of responsibility. While 55 to 72% of the responses to the dilemmas made by the alternative school students were in the responsibility mode, only 7 to 18% of the responses made by regular high school students were classified in this mode. The median stage scores for deontic and responsibility reasoning on the school dilemmas indicate that in both modes the regular high school students' reasoning was one-half to one stage lower than the stages used by democratic alternative school students. This is striking because the median classical moral judgment scores were the same within comparison and democratic samples in each pair of schools. Again, we feel the democratic process and the explicit valuing of community led to these results. Thus, the students in the democratic schools offered more prosocial solutions to the school dilemmas and formulated their reasons for their choices in the responsibility mode, that is, seeing the welfare of the other as a sufficient condition to activate them to offer help within the context of a strong sense of community. It seems to us that the development of conscience includes within it the idea of the development of judgments of responsibility, those judgments that are in the minds of the people making them commit themselves to doing the good or right as well as discerning what it is in any particular situation.

Turning to the moral atmosphere results, we can summarize the results quickly. The democratic school students perceived their alternative schools to be strong communities in which students consciously held collective norms, expressed strong commitments to upholding them, and formulated the reasons underlying the norms at their highest level of moral judgment competence, Stage 3/4. The comparison groups of students perceived their high schools to be lacking any sense of community and questioned whether their schools even fulfilled the obligation of an academic institution, to promote learning. Also these students perceived the general anomie in the normative structures of their schools; they thought their schools had no prosocial collective norms but rather that there existed a peer culture of negative or counter-norms, such as not helping out an unpopular student. The level of reasoning underlying the individually held prosocial norms and the recognized peer culture counter-norms was lower than their level of moral judgment competence. In other words, the comparison students characterized their social environment using the logic and language of Stage 2/3 or 3, transitional from pre-conventional to early conventional reasoning. This is a half to whole stage lower than the average level of individual moral reasoning for the same students in the classical dilemmas which is Stage 3/4.

In summary, the democratic school students were more socially responsible than their regular high school controls in the content of their school dilemma choices - favoring prosocial responsibility, in their mode of judgment - making judgments of responsibility, and in their stage of judgment. We believe that these differences reflect real differences in moral action in the schools, and demonstrate one useful way to operationalize and analyze the development of conscience in students. We interpret the differences in school-related moral judgments as due to the differential moral atmospheres of the democratic and traditional schools. The democratic schools have a strong sense of collective prosocial norms and a strong sense of community; the traditional schools have neither. The methodology that we have described is useful not only for studying the moral atmosphere of the school but also that of the workplace and the family and their influences on the development of judgments of responsibility and of conscience.

Harvard University, Graduate School of Education

* I wish to acknowledge my colleagues in this research project, Prof. Dr. Lawrence Kohlberg, Dr. Clark Power, and Dr. Joseph Reimer. The conceptualizations and insights in this paper are the results of our collective efforts.

BIBLIOGRAPHY

Durkheim, E.: 1973, *Moral Education: A Study in the Theory and App-lication of the Sociology of Education*, Free Press, New York.
Kohlberg, L.: 1980, 'High School Democracy and Educating for a Just Soc iety' in R. L. Mosher (ed.): *Moral Education: A First Generation of Research and Development*, Praeger, New York, pp. 20-57.
Kohlberg, L.: 1981, *Essays on Moral Development,Vol. I: The Philosophy of Moral Development*, Harper and Row, San Francisco.
Power, C.: 1979, *The Moral Atmosphere of a Just Community High School: A Four-Year Longitudinal Study*, unpublished doctoral disser-tation, Harvard University.
Ruma, E. and Mosher, P.: 1967, 'Relationships Between Moral Judgment and Guilt in Delinquent Boys' in: *Journal of Abnormal Psychology*, 72, pp. 122-127.

DISCUSSION

Josef Fuchs SJ, Ann Higgins, Lawrence Kohlberg,
Georg Lind, Heinrich Scholler, Hans Strotzka, Günter Virt,
Paul Weingartner, Thomas E. Wren, Gerhard Zecha

SCHOLLER: I would like to start my question with this ex-ample. Did you differentiate in your research between classes of schools composed of very different groups: Blacks or other mi-norities or of Polish background, because if you have schools composed of minorities, they certainly have within their group norms of responsibility of racial background which will not function between them and the others. So they are hiding their own norms and you have a kind of vacuum in your whole set, because these groups are not interacting. So, I suppose if you can relate those hidden, unknown norms of cooperation to cer-tain groups, I would better understand.
HIGGINS: Yes, we did find the same thing that you're sug-gesting in the schools, the Cambridge High School and the Cluster School, the schools in Cambridge, Massachusetts, that exemplify this problem. They are both racially mixed. In the Cluster School the norm of helping your own kind was inherent

in each sub-culture, "The Blacks help other Blacks", and "Whites help Whites". The idea that Blacks and Whites should and would help each other came into existence only out of the effort of the just community intervention to build a common idea of community and a collective norm of helping any and all community members.

The students who weren't in the democratic just community schools said, "Sure, I'm a nice person, I would help so and so". But then we asked what their peers would do, and they said, "No, no one else here would help". That's what I am calling "pluralistic ignorance". I think one educational implication is apparent. The students have these ideas in their heads about themselves being good people, and everyone else being selfish or uncaring. We would maintain that to bring those students into a democratic explicit discussion about the ideas and stereotypes of others that they hold would bring this kind of hidden cooperation into the open and make it explicit and then they would see what they share with each other, with others outside their own subcultural groups.

SCHOLLER: Is there a difference between the situation in governmental public schools and schools run by churches? Can they enforce a higher degree of interaction among the pupils, the students of different ethnical backgrounds, or is the problem with the governmental schools more obvious, since there is not such a moral philosophy in the schools like in a church school?

HIGGINS: I would say that both things are a problem. One is that there isn't such a moral philosophy in the public schools and also that they are more ethnically diverse. The religious schools are both more ethnically homogeneous and I think people feel if it's a religious school there can be some teaching of content or of virtues according to their own religious precepts.

LIND: I wonder how much the type of school system has influenced the opportunities for participation and subsequently for developing higher moral judgment competency. When I compare the German and the American system, at least the German system as it used to be in my days, we have this classroom teaching, we stayed in our classroom and there was from the beginning a formal organization to which we were moulded; we had to cope with the requirement of a formal organization. While, as I experienced it, in American high schools the course system is a much more informal one. I have attended both schools and I know what it's like, teachers made me sit down in Germany beside a student which I didn't like. I had to get along with him the whole year. In America the course system enables students to go more with your friends, with those you like and you all build informal groups: a friendship setting.

HIGGINS: This is also a difference in the private schools and religious schools in America, where the group stays together much more in each class. In a normal public or government high school you see a particular other student for one course and then you do not see that same person again until three days later when you have the same course again. So, the notion of anonymity it a fitting one when many Americans think about their own high school experiences. Anonymity is the other side of the informal friendship structure of American public schools.

WREN: It was my understanding that your original thesis was that the binding force in the alternative school was not that they were from the same social group or otherwise inclined to be friendly to one another, but that it was the community discussion which was the source of this particular caring relationship that you described. Now I wonder if we might not be getting into another issue, if we talk about other sociological factors that would account for the students taking good care, or not taking good care, of each other.

HIGGINS: Yes, in terms of our theoretical focus it has been our aim to prove this hypothesis: that it is the creation of the sense of community by the students that fosters the creation of positive norms about caring, about trusting etc. Belonging to the same social or ethnic group cannot account for the differences between the democratic and traditional high schools since one pair of schools in our study was racially and economically mixed and one pair was homogeneous in these regards. We had another school identified which was a "traditional free school", a kind of American 1960's alternative school. It was very individualistic, students were encouraged to do their own thing; it was a very laissez faire operation. We had one of these schools in our research study thinking we would then control for such things as size and even student interaction; but that school folded in the first year of our study, so we were unable to address some of these issues in the research in the way that we had hoped.

LIND: Just a thought experiment: Could you think of a just community in regular classes with two or three thousand students?

HIGGINS: There is one conceptual problem: We have placed a lot of importance on direct participation. How do you have direct participation with three thousand students? One of our colleagues, Clark Power, took a job in the Brookline High School for a year after this study was completed to try to answer that question. They created a representative community meeting of teachers and students and also support staff in that case. But one important thing he did was to keep direct participation of all students in terms of the building up of norms by having all classrooms discuss and vote on new rules, then having classroom representatives at the community meeting vote on one version, and finally having all students in every classroom rating the final version of a rule. Whether these rules represented binding norms is difficult to say without some research. This might seem like a long and clumsy process but in the first year several rules were made this way. This school continues to run as a participatory and representative democracy in the present.

VIRT: I have a question about the moral atmosphere of the subculture. For about nineteen years I have been doing work in communities and a parish. I found a group of young people that were dependent on drugs. They had built up a sub-culture with very strict rules. We tried to get them out of this atmosphere and brought them to our parish. Then they were 'clean'. But we had another experience: They were much more obedient to the rules we had in the parish than other young people.

My question: Is there any research about the maturity of judgment of young people who are drug-addicts?

HIGGINS: The just community democratic schools were more or less successful in creating an environment where there wasn't any drug use. None of the students in any of these schools could be characterized as drug-addicts.

KOHLBERG: We talked about Scarsdale, Brookline and Cambridge democratic schools: The norm for most of the students was to use marijuana during the school day. What happened in the alternative democratic schools was that because of discussion in the just community they would not use drugs in the school because they developed a norm against that which was specifically school related, but many of them would continue to use drugs outside of school on the weekend at home. Their parents did not seem to object to this practice particularly. A norm was built up that you could not be a good member of the school if you were "high on drugs", as the students say, and you could not participate in your classes and community. However, they would not transfer this norm to the idea that, in general, they should be drug-free. So, getting back to the question Mr. Virt raised about the stage of moral reasoning we would have to say that in our groups there was not a specific lower stage in the moral thinking of students who smoked marijuana. In other studies we have found delinquents were lower stage in their thinking than their non-delinquent peers. That is, those who commit anti-social or illegal acts are typically Stage 1 or Stage 2.

VIRT: For my group I had the impression that they were on Stage 3: total identification with the group.

KOHLBERG: So, you were more successful than we were in changing the norm of the group with regard to drug usage apparently. This is one of the things we were less successful on than on some of the other things.

HIGGINS: It is difficult to know what stage the children were in your group because even this kind of group solidarity certainly exists with groups of people who are basically reasoning at Stage 2. You see it on the streets and you see it in the prisons, so there can be this kind of group solidarity and loyality at several stages. Certainly at Stages 2 through 4 groups can develop the kind of in-group/out-group and exchange of goods that can bind people together. Just by the fact that they have a strong group you don't know the stage of reasoning of the group members.

WEINGARTNER: My question is this: How much did this community also depend on the relation of the students to the teacher? What I have in mind is this: You mentioned the authority and the kind of authority the teacher has or is for the students and this, I think, is an important matter. There are very different kinds of authority: On the one hand the kind of, so to speak, administrative authority which a teacher gets just because he holds a position at a school or university. And on the other hand an authority like a leader of some criminals, that means: the authority that is freely given by the children to the teacher because they find out that he is very clever, he knows a lot and so on. Now I could think that this makes a lot of difference.

HIGGINS: Yes, I would agree with you that the teacher should have both kinds of authority, however, we would say also that the teacher should have a third kind which somehow mitigates some of the charismatic or personal authority. And the third kind I just referred to is the teacher as an *advocate* for the welfare of the group: That part of the authority comes from the fact that the teacher is a spokesperson for what will help the whole group progress or what will make the school a better place for learning.

WEINGARTNER: When you speak of responsibility, then you say that judgments of responsibility go beyond deontic judgments. Now concerning authority of the administrative kind: Couldn't we speak here also of some responsibility? This would then mean that in this case it would not go beyond. But in the case of an authority which is freely chosen your claim, judgments of responsibility go beyond deontic judgments, is very well justified.

HIGGINS: That's a good point and I would agree with you. I would agree the teacher has authority that includes both aspects, deontic and responsibility reasoning; that is, to advocate what should be done and to act consistently.

ZECHA: You said the central point of your findings was that students in democratic schools made more responsibility judgments. My question is whether these responsibility judgments involve some sort of morality or moral philosophy. Because if that is not the case, if the only criterion involved are the needs of the other person, then I would say these responsibility judgments are purely relative (to the students). But if you have some other criterion that are beyond the needs of the students, then what are these?

HIGGINS: We have worked out a philosophic rationale for non-relativistic deontic judgments of justice. Our conception of judgments of responsibility are more tied to the person's perception of herself as a moral agent in relation to other people in the community. And moreover, in ways that are yet to be spelled out, judgments of responsibility must rest on deontic judgments or somehow be inclusive of them in order to "go beyond" deontic judgments. However, we do not yet have a clearly defined rationale for universalizable judgments of responsibility.

KOHLBERG: We are still philosophically vague about the greater adequacy of higher stages of judgments of responsibility and of a Stage 6 in such judgments. It's much clearer in judgments of justice what the stages are.

ZECHA: But are you aiming at such a non-relativistic view or don't you mind?

HIGGINS: Yes, I think so. I think maybe Dr. Kohlberg and I differ somewhat on this. I really see this concept of judgment of responsibility as useful when put more in terms of sociological and psychological research, or social-psychological research. When looking at what happens in social groups, you can break things apart in a way that this aids understanding, particularly between the relation of someone's judgments about what is right or good and their acting consistently or not with that judgment. The kind of longitudinal data we have about that I didn't really present.

KOHLBERG: I'll present a case when it comes my turn to talk tomorrow; a little of a principled sense of responsibility that I think would be universalist.

STROTZKA: Your criteria are very difficult criteria to judge ways of commitment of students to the institutionalization of norms. How do you find out this commitment? It could be done either by participant observation or by interviews of teachers and administrators probably. How did you do it?

HIGGINS: Thank you for asking. We did it in both of those ways but we started out with direct observation. I spent many hours audiotaping community meetings in these different schools, as well as did some of Dr. Kohlberg's students. First we used a rather ethnographic approach, mostly with students, but some with teachers, asking them how the school functioned and how the people treated each other. Then, after two years, we started writing these dilemmas that I presented - The Caring Dilemma - "Should Billy drive Harry?" All of these came out of particular incidents that had happened in one of the schools. The movement in that direction has been an effort to provide some kind of measure of moral atmosphere that people could use in different schools. One question is how different is the school before you have to get a new dilemma with a new norm. You do have to know enough about a school to know that the norms in the dilemmas are central to it or your analysis won't make sense. What I reported today is based on the latter aspect: interview data on these dilemmas. For different schools there could be different probe questions that would be sensitive to particular aspects of a school and still be analyzed in terms of our major concepts.

WREN: My curiosity is whether there has been some work in the kibbuzim that would be parallel to the just community model and these kinds of questions - I don't know if the data collection procedures would have to be the same. But do you see any analogies between what you've presented here and what other researchers have done when they're gone into the kibbuzim in Israel, using the Kohlberg scoring procedures? In other words, I'm looking for just communities in the kibbuzim.

HIGGINS: Yes, but I'm really going to let Dr. Kohlberg answer this because he conducted a longitudinal study on a kibbuz, just to look at individual moral judgment development. Out of that study came some of the ideas for this kind of educational intervention.

VIRT: When you talked about ethical principles, I heard responsibility and justice. Now I would like to ask for a definition of "justice"; for instance, when I remember Aristotle, I remember it's "a habit to act according to the law", and then you

can do the greatest injustice according to the law. It is a problem when justice is the highest principle. In this sense I would
say, "No, charity is the highest principle". We always have to
correct justice but I think you will take "justice" in another
sense. I want to hear in which sense "justice" is for you the
highest principle and the highest measure for all your items.
HIGGINS: Justice we take to be of a different order than charity, although I think that charity is a very good idea. Dr. Kohlberg's whole theory takes justice as the core of morality. It's not
that we take justice to be the highest virtue, but that the understanding of morality comes most clearly through reasoning
about justice issues.
KOHLBERG: Just going back to Aristotle for a moment: Of
course he has two definitions of justice, one in terms of legality
and one in terms of what I call "fairness". He distinguishes between the two. Within fairness he distinguishes between distributive, corrective, and commutative justice. To some extent the
dilemmas I started using back in 1958 in these longitudinal and
cross-cultural studies were somewhat of a tilt towards asking
questions of distributive, commutative, or corrective justice. I
have tried to formulate the stages in terms of a variety of theories of justice. Rawls is one example, helping to find higher
notions of justice. I think we focussed on justice partly because
of the rational or cognitive focus of the research program. There
is a sense in which you could rationally articulate justice at its
various levels more clearly than you could other virtues. What
Dr. Higgins has been talking about in terms of responsibility we
looked at as something going beyond justice, or as expanding
the notion of morality beyond the justice notion, although the
cognitive developmental theory of morality has been most easily
formulated in terms of justice. I followed a tradition that you can
find in Aristotle and in Piaget; so that we tried to define for each
stage the characteristic, what we called "justice operations".
These would include reciprocity, equality and equity, but these
are differently conceived at each stage. For instance, at Stages 1
and 2, reciprocity is represented by the fact that - let's say you
ask a child at that level, "Tell me the Golden Rule", and they
say, "Do unto others as you would be done by them". Then you

say, "If somebody comes up and hits you what does the Golden Rule say to do?" And they say, "Hit 'em back! Do unto others as they do unto you!" So this is one notion of justice as reciprocity. At Stage 3 for the first time the child understands the Golden Rule and, for instance, one child who was just coming to this awareness said, "That's really hard". He was an eleven year old boy and was asked about somebody hitting him. He said, "It's sort of as if your brain has to leave your head and, like it's in the other person's head. You see it from the other guy's eyes, but your brain comes back into your own head, but you still see it from the other guy's eyes but you see it from your own eyes, and then you go back". He was struggling to articulate the operation of the Golden Rule as a norm of justice, or you could call it something broader. In some ways it can be extended to "Love thy neighbor as thyself", so that we're a little sloppy about justice. At least that gives some sense of the cognitive core that we focussed on, and why we wanted to tie it to justice.

SCHOLLER: Thank you. I would like to come back to a question I put forward earlier this morning. What is the numerical relation of students to teachers in those schools you observed? I heard at the ordinary schools we have, I suppose, 1 to 20 teaching and listening persons. I would like to know what kind of numerical relation? As I understand the development of moral teaching was also related to a kind of family sized relation. So, possibly the family sized group can walk and talk at the same time to a large group of people. The same is true for Jesus and his twelve apostles, a small group walking and teaching. I suppose it has to do with numbers.

A second question: The basic idea of Piaget was to relate games to moral development. To what extent in your schools do sports and games play an important role on different levels of moral stages for the development of moral judgment?

HIGGINS: First of all, the ratio of student to teacher is approximately 1 to 15, one teacher for fifteen students. There would be five to seven teachers in a group for 70 to 100 students. I think in some places in American public schools the ratio is about 1 to 20, and in some schools it's about the same, and in private schools, it might be better, 1 to 10. To answer your second question about sports, we have not particularly emphasized sports in these schools.

Remember each school is attached to a large high school, so the students who are interested in sports can get their sports through belonging to a part of the large high school. One of Dr. Kohlberg's students now has just developed the idea for a dissertation and has opened a sports camp for boys. He's running the sports camp for the first time this summer based on these ideas about just community. Hopefully he will do some research about the relation of cooperation to competition.

FUCHS: I am interested in the following: You go to these people at different schools, and you try to find out: How can we foster the cognitive moral development and, correspondingly, also personal morality within the group? This is excellent. I have a question. In all this activity, you suppose you know what morality is. What is your concept of morality in all of your research? Why do you say, for instance, and I agree with you, that the Golden Rule is excellent? But how do I see that it is excellent? You suppose it, I suppose it. These are topics of the highest importance; therefore it is our question: Where are these coming from? We do not have a special source for this. Do you have an answer for this?

WREN: Since we are nearly out of time, perhaps it would be well to ask if there are other questions, so Dr. Higgins can answer them as a group.

LIND: I've been very much interested in what is called preferences for moral principles, for moral stages of arguing these things. I've reviewed some literature and I've done some research on this, and it's really fascinating that almost all people have a sense of these even if they don't apply it. They have intuitions or feelings that some kinds of reasoning, some kinds of principles are better than others. I don't know where it comes from. Is it inborn or culturally adopted? In communist countries, the hierarchy of preferences is the same, even in young children, as I learn from studies. Even in very young children we find already a sense of qualitative differences in moral argument.

WREN: Was there another question to this theme? Because this would be a good occasion to ask for a summary statement from Dr. Higgins.

HIGGINS: A summary statement that won't answer this question!? I really do ask myself this question, but I also go into the schools and talk with the teachers and the students. We have proceeded without really answering the question of the human source of morality. I think one other partial answer as a psychologist is that I'm really quite convinced that there are developmental stages of reasoning about issues of justice or morality. Given the goal of education, somehow the ultimate question doesn't have to be answered, working with children or adolescents.

FUCHS: Can I give an answer?

HIGGINS: Yes, please do.

FUCHS: If I were you, I would say that we are doing a work that is very important. We should know more about the use of the contingent concept "moral", but this is not our speciality. We suppose it. And I'm sure we have it. We know what morality is, but we do not reflect on this here. It's other people, other sciences (ethics) that ultimately do it. But fundamentally, all people think we have not to reflect on everything we do. So this is one point in our research: We do not reflect on what morality is, but we are sure there is something. Maybe other people, Mr. Virt for instance, should study about this. I would be pleased with this answer, although you gave a description of "justice", "fairness", a few minutes ago. I think it is nothing other than a description of morality. For me, as a model, it is quite interesting that we agree that we have something. I would not say it is inborn, not innate; but I would say all human beings have a certain possibility to understand it.

HIGGINS: I would say, we ask the children to think, to be reflective about what they think is moral. If we ask them to reflect, then we should also reflect. I don't think I can be quite as comfortable with your answer. That's what the cognitive developmental approach is. There are limits to that and there are necessary philosophic bases on which that approach must rest but it is an attempt to study and understand the phenomenon to

which you referred, that all human beings have a certain possibility to understand, or intuitions about, morality.
<u>WREN</u>: Unfortunately, there are also limits of a practical sort
which must be put on this discussion, and we have now reached
them. Thank you all very much.

End of discussion.

PART 3

CONSCIENCE: SPECIAL TOPICS

GÜNTER VIRT

CONSCIENCE IN CONFLICT?*

1. INTRODUCTION

The conscience in conflict with theory and practice, with various ideologies, in conflict with practical interests - these are statements concerning the problems of conscience in our society. Considering these manifold problems, we have to ask the question, whether there is any reliance on the conscience.

1.1 *Claim on the Conscience*

Our present-day society is by no means short of claims and publicity for the conscience. For many young people, military service, for instance, is inconsistent with the voice of their conscience while committing civil offences. Through their recent law reforms, modern states have increasingly shifted the responsibility concerning problems of morality on the citizen's conscience, for example, the questions of divorce, abortion etc.

The bishops of Austria and Germany have emphasized their respect for members of the Church who base their decision about points at issue like methods of contraception on the sway of their conscience.[1]

In the worlds of politics, research, trade, technology, administration etc. as well as in the Church it is impossible to overhear the call for conscience. The field and the necessity for an individual decision based on the conscience have obviously expanded. However, this increased area of moral competence proves to be in a state of ambivalence.

On the one hand, the competence of our conscience is challenged, whereas on the other hand we find human behavior in the industrial society to be controlled in many ways: quite openly in the Marxist states, more subtly in the Western world. This exerts pressure on the people, so that they are likely to find a safety valve in the questions of ethics.

165

G. Zecha and P. Weingartner (eds.), Conscience: An Interdisciplinary View, 165–200.
© *1987 by D. Reidel Publishing Company.*

1.2 *Privatization of Conscience*

The result of making our conscience an increasingly personal matter, simply as a means of running away, does not, however, provide a good basis for the development of a true competence of conscience. On closer examination these apparently personal decisions of the conscience turn out to be far too often dependent or - even worse - counterdependent upon social trends. A decision based on the conscience is not justified simply by referring to the emancipation[2] conventional morality, but rather by defining its interest, the ethical meaning of which has first to be made clear.

In a social climate, where the influence of the conscience frequently carries weight when personal needs are at stake, hidden group-coercion appears or individuals behind the scene are manipulating certain interests, a truly independent and individual conscience is obviously very difficult to attain.

Nevertheless the conscience asserts itself also in a secularized society. But in which way does the conscience assert itself? This is one of the most important questions we shall have to discuss. Is it a reflection of modern trends and a means of conforming them as internalized principles of social manipulation or as a means of disguising the own interests or even extreme group-interests which aim to destroy the structure of society by force in the name of conscience?

Recalling the words of Arthur Schopenhauer, this problem obviously has been realized before our days: "Many a person would be amazed to see the actual structure of his conscience, which he believes to be quite respectable: it consists of about one-fifth human fear, one-fifth fear of idols, one-fifth prejudice, one-fifth vanity and one-fifth sheer habit, which makes him basically no better than a certain Englishman who flatly stated that he could not afford to have a conscience. And yet, is the entity, to which we are keen to appeal and whose help we so often seek, in any way identical with the principles of the traditional doctrines of conscience?" (transl.)[3]

1.3 *The Relative Lack of Reflection on the Question of Conscience in Recent Moral Theology*

The conscience is undoubtedly one of the most important issues of Christian ethics. It is thus all the more surprising that eminent works on moral theology and philosophical encyclopediae of recent times have made no reference to this matter where a detailed discussion would have been expected. Occasional committee reports[4], a systematic synopsis in the encyclopedia entitled *Christlicher Glaube in moderner Gesellschaft* [5] and some sporadic essays[6] prove to be rather the exception. Less surprising is the missing of the key-word 'conscience' in works of Marxist philosophy, since in a totalitarian regime it can hardly be expected that anyone is interested in developing an independent competence of the conscience.

1.4 *Challenge by the Humanities*

How can it be that the immensely increased insight of the humanities into the development and legitimacy of moral judgment stands in direct juxtaposition to the lack of philosophical and theological reflection about the conscience? A first consideration refers to the practical impossibility to digest the immense overflow of knowledge of the humanities in regard to the phenomenon we call conscience, from the point of moral theology. It seems that the denial of the autonomy of the conscience by both psychologists and sociologists results in a certain feeling of helplessness for moral theologists.

1.5 *Vagueness About Our Own Tradition*

However, a further consideration leads us to the unsolved problems of our own tradition. The term 'conscience' is one of the most vaguely to define. In 1963 J. Stelzenberger established in his monography about the history of the term 'conscience' "a gross incongruity between the frequency of use and the transparency of the substantial conception." (transl.)[7]. Yet, what are the possible meanings of this term?

1.6 *Ambiguity of the Term*

With logical precision, Bruno Schüller differentiates four ways in which the word 'conscience' is used.[8] In phrases like 'that's a matter of conscience for me' or with the adjective 'conscientious' we understand that we are looking at a matter from a moral and not from a legal or a political point of view. In this *first* meaning 'conscientious' is synonymous with 'responsible' or 'humane'.

In a *second* usage the term 'conscience' corresponds with the abilities of cognition and judgment, for instance, when we speak of the development of conscience. In philosophical treatises this meaning is frequently expressed as 'practical reasoning' which in turn presumes that ethical statements can express the truth and are not simply a matter of emotion or a reflection of irrational dependency.

The third meaning of 'conscience' introduces man's original experience of judging himself: He has an ethical relationship to his inner self, thus enabling him to tell himself, 'You must do this now' or 'You may on no account do that'. My conscience admonishes me, warns me, judges me, declares my innocence or my guilt. This authority of an imaginary inner judge can ultimately pass sentence only upon myself. It would be nonsense to say, for example, my conscience condemns those who produce weapons. A good conscience gives approval, a bad conscience can only condemn myself. Yet, whose voice is speaking here? Certainly not God himself, for God can never be wrong, whereas we know from experience that the conscience can indeed be wrong. Is it the voice of the true self? Thus the question arises: How can it be possible to pass sentence upon myself? Should it be an inner voice of authority, from my childhood, then 'the voice of conscience' means nothing but outside decision and spiritual outside guidance.

Finally 'conscience' can have the fourth meaning of the 'ethical subject', insofar as it continually draws the line between 'good' and 'evil' when faced with an ethical challenge. Thus we can read in 1 Timothy 1,5: "The goal of this command is love which comes from a pure heart and a good conscience and a sincere faith." In this sentence the words 'heart' and 'conscience' both refer to man as a free ethical subject. 'Conscience' then simply means the same as 'conviction'. Used in this sense the word 'conscience' no longer remains on the level of practical reasoning, but rather on the level of will.

Thus we have:

'Conscience' simply in the sense of 'moral';

'Conscience' in the sense of practical reasoning and the ability of moral judgment;

'Conscience' in the sense of an inner master and judge;

'Conscience' in the sense of heart, conviction, will or ethical subject.[9]

These and perhaps some more meanings of 'conscience' make us consider man's ethical life from manifold aspects. Therefore Schüller (1980, p. 56) draws the conclusion that the concept of conscience is a proposal which can also be rejected, as there are synonyms for the actual word 'conscience'.

1.7 Three-Step Construction

A historical survey could show that the concept of conscience is a specific achievement of the so-called Christian Occident. Nevertheless the manifold interpretations of the word lack for unity.[10]

This survey, amply covered by competent works of lit-erature, would of course be beyond the scope of this lecture. However, I would like to refer briefly to Thomas Aquinas' ideas of conscience and to summarize the main instants when this tradition has been denied in modern times. I shall then make references to Thomas in the following attempt of developing a concept of conscience which is able to do justice to the Western tradition, while at the same time incorporating the aspects of some points of justified denial of this tradition in contemporary society. This systematic attempt will have to prove useful in a concluding third step - that is to say, by solving present-day problems, such as the scrutinizing of conscience, and by finding suitable criteria which help to distinguish between the correct and the improper way of calling upon the conscience.

2. A HISTORICAL SUMMARY

In the writings of Thomas Aquinas we already find a differentiated concept of conscience. Through a presumable mistake in Hieronymus' Commentary on Ezekiel (or in the tradition of this text) (PL 25,22), the Greek word 'syneidesis' used in the sense of 'conscience' or 'moral self-awareness' was changed to 'synderesis'.[11] This mistake faced the scholastic writers with the problem of defining the connection between the two concepts of conscience; that is to say, between the Ancient Greek concept of 'syneidesis', translated into Latin as 'conscientia' and into English as 'conscience' (German: *Gewissen*), and this new concept of 'synderesis', which stood for an original force.

2.1 *Synderesis*

Thomas used the word 'synderesis' for man's original moral capacity, which is an integral factor in every ethical consideration and decision, and which cannot be experienced or manifested separated from the actual moral act. Man's original understanding of 'good' and 'evil' and the absolute demand for doing what is good and avoiding what is evil, does not yet offer a certain content. It, however, gives us a blank system of coordinates which only makes it possible to experience whether something is good and humane, or evil and inhumane. This is consistent with the highest principle of moral reasoning - to do the good and to avoid the evil[12], a principle of practical reasoning to avoid contradiction. It implies that an action cannot possibly be considered both good and evil in the same respect. As much as this to Thomas' views on 'synderesis', the nearest English translation for which being 'basic conscience' (German: *Urgewissen*) which is infallible, since it defines the principles of the structure of moral acts, a structure from which none of us can possibly escape.[13]

2.2 *Conscientia*

With the word 'conscientia', literally translated as 'joint knowledge' (German: *Mitwissen*), Thomas expresses what we would call a 'functional conscience' (German: *Funktionsgewissen*), for we draw upon the standards of our original understanding of good and evil in our everyday ethical considerations. Those considerations which lead us to our final judgment of 'I should do this' and 'I should avoid that' even though I may be solely tempted to do it, are guided by this original understanding of good and evil. However, we do not only form our decisions in this way, we also put them to test. We modify our judgment and our actions according to the standard of this highest principle. This complex structure of moral planning and testing our actions, which refers to the original understanding of good and evil, Thomas thus calls 'conscientia' which is as much as 'joint knowledge'. Everybody will certainly know from his or her own experience that this process of linking up the realities of our life-situation and our moral outlook with this highest principle of original understanding of good and evil is bound to leave ample loop-holes for mistakes to creep in (e. g., by the influence of passions, of social prejudices, extraordinary circumstances, etc.).

Thomas decides precisely as to whether we should obey the superior or our own conscience in a case of conflict: The verdict of conscience must be followed, even if it is objectively wrong.[14] It is better to be burnt at the stake than to act against the dictates of conscience.

Romano Guardini once summarized the traditional concept of conscience with the following words: "What is good affects me deeply. There is something inside me which naturally responds to goodness, as does the eye to the light: my conscience." (transl.)[15]

It is exactly this interpretation of conscience as a sensory organ for goodness, which, as it were, grows and develops out of its own accord, which is widely disputed by modern humanities. In these contemporary humanities there obviously is no place for what was called 'conscience' in former Christian tradition.

2.3 *Contemporary Humanities*

2.31 Biological Conscience
Modern studies of the humanities employ methods of research
based on the ideal of precision such as seen in the natural sciences. They offer the chance of investigating established causal
laws, but not manners, which are formed by a conscious attitude towards these determinate laws. From his studies in
brain-research C. von Monakow[16] assumes man (as a gigantic
protoplasm) to possess a physiological compass which stands
on behalf of the organism in the world in an optimal way and
which directs him towards his aims in life. This biological 'syneidesis' is already present as a seed in the embryonic stage and
forms a basis for ensuing developments.

2.32 Psychological Conscience
The question of how the concrete ethical standards of a society
can become an integral part of the individual personality cannot
be answered by means of brain-research. Sigmund Freud's
psychoanalysis, which has since been further developed in various directions, traces the mechanism of the psyche, with the
help of which a superior authority, the so-called Super-Ego, is
set up above the self in the own person. Anyone who asks
children at an Infant's School if they have ever heard the voice
of their conscience will easily realize from their response that
they are speaking out of the inner echo of parental influence.

During the so-called Oedipal Stage, children solve existential
problems with authority by 'swallowing' psychically, as it
were, this very authority.[17]

Since the process of personal integration is not yet settled at
this age, this inner voice of authority can still be seen partly as
an alien voice within the actual self. Later in life, the demands of
the Super-Ego are mostly unconscious. However, only the
process of controlling the actions and intentions of the self,
which originate from this Super-Ego, is called conscience by

Freud.[18] Nonetheless, it is impossible to make such clear decisions about the moral correctness of inner attitudes, which are assimilated from the small field of the family group.

2.33 Sociological Conscience

Human behavior is not only controlled by the small family circle, but by all social procedures collectively and especially by their institutions. From this angle the conscience is seen as a meeting place for social standards. It makes us realizing it when we neglect social duties or in case of a confrontation between irreconcilable yet equally acceptable standards.

A. Gehlen says, "Thus, the conscience can act neither as a relatively reliable pathway of survival, nor as a competent organ of perception, where no perception is possible." (transl.)[19]

And he agrees with Max Scheler, when he says, "The principle of freedom of conscience, according to which anyone should have the right to decide what is good and what is evil, can be seen only as an expression of inner moral anarchy." (transl.)[20]

Gehlen concludes, "Thus the sacrifice of the own 'ego' and perhaps even of the own conscience may be worthwhile as a means of maintaining order." (transl.)[21]

All theories about conscience which are built only upon these indisputable causal connections have one thing in common:They look upon the conscience as to be at mercy of certain given powers. We cannot, however, depend on such a conscience. It has in no way an independent competence.

The precisely verifiable moments of modern theories of conscience can be summarized in a triangle comprising the biological, psychological and sociological conscience, which indicates the determinant factors of human behavior.

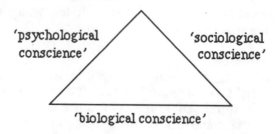

'psychological conscience'   'sociological conscience'

'biological conscience'

Diagram I

The original experience of conscience cannot, however, be en-
compassed simply in a two-dimensional form, as conscience
does not only mean an organ of perception for biologically, psychologically, socially, and also ecclesiastically prescribed standards, which mark out the boundaries of human behavior. Thus
it is impossible to define the form of conscience by means of
univocal terms. For 'conscience' essentially means man's relationship to himself - a relationship adapted by man himself according to the existing relationships within the self.

In order to do justice to the entire human experience of conscience, our diagram would have to rise above the two-dimensional form and point out the various dimensions of human
existence, between which the conscience acts as mediator in this
relationship to the self.

To achieve an understanding of such a complex phenomenon as the conscience, we must discard this single-minded,
clear-cut and thus univocal concept and adopt an analogous, referring view. Forms and concepts which do not only represent
objects, but also encompass other meanings and implications of
experience, and which thus express a relationship between various levels of meaning, are known as symbols.[22]

3. SYSTEMATIC DEVELOPMENT OF THE NOTION OF CONSCIENCE AS A SYMBOLIC CONCEPT

Therefore, in the systematic section I propose to regard the concept of conscience as an analogous symbolic notion, and to further elucidate this by proceeding with our diagram. We shall now try to develop the elements of a theory of conscience mentioned so far with the help of categories which indicate a hermeneutic understanding of symbols.

Concepts without conception are void. Therefore we shall build up a model which is able to integrate all the various elements called 'conscience' in the following sense: the biological, psychological and sociological standard experiences, the planning and investigating of our own actions, and the interpretation of the absolute moral demand which is constitutive for the conscience. To Paul Ricoeur, a symbol is an expression which refers by means of an immediately obvious sense to a hidden and indirect sense. Ricoeur illustrates this hermeneutic structure of symbols with the example of the dream. Actions in a dream often seem to be senseless and it is quite a piece of difficult interpretation to make out the sense behind. Dealing with the symbol we have to realize not only the dualism between sensuous sign and meaning or the dualism between meaning and thing, but also the dualism between 'sense' and 'sense'.[23]

We must now consider the conditions enabling man to get a true relationship to himself, and not merely an apparent relationship as suggested by Freud. For man's Super-Ego is plainly an alien, heteronomous structure which finds its way through the defence-mechanism of introjection into the person himself. Such a derivative structure cannot justify the basic right of freedom of conscience. A true relationship to the self is based on the condition that man rediscovers his inner self through a true and real entity, and so finds his own identity.

3.1 *"Self and I"*

Modern anthropology, e.g., G.H. Mead's symbolic interactionism, regards this entity as identical in many respects with the image of myself as seen by others. The reflected image of the self, that is to say, how others see me, is the focal point over which the mature, spontaneous self can rediscover its essential being in reflection, thought and deed throughout the course of life. From this explanation of man's relationship to his inner self we can derive a great deal of concrete and detailed knowledge, but we are not enlightened about man's capability to differentiate between 'to be or not to be' and between 'good and evil'. For all relative and finite realities can have only a limited, but never an absolute influence on man. Man experiences himself in his relationship to his self absolutely challenged by the moral claims of conscience. However hard one may try to explain away this awareness as a derivative phenomenon, it remains a hard fact which cannot be refuted. Man's capacity and also his need to make judgments such as 'this is so', or 'that is in fact not so', or 'this is good and that is evil', must therefore be founded upon a structure within himself - a structure which enables him to make such judgments.

In a next step we have to look for a concept which is suitable by reason of its implicitly comprehensive nature as a mediator between concrete experience and the original experience of absolute goodness as a precondition for successful human existence (i.e., in philosophical terms: a mediator between the categorial and the transcendental level).

3.2 Basic Trust

An unlimited amount of trust is required for a person to venture to try and meet the expectations imposed upon him by his environment, before he has even begun to speak in terms of 'I': In the jargon of modern anthropology, this means the acceptance of the self and the subsequent development from his self to an autonomous, independent self. In this connection Erikson speaks of a basic trust which, experienced in the first months of life, is a precondition for further successful steps towards maturity. The question about the beginning is accompanied by the question about our origin. Basic trust is the attitude towards ourself and towards the world as based on the experiences of our first year of life. With 'trust' Erikson wishes to express a feeling of being able to utterly rely on the credibility of others and on the own trustworthiness.[24]

In order to be able to rely upon an image of myself different from the one presented to me by society, I must first find a sound footing on a different level. Such absolute trust, however, cannot possibly originate from limited mortal beings, no matter how 'good' they may be. It is important to make a clear difference between what is mediated and the process of mediation. Basic trust can at best be mediated through people but never produced by them. Whosoever may venture to establish an identity, whether it be in the form of a decision about profession or of a seemingly insignificant yet true decision to be loyal in everyday matters, can only dare to do so if he builds upon a sound foundation, a foundation of reality which can be trusted in as one of essential goodness.

In every real decision of conscience man realizes his contact with the infinite and incomprehensible mystery which the Jew and the Christian haltingly call God and Father, and for which the agnostic has no name at all. He too, however, relies on the existence of this 'mystery' as a vital condition for venturing to devote himself to the cause of goodness. From a strictly theological point of view, an ethical decision as based on man's readiness to believe in the good Creator of a good creation. This chain of reasoning can provide neither an anthropological nor an ethical proof of God's existence; what it does provide, however, is the basic foundation-stone upon which to build up one's identity. Through this realization we are unavoidably faced with the religious quest for the deepest meaning of life and for the experience of the highest principle of practical reasoning which at first sounds very formal: 'Do the good and avoid the evil'.

Thomas called this principle 'synderesis' which is part of every judgment of conscience. This basic awareness of conscience is present when we place confidence in the absolute goodness, which thus makes it clear that in every ethical question I am necessarily obliged to differentiate between good and evil. This obligation of choosing what is good cannot be explained from choices made with a limited sense of value. Our obligation is based on absolute faith in absolute goodness.[25]

We now have to add this viewpoint to our diagram.

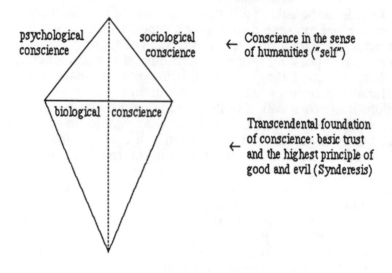

Diagram II

3.3 *Ontological Foundation for the Highest Principle of Moral Judgments*

This basic trust can neither be arbitrarily chosen nor have we accidentally inherited it from our parents. It rather is an onto-logical condition present in every ethical decision. A moral effort which does not concur with this basic structure present in all practical propositions is simply inconceivable; otherwise we would contradict ourselves, which means we would desire something because and inasmuch as it is not desirable, i.e., good.

The connection between the heteronomous structures of our existential conditions, paraphrased in our triangular sketch as biological, psychological and sociological conscience and our basic sense of conscience can be expressed by the prefix 'con-' (meaning as much as 'together') in the sense of '*conscientia* ', that is 'con-science'. This 'joint knowledge' of both levels manifests itself in an act of conscience in two different ways. Firstly in planning and considering an action in a final practical judgment, secondly in testing this judgment. In my opinion there is no reason for excluding either of these points from the symbolic concept of conscience.[26]

3.4 *Reasoning in Planning and Testing*

The phenomenon of conscience encompasses two directions: the direction which guides our actions and which declares the concrete action directly founded on this basis to be good; secondly, the direction which tests our decision by examining the concrete action in harking back to the highest moral principle as to whether the concrete decision of conscience can really stand in the face of this highest principle. The complex task of our conscience consists in connecting our will, which determines our actions, with the highest principle of practical reasoning; that is, by making sure that a concrete action can possibly be justified in the face of moral reason, and by deciding whether a certain action is an aid for the realization of human life.

The testing of a completed action does not relate directly to the act itself, but rather to the question of whether I can justify the reason for any action to myself. In which way practical reasoning achieves this mediatory task is a question of the establishing of norms.

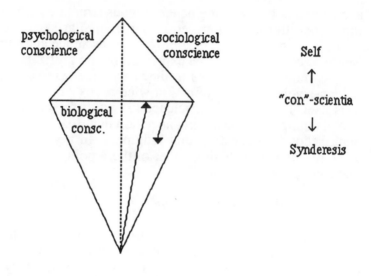

Diagram III

3.5 *Conscience and Feeling*

Taking this model as a starting point, every interpretation of
'conscience' through will, through emotions and through the
direct insinuation of an alien voice must be eliminated. Precisely because reason is the only possible power within the
conscience, which is capable of relating all the individual actions
to an ultimate unity, that is, to a successful human existence
based on a firm foundation. Such a judgment of reason manifests itself in man's total involvement.[27] The involvement of our
life as a whole and of our own identity are manifested through
the medium of 'feeling'. Even the 'unconscious' is activated
when the conscience is at work. The echo of this emotional
sway shows us whether our own will can justify its existence or
not in the face of moral reason. This also is the practical reason
why authors continually refer to the conscience as the impulse

of a particular instinct, as an expression of emotions, as an act of will or as an inner voice.

3.6 Summary

This model of conscience as seen symbolically can, in my opinion, demonstrate the source of our knowledge of an absolute moral obligation and the place where our religious involvement of conscience can exist. Yet, not only this, it can even show why the agnostic nevertheless has a conscience. This model ties in with the great Christian tradition, but it can also integrate our more recent insights and investigations. We can further use this model to specify the origins of doubts and errors of conscience.

The basis on which conscience is built, that is, basic trust, is indeed firm and infallible and is expressed in the highest moral principle: 'Do the good and avoid the evil.' However, the connection with the concrete, environmental and social conditions of my life remains open to error and doubt. Conscience does indeed stand on firm ground; and yet it is not infallible in its concrete role of a mediator, and hovers, as it were, in a state of perpetual motion. Since 'will' and 'feeling' are bound by what 'reason' presents to them as good or evil, the invincibly erroneous conscience is also absolutely binding.[28] Acting according to the conscience is only realized if we agree to an action judged to be good and right by our reason, that is, rational.

"When reason determines will, the bond of conscience to what is recognized as good is not the sole demand incurred, but also the forming of conscience which assures the demand of truth of this realization." (transl.)[29]

4. PRACTICAL QUESTIONS

With these considerations we have now arrived at some concluding practical questions with which the suggested model has to be tested.

4.1 *Testing the Conscience*

The legal right of freedom of conscience is anchored in the majority of Western States. The Supreme Court of the Federal Republic of Germany considers the judicial evaluation of a decision of conscience concerning right and wrong to be incompatible with the basic guaranteed right of freedom of conscience.[30] The same judgment, however, insists upon the mediation of the decision of conscience and states that it is permissible and necessary to verify whether there is a decision of conscience at all. Thus there must be a straight line between the decision of conscience and decisions of a different nature. It should be made clear that this delimination is only possible by accounting for the specific moral rationality of a decision or of a judgment; a rationality which we have attempted to show in its basic structure. Therefore there is a fundamental distinction as to whether this is a case of a real 'conscientia' or 'joint knowledge' in the form represented as a moral relationship to the self, or on the other hand a case of 'remote control' or even of hidden pressures. In the latter case, it would not be a matter of man's self-determination whose protection is supposed to be the basic right of freedom of conscience, if man could not justify his actions and likewise the consequences of his decision of conscience both to himself and to others. An arbitrary decision of a purely emotional, instinctive reaction would be the opposite of a decision of conscience - heteronomous, 'remote control' or a product of chance.

In the final reckoning, each of us is individually responsible for the development of his own conscience in view of the many possibilities of error and manipulation. Each error in the sphere of ethics, in which the success of humanity stands or falls, can have disastrous, inhuman and brutal consequences.

On the publication of the encyclical *Humanae Vitae*, 1968, the Austrian bishops stated, "There is indeed freedom of conscience - but not freedom in the development of conscience." (transl.)[31]

Any omissions in the development of conscience impair the free functioning of conscience and thus make a person susceptible to errors and manipulation of conscience. An uncultureed conscience is easily manipulated. If the conscience were called upon to act as a cover for indolence, egoism and withdrawal from the solidarity of society, this would lead to the long-term effect of disregard for the legitimate right of freedom of conscience in our society, and hence lead to a totalitarian regime.

The possibility of abuse is perhaps greatest in calling upon the own conscience. This makes the continual development of the conscience all the more important. But how?

4.2 Development of Conscience

As we have already seen, the heteronomous view of my own self as given to me by others is present at the very beginning of life. In the 'Super-Ego', the pre-form of conscience, the social standards and expectations concentrated in the persons nearest and dearest to us become an integral part of the person in his development towards an individual personality. And yet, "education of man, as distinct from 'training' in the social sense, does not solely aim at directing our behavior towards acceptable standards, but also at constructing an independent sense of responsibility in young people." (transl.)[32] Conscience then reaches a state of maturity when it can stand up to the test of reality.

During the course of life most people depend on the directional help of those standards which expound the demands of reality, and in which the experience of a well-proved and successful way of life is preserved and further developed. This is not necessarily a bad thing; moral norms may at first be experienced as having an alien moral content, which not necessarily signifies the heteronomy of conscience itself. Maturity of conscience is proved directly by its continual preoccupation and endeavour towards the humanely, and in this sense objectively correct normative insight, and by developing through these standards. Ethical norms have no pretensions towards keeping man in a state of continual dependence, but rather have the aim of showing man the way towards a truth in which he can grow and develop beyond his previous limits and hence towards an autonomous conscience by experiencing himself as identical with his inner self. To impart trust is the decisive factor of each step of this pathway towards the development of a mature conscience. Only from the basic foundation of trust man is able to succeed in his venture of gradually differentiating his independence from the given image of the self and from the prescribed social roles, and hence to assume independent responsibility for his actions.

The formation of conscience, however, is not achieved primarily through norms, but mainly through the relationship to concrete persons.[33]

4.3 *Criteria and Example*

The conscience is good insofar the will, that is to say a person's motivation and intention, is good. The conscience is right, if it touches man's humanity in a concrete situation. Goodness and correctness can be differentiated as the case may be. Bothering about ethical correctness is part of the goodness of conscience and therefore part of every truly engaged conscience. However, what is the 'measurement of humanity'? How, after all, to find the optimal humanity in a certain case - also then when norms are useless because of their formulation? Through these questions we become aware of the dilemma of a merely formal definition of humanity as given by the Categorical Imperative or the Golden Rule. Criteria in principle are necessary, but they are not sufficient as points of a definition of ethics. Concerning concrete criteria we have to refer to the historical models of ethics and to the experience of life drawn from them. The individual can only realize the humanity he seeks for in a sectional perspective. Development of conscience by trying to emulate the personality of an individual ideal means altering the original and most personal destination of a person, and hence reverts to being motivated and guided by outside influences. Only a figure capable of simply giving an expression of humanity and not asserting an individualized role in his moral existence could orientate the development of conscience.

Christians believe that this concept has become reality in Jesus Christ's total devotion to an unrestricted labor of love; a reality unattainable through purely human morality. Thus Jesus is qualified to demand the imitation of his example. The aspect of a specifically Christian morality does not originate from isolated norms or abstract principles, but from the person of Jesus Christ. The Christian forming of conscience[34] is thus achieved most precisely by listening and praying to Jesus Christ.

Continual contemplation about the Gospel with all the powers of the psyche engages and develops powers of decision and hence man's independence at his deepest personal levels; this is achieved far more effectively than through purely logical deliberations. Testing the harmony between our own principles of acting and Jesus' way of life as presented to us in the Gospels, we find the most crucial criterion for the distinction between the legitimate appeal to a conscience formed by Christian norms and an improper appeal to a 'self-relationship', which is marked by self-orientated or exclusive group interests. Anyhow, we may have faith in a decision of conscience which is tested by prayer in the light of the Gospel, which has undergone a critical 'discretion of the spirit', and which, finally, is not advantageous solely to ourselves.

The most specific presentation of these more concrete criteria seems to be the Christian tradition of the so-called 'discretion of the spirit'. As far as I know, secular ethics has nothing to put on the same level.

G. Greshake recently attempted to formulate a code of rules from this tradition, which I shall now repeat slightly modified.[35]

1) When conscience makes a word of the Bible relevant to a specific situation in my life, this is the doing of the Spirit of God. (This rule has to be seen together with the following rules.)

2) The will of God is rational, i. e., not simply in the sense of social plausibility but rather in this way that God's call is heard within the rational structure of reality and not in an imaginary enlightenment.

3) A decision of conscience is proper if it can be proved to be rational in the light of motivation, origin, aim, and methods. If one of these aspects is unsatisfactory, the decision of conscience has to be further considered, for instance, the motive has to be altered. A serious claim of conscience must not miss one of these moments.

4) A decision of conscience is proper if it is accompanied by the experience of inner consolation, joy, confidence, and hope. Inner harmony with the self, i. e., with my own identity, is a sign of a good decision of conscience.

5) A true decision of conscience will never let me feel overcharged. Excessive demands and stress originate in the 'Super-Ego'.

6) A decision of conscience must consider the question: How can I improve in doing good? More justice is not always sufficient. True goodness often requires an excess of charity. A decision of conscience is true if my life and the life of others are improved.

7) God's claim upon one's conscience is always concrete. All vague impulses about 'somewhere - or - other' or 'sometime - or - other' cannot be reckoned as true decisions of conscience.

8) A true decision of conscience is always open to the judgment of others. The correctness of a decision of conscience can only be clarified in communication, deliberation, prayer and argument.

All these rules must never be applied in a static way. The 'discretion of the spirit' can never be applied as to giving an absolutely certain statement about the state of conscience. Conscience is by no means an isolated and isolating entity, but rather an essentially social structure in man, who is related to other persons.

4.4 *Development of the Teaching of the Church*

In the Second Vatican Council the teaching of the Church has taken into account the increasing feeling that the mature conscience is creative and independent and not simply a receptive organ for ethical norms. The change in the moral doctrine of the

Church, also in fundamental areas, can be seen very clearly in the comparison between the text prepared for the Second Vatican Council about moral order - *De Ordine Morali* - and the text which subsequently became the obligatory Council text in the Pastoral Constitution of the Church in Today's World.

De Ordine Morali:

In the scheme prepared by Neo-scholastic theologians it was in 1962 still accepted that, "Christian moral order guides the Faithful by the conscience of the individual" (transl.)[36] This means that the conscience is merely a receptive organ for religious and ethical norms and standards. Consequently, this text continued thus on the theme of appeal for freedom and dignity of the conscience: "Such a right, such a freedom, such dignity of conscience exists neither in human nature nor in man himself, being an individual person." (transl.)[37]

Accordingly, the encyclical of Gregor XVI is cited once again, where freedom of conscience - perhaps understandable from the circumstances at that time - is called *deliramentum* (madness).[38]

In Number 16 of the *Pastoral Constitution of the Church in Today's World*, we find the text which has been worked on and altered right up to the last moment: "Conscience is the most secret centre and sanctuary in man, where he is alone with God ... Through loyalty to the conscience Christians are united with all the other people in the search for Truth and for the true solution to the large amount of moral problems which arise in the life of the individual as well as in the life in society. And so, as the true conscience asserts itself more and more, groups and individuals can increasingly desist from all arbitrariness and strive to regulate their behavior in accordance with the objective norms of morality. Conscience can nonetheless be in error due to unavoidable ignorance, without losing its dignity." (transl)[39] This text has also been widely criticized.[40] It represents a piece of compromise, which nevertheless recognizes the essential difficulties and which points out a direction for Christian ethics and moral education.

5. CONCLUSION

Christian ethics as an integrating science is faced with the challenge of preserving the continuity of its own great tradition, and
of linking this up with the legitimate insights and problematic
questions of modern anthropology. Obviously is this set of
problems of particular urgency in the matter of conscience. For
only a theoretical understanding of the conscience, which on the
one hand places the relationship to the self on a firm foundation,
but still includes the detailed knowledge of human behavior in
the midst of ever-changing life circumstances, can create the
pre-condition for the development of a mature conscience. This,
however, is the only way of forming the conscience, which, in
the midst of increasing socio-technical manipulation, enables
man to constantly develop his autonomy and prove his dignity.

University of Salzburg

NOTES

* Translated from the German text by Sheila Bumerl and Nora Schön-
fellinger.

1 Königsteiner Erklärung der deutschen Bischöfe vom 30. August 1968 Nr.
16 und Erklärung der österreichischen Bischöfe zur Eheenzyklika *Humanae
Vitae*, Wiener Diözesanblatt Nr. 2, 1.10.1968.
2 Mieth (1981), p. 166.
3 Schopenhauer (1950), p. 192.
4 E. g., Fuchs (1979).
5 Mieth (1981), pp. 138-184.
6 E. g., Rahner (1984), pp. 11-25.
7 Stelzenberger (1963), p. 13.
8 Schüller (1980), pp. 40-57.
9 Fuchs, 'The Phenomenon of Conscience: Subject-Orientation and Object-
Orientation' in this volume.
10 Reiner (1974), pp. 574-592. Stelzenberger (1963), pp. 81-84.
11 Stelzenberger (1963), pp. 81-84 and Leiber (1912), pp. 372-392.
12 *Summa theologiae* I-II, q 94 a 2.

13 Thomas A., *S. Th.* I q 79 a 12 and *De Ver.* 16,1.

14 Thomas A., *Sent* II, d 39 q 3 a 3. S. Th. I-II, q 19 a 5 and 6; *Quaestio disputata de veritate* q 17 a 3 and 4; *Quod.* q 12 a 2. Cf. also Golser (1975), pp. 43-47. Obviously, Thomas did not yet realize the dignity of the erroneous conscience as we do in modern times. The indisputable axiom of '*bonum causatur ex integra causa, malum autem ex singularibus defectibus*' will not permit him to regard an action based on an erring conscience as basically good. And yet one's will, which is unable to control reason, is always obliged to obey reason, even if the conscience is in error. If will is not subordinated to reason, then it is indisputably morally bad.

15 Guardini (1962), p. 11.

16 Von Monakow (1966), pp. 1-37.

17 This psychic pattern is reflected in a child's habit of putting things in its mouth; this engenders pleasure, aggression is reduced, and finally the fear of separation is overcome.

18 Freud (1972), pp. 495.

19 Gehlen (1969), p. 174.

20 Ibid.

21 Ibid., p. 175.

22 Ricoeur (1974), pp. 30 s; Virt (1983), pp. 123-131.

23 Ricoeur (1974), pp. 21-32.

24 Erikson (1973), p. 62.

25 Kueng (1978), pp. 490-526; Pannenberg (1983), pp. 173-235.

26 Thus see for example: Honnefelder (1982), p. 26.

27 Ibid., pp. 32 s.

28 Ibid., p. 34.

29 Ibid., p. 35.

30 Ibid., p. 20.

31 See note 1.

32 Griesl (1970), p. 12.

33 Biemer/Biesinger (1983); Stachel/Mieth (1978).

34 Virt (1981), pp. 107-120; also Stachel/Mieth (1978).

35 Greshake (1984), pp. 62-85.

36 Golser (1975), p. 21, note 29.

37 Ibid., p. 23.

38 DS 2730.

39 *Vat. Conc. II*, *Gaudium et spes*, Nr. 16, passim.

40 Ratzinger (1968), pp. 328-331.

BIBLIOGRAPHY

Biemer, G./Biesinger, A. (eds.): 1983, *Christ werden braucht Vorbilder*, Mainz.

Denzinger, H./Schoenmetzer, A. (eds.): [36]1976, *Enchiridion symbolorum definitorum et declarationum de rebus fidei et morum*, Herder, Freiburg.

Erklärung der österreichischen Bischöfe zur Enzyklika *Humanae Vitae*, 1. 10. 1968, Wiener Diözesanblatt Nr. 22.

Sacrosanctum Concilium Oecumenicum Vaticanum II: 1966, *Constitutio pastoralis de ecclesia in mundo huius temporis* in: *AAS* 58, pp. 1025-1115.

S. Thomas Aquinatis: [6]1929, *Scriptum super libros sententiarum*, R. P. Mandonnet, O. P. (ed.), P. Lethielleux, Paris.

S. Thomae de Aquino: 1965, *Opera Omnia*. Iussu Leonis XIII P. M. (ed.), Sanctae Sabinae, Roma.

Wort der deutschen Bischöfe zur seelsorglichen Lage nach dem Erscheinen der Enzyklika *Humanae Vitae* 1968, in: *Enzyklika Papst Pauls VI. über die rechte Ordnung der Weitergabe menschlichen Lebens*, Sekretariat der Deutschen Bischofskonferenz (ed.), pp. 63-71.

Erikson, E. H.: 1973, *Identität und Lebenszyklus*, Suhrkamp, Frankfurt.

Freud, S.: [5]1972, *Gesammelte Werke*, 14, S. Fischer, Frankfurt.

Fuchs, J. (ed.): 1979, *Das Gewissen. Vorgegebene Norm verantwortlichen Handelns oder Produkt gesellschaftlicher Zwänge?* Patmos, Düsseldorf.

Gehlen, A.: [2]1969, *Moral und Hypermoral*, Athenäum, Frankfurt-Bonn.

Golser, K.: 1975, *Gewissen und objektive Sittenordnung. Zum Begriff des Gewissens in der neueren katholischen Moraltheologie*, Wiener Dom-Verlag, Wien.

Greshake, G.: 1984, *Gottes Willen tun. Gehorsam und geistliche Unterscheidung*, Herder, Freiburg.

Griesl, G.: 1970, *Gewissen, Ursprung, Entfaltung, Bildung*, Winfried-Werk, Augsburg.

Guardini, R.: [5]1962, *Das Gute, das Gewissen und die Sammlung*, Grünewald, Mainz.

Honnefelder, L.: 1982, 'Praktische Vernunft und Gewissen' in *Handbuch der christlichen Ethik*, III, Herder, Freiburg, pp. 19-43.

Kueng, H.: 1978, *Existiert Gott?*, Piper, München-Zürich.

Leiber, R.: 1912, 'Name und Begriff der Synteresis in der mittelalterlichen Scholastik' in *Philosophisches Jahrbuch* 25, Fulda, pp. 372-392.

Mieth, D.: 1981, 'Gewissen' in *Christlicher Glaube in moderner Gesellschaft*, 12, F. Boeckle/F.-X. Kaufmann/K. Rahner/B. Welte (eds.), Herder, Freiburg.

Monakow, C. von: 1966, 'Die Syneidesis, das biologische Gewissen' in N. Petrilowitsch (ed.), *Das Gewissen als Problem*, Wissenschaftliche Buchgesellschaft, Darmstadt, pp. 1-37.

Pannenberg, W.: 1983, *Anthropologie in theologischer Perspektive*, Vandenhoeck & Ruprecht, Göttingen.

Rahner, K.: 1984, 'Vom irrenden Gewissen' in K. Rahner, *Schriften zur Theologie*, 16, Benziger, Zürich-Einsiedeln-Köln.

Ratzinger, J.: 1968, *Pastorale Konstitution über die Kirche in der Welt von heute. Kommentar zum I. Kapitel* in *Lexikon für Theologie und Kirche*, Ergänzungsband III, Herder, Freiburg-Basel-Wien, pp. 313-354.

Reiner, H.: 1974, 'Gewissen' in *Historisches Wörterbuch der Philosophie*, 3, J. Ritter (ed.), Schwabe & Co., Basel-Stuttgart, pp. 574-592.

Ricoeur, P.: 1974, *Die Interpretation. Ein Versuch über Freud* , Suhrkamp, Frankfurt.

Schopenhauer, A.: ²1950, *Grundlage der Moral*, Sämtliche Werke, 4, Brockhaus, Wiesbaden.

Schüller, B.: ²1980, *Die Begründung sittlicher Urteile*, Patmos, Düsseldorf.

Stachel, G./Mieth, D. (eds.): 1978, *Ethisch handeln lernen*, Benziger, Zürich.

Stelzenberger, J.: 1963, *Syneidesis, conscientia, Gewissen*, Schoeningh, Paderborn.

Virt, G.: 1981, 'Das spezifisch Christliche in der Gewissensbildung' in J. Reikerstorfer (ed.), *Glaubenspraxis*, Wien, pp. 107-120.

Virt, G.: 1983, 'Sittliches Handeln als Symbolgeschehen. Die Bedeutung des psychoanalytischen Symbolbegriffes für eine ethische Handlungstheorie' in *Theologische Quartalsschrift* 163, pp. 123-131.

DISCUSSION

*Josef Fuchs SJ, Lawrence Kohlberg, Georg Lind,
Heinrich Scholler, Günter Virt, Paul Weingartner,
Thomas E. Wren, Gerhard Zecha*

WREN: I have a question which refers to the passage of your paper: "In every real decision of conscience man realizes his contact with the infinite and incomprehensible mystery which the Christian haltingly calls God and Father". I would like to know the status of this claim. Is this your definition of what a real decision of conscience is? If so, then suppose I came to you and I said, "Yesterday I had a decision of conscience, but I did not realize my contact with the infinite and incomprehensible mystery which the Christian haltingly calls God and Father". I would expect you to say, "Aha, that was not a *real* decision of conscience". If I am right so far, then could you please tell me, since it is surely not merely a stipulative definition but rather a definition that actually describes the notion of decision of conscience, what is your evidence for the claim that conscience is like this?

VIRT: The decision of conscience has a moment of absoluteness.

If I were forced to act against this decision of conscience, I would be breaking with my identity: It is an absolute claim. But where can an absolute claim come from? Certainly not from relative norms or contingent values. So, to answer this question, I tried to explain that in each conscience decision there must be a complex setting, consciously or unconsciously. It's a question of transcendental interpretation, a question of the ontological presupposition of experience. I realize the absolute claim....

WREN: Wait a minute. Perhaps this is where I am having trouble, because the English word 'realize' can be used in two ways: psychologically, to mean a hightened form of experience or awareness, an *Erfahrung* (or *erfahren*) which is actually your own term in the original German text, and causally or even ontologically, as meaning to make real (*in Wirklichkeit bringen, verwirklichen*). As your own use of *erfahren* makes clear, you are using the word 'realize' in the psychological sense of 'to experience'. In other words: Your sentence, "Man would realize his contact with the infinite and incomprehensible mystery" appears to go beyond the data, because it suggests that a person can have what he or she thinks is a real moral decision of conscience without any transcendental experience whatsoever - or is it a religious experience?

VIRT: You cannot have the experience separately from the experience of the acting conscience. That's a question of the presupposition and interpretation how an absolute binding claim can be realized.

WREN: I hope my question is clear to the group. My question is that I am challenging this claim of a conceptual linkage between the decision of conscience and the religious experience. I want to say, on the contrary, that one can have a thoroughly secular moral experience. Now you say, "In every *real* decision of conscience". It seems to me what you are doing here is saying that there are two kinds of decisions of conscience: the real ones which have this reference to the transcendent and the unreal ones which do not.

VIRT: No, I tried to say that the moment of an absolute claim is constitutive for conscience.

WREN: Well, then I go back to my previous question: 'What is your evidence for this claim?'

VIRT: I can't give you the evidence, I can give an interpretation.

WREN: There is no evidence?

VIRT: You have to ask for the source where an absolute binding can come from, if all the things we have to decide are only of limited value. I tried to explain it in a philosophical way ...

WREN: No, you explained it in a psychological way! You say there is an '*Erfahrung* ', there is a realization.

VIRT: Maybe the word 'realize' is not correct; I should better say: In the decision of conscience man is in contact with an absolute goodness, whether he is aware of it or not.

WREN: I challenge the data, or rather its supposed universality. I say for many people there is no such awareness.

FUCHS: I think he uses 'realizing an experience' in a psychological experimental way. We are thinking of this, but our awareness is not only an awareness in thoughts. We have a much deeper experience that is not in thoughts, not in concepts: This is the deeper experience which you cannot control by thought. You can only make an interpretation of yourself. Can you understand this experience of an absolute without supposing that you have this deeper realization with or without your reflection? This is a concept of transcendental philosophy.

ZECHA: Maybe a simple distinction can help. What Prof. Wren has in mind seems to be - as far as the experience goes - a descriptive definition of "conscience". That would be: I ask several people for their judgment of conscience. Then I can describe them, I can try to find a common denominator and then I will have a descriptive notion of conscience.But what Prof. Virt seems to be using in his paper is a normative definition of "conscience". So he would say, "Just a descriptive notion is of no help, because then we are left with the possibility of an arbitrary decision or judgment of conscience", and this we do not want. What we want is a more objective or more anti-subjective decision and the root of such a decision somehow lies in what we call God or a transcendental being: that's a stipulation of a normative concept.

VIRT: I thank you for this explanation.

WREN: Now I understand, but I gather you want to say it is more than a purely normative statement, that it is - as Prof. Fuchs said - a transcendental claim about the very possibility for the conditions of there being any moral experience whatsoever. Now, it is not necessary for me to insist that the experience of conscience must have a lot of linguistic sharpness, but what I am asking about in the present context is the experience of the infinite mystery which would have been phenomenological in the non-Husserlian sense in which American psychologists use that word. What I gather from your response is that it is not even necessary that it is a phenomenological experience; that it could be an unexperienced experience as it were. I now see that you have reversed the *Cogito* as far as religious experience is concerned. Instead of saying, "*Cogito, ergo sum*", one would say, "I am a moral agent, therefore: *cogito*". (I am having religious experiences.) I think that's a very extreme position.

VIRT: I think this is quite a different point of view concerning 'experience'. In the scheme of the different levels of experience and meanings of experience of conscience which I presented in my paper, I tried to link your question with mine.

LIND: You say the conscience can be determined by an unconscious drive or by social pressure and the like, so here you have the problem to single out 'real conscience' from 'only conscience'. How would you relate this to a real problem like the conscientious objector?

VIRT: My answer would be: I cannot do it directly, because I have no direct insight into the conscience of another person. Mr. Scholler mentioned this problem.

KOHLBERG: Back to the question that Tom Wren raised. There seem to be intuitions that we keep coming back to, one as right and the good and the other as the issue of the transcendent in conscience. I try to understand the analogy between the definition of justification that you have given to the kind of Kantian appeal to a transcendental reason, that is, that behind every act of conscience according to Kant there is an awareness of the individual's noumenal nature as a rational being. You see the kind of arguments or stipulations are similar, but still the ways of argument derived from Saint Thomas and the one Kant made differ from each other. Kant tried to derive the experience of conscience from something transcendental or from transcendental reason.

VIRT: Kant asks the question, 'Where can absolute binding come from?' And then he says, 'It must be an infinite judge - I cannot say it is God. But what is it? It must be an agent or an instance'. And he says, 'You cannot prove it in this way, that's impossible; it is only a postulate of moral life. You assume this agent'. I think upon this point Saint Thomas and Kant agree, but the difference lies in the interpretation of this absolute binding.

WEINGARTNER: I did not understand one thing: Why did you stress the symbolic concept - conscience as some kind of symbol? First of all, it seems to me that it does not occur later in your paper nor does it give you any new point, and secondly, I didn't get this: According to Ricoeur, you said, conscience is a relationship between various levels of meaning. What would be the concept of conscience then? A relation between concepts? Which levels of meanings? Which meanings? Further you mentioned Thomas' first principle: 'Good should be done, bad should be avoided'. How would you interpret 'the good' or 'the bad' here? Referring to this very important distinction Prof. Fuchs differentiated between right and good. My last point: In your paper you talked about the erroneous conscience. In *De veritate* St. Thomas answers the question, 'In what sense does the erroneous conscience bind?' I just wonder why you left that out. He says, it does bind in the sense that if you don't follow it you sin in some way, but it does not bind in the sense that if you follow it you are morally correct.

VIRT: May I reverse the sequence of points and start with answering the last question. Yes, that's a crucial problem: A will which is moral can only be a will which is not against reason. We talk about the invincible erroneous conscience; but this raises the question if there is an invincible erroneous conscience at all. That's a question of cultivating one's conscience. We are responsible to try to get to the next stage, it is a moral responsibility not to stay at Stage 1 throughout my life. And when I have no other insight, then my will is only moral when it acts according to reason.

Now I have to distinguish between goodness and rightness. I talked to Mr. Kohlberg about the root where both of them come from. I think they both are together in one essential root. And the first principle, I think, is this root. The elements of a moral act are separated later.

Why the concept of symbol in this context? I found that there are a couple of possibilities how 'conscience' is used in the literature: biological syneidesis by Constantin v. Monakow, psychological by Sigmund Freud, sociological ... etc. Also practical reasoning and the four meanings I quoted from Schüller. This author says, it's better to use the term 'conscience' no longer, because too many different meanings are being attached to it. Against this position I say: No, there is a real meaning of conscience. Not only the single moments are called 'conscience', but the whole is called 'conscience'. How can I bring all these moments together? I tried to find out how to integrate them and then I found this definition of 'symbol' in Paul Ricoeur's *De l'Interpretation. Essai sur Freud.* I have a good access to this experience in everyday life from dreams. Also all our actions are a symbol for our inner habit, for our way of life. A crucial problem is that human freedom has several levels, not only the freedom of choice. And to combine all these levels of freedom in the best way is to explain this with this concept of symbol I found in Paul Ricoeur's book. From the point of transcendental philosophy would you say that it is a trivial problem to ask the question: Where does absolute binding come from if not from norms? We can experience that there are norms, but there is no explanation of the absolute binding. And I think in the constitutional law exactly this is protected. We protect a thing which is a paradox. My reaction to this paradox is the question about presupposition.

WEINGARTNER: Going back to more basic principles. I would not call them 'transcendental'. The transcendental question would be: What are the conditions of the possibility of knowledge at all? (*Bedingungen der Möglichkeit für Erkenntnis überhaupt*). Here transcendental philosophy comes in. But there is not much gained by that. All you have described is quite familiar to me and much more concrete than any condition or mere possibility of ... whatever that may be. For these more concrete facts I would not use that name.

VIRT: For me it's not only a question of going back to abstract principles. I also asked for the experience: What kind of deeper experience could be behind this principle? I think there are also consequences. When I go back to the presupposed experience in the first principle: This means that the first condition of a good moral education is trust: that would be the consequence.

WEINGARTNER: This I understand very well. There are necessary conditions for having conscience. All right, this is very important, but is not on the level of, say, Kant's philosophy. Kant's philosophy goes at least one step further: Concrete conditions are not interesting to him. You must ask again: What are the conditions of the possibility of having such a thing? But such questions are probably not much rewarding, as long as we do not know the "space" of possibilities here, and the respective claims (that there are such conditions of possibility) are then quite weak and trivial.

SCHOLLER: My remark has to do with the idea of the symbolic nature of conscience. I would say we are basing our concept of conscience on analogies; and if you take, for instance, the quotation of Romano Guardini of your text, that is a wonderful experience. He uses this definition in three different senses. He is touched by this experience of conscience, he is responding (= auditive dimension), and then he says, 'Conscience answers like the eye to the light' (= visual dimension): one expression and three kinds of analogy. Do you mean this or do you mean by 'symbolic' something else? I am not quite sure.

VIRT: With the term of analogy I tried to interpret what I mean by "symbolic". To me an analogy is a structure; a symbol is a figure in order to get an idea of this complex relationship of what is working together when we speak of conscience.

SCHOLLER: All actions, all gestures are a kind of symbol of something which is behind. - That's a different level of symbolic analogy. I just referred to the process of experience. This process of experience is described in all kinds of books either as experience in the shame-culture or as experience in the guilt-culture. I don't know to which culture you refer. It's a way or different attempt of man to express the inner process by referring to some kind of sentiments, of feelings, of wishes.

VIRT: Expressions of guilt, as Ricoeur pointed out, are always symbolic expressions. And symbolic expressions may also refer to tactile experiences. The first and maybe the oldest symbol of guilt is spots, spots of dirt; to get in touch with some unclean thing. We cannot approach to the very experience of guilt other than through such symbols.

SCHOLLER: Similarly we say, "I hear the voice of my conscience". Conscience is a visual concept; now 'hearing the voice of my eyes' is nonsense, if I would attach it to physical experience. But we are combining a kind of analogy by vision and by auditive experience. It's a mixture of analogy. It's very far from all other experience.

VIRT: Yes, we don't have any other approach, but this indirectly approaches the question: What is moral goodness?

ZECHA: I wonder what role the emotions play when my conscience is at stake. As far as I understand there are two functions: Emotions can warn me, but on the other hand they can give me happiness, satisfaction. What is the precise role of emotions in relation to conscience?

VIRT: In the middle ages there were two schools. It was not a matter of course that St. Thomas linked conscience with reasoning, as other schools said conscience is a question of will, a question of emotion and so on. I have chosen Thomas and I tried to explain from this point of view that in moral decision, when I try to direct my will according to the best of my reason, the entire person is involved. And all the person's levels participate in this process too. It is a feeling of harmony with the deeper levels of the person, for instance, the harmony between my practical reasoning, my unconscious, and all my life-experience.

HIGGINS: Would you have the same feeling of harmony and joy in the case of the invincible erroneous conscience? Are the emotions the same for this person?

VIRT: I can't say they are not. Maybe so, but I cannot imagine that they are.

HIGGINS: But you are saying it could be, what would help us to differentiate?

VIRT: Emotions can be an important criterion for personal decision, but only in connection with a person's willingness to give as much rational account as he is able to give at the moment.

STROTZKA: Two remarks: You are quoting a declaration of the Austrian bishops which is in my translation, "There is freedom of conscience but not freedom of the development of conscience". I have difficulties to understand this sentence; I would have understood easily if the bishops said, 'There is freedom of conscience, but here is a permanent obligation to work on one's own conscience'. But what the bishops say, that there is no freedom of developing the conscience seems to me to be a total nonsense, because this process starts with the parents, the schools and so on - and the children and adolescents have no freedom of choice? They are forced into these situations? This is my first question. The other remark: Do I understand the symbol problem correctly in this way: If I make a decision out of conscience-reasons to go to a demonstration against atomic war. And then I go, and I possibly appear on television. If someone afterwards says, "What really happened was a symbol of my exhibitionism", but I myself never thought about that, so I did it on unconscious reasons. Is that what you mean or is it something else?

FUCHS: Could we see it very briefly in this way: Conscience - this is me. In a certain way everybody is aware of what he is. This is me, I am aware of myself by emotion. Therefore, morality will always have to do with emotions.

Second, morality - we had distinguished between goodness and rightness - participates in freedom. Freedom, oh yes, depends on me, but not freedom for arbitrary decisions. If I am acting, I should act out of moral goodness. Moral goodness is the harmony between my decision and the reason I have. This harmony makes me happy.

Now, suppose the good is also a certain degree of rightness, but you did not do good except by a symbol. So, you were good by doing the right thing; you are happy both because you are good and because you did the right thing. In the erroneous conscience it could happen, that you are good, and therefore you are happy.

VIRT: Let me briefly say to Mr. Strotzka: You are right, because here is an ambiguity in the sentence of the Austrian bishops. In the first sense, 'freedom' means 'freedom of conscience' in its original sense, and in the second remark about freedom, 'freedom' is the same as 'you are responsible for fostering your conscience'. I think there is an ambiguity.

To your second remark: I would distinguish between symbol and symptom. A neurotic symptom, for instance, is a sign of conflict in a person's unconsciousness. Persons cannot understand themselves, and other people cannot understand them either. This is Sigmund Freud's most helpful approach to help to understand things we were unable to understand before: the lowest level of a symbol - a symptom.

End of discussion.

PAUL WEINGARTNER

AQUINAS' THEORY OF CONSCIENCE FROM A LOGICAL POINT OF VIEW

1. AQUINAS' THEORY OF CONSCIENCE IN GENERAL

1.1 *Thesis 1*

Aquinas' theory of conscience[1] has a very simple logical structure: Every statement of a correct conscience is a conclusion of an argument such that the following conditions are satisfied:

(1) The argument is deductively valid (a valid logical inference), i. e., the conclusion follows logically from the premises.

(2) The premises are true (valid).

(3) The first premise is a law-like statement.

(4) The second premise is an instantiation of the antecedent of the law-like premise; both premises together imply the conclusion, which is an instantiation of the consequent of the law-like statement.

The epistemological and psychological aspect of the matter is roughly this:

(5) The law-like statement is habitually known in the sense that it is known without investigation and that it is available whenever needed.

(6) The second premise is not known habitually. It has to be found out by reasoning and investigating and it depends on the concrete situation.

(7) Whereas error is not possible in respect to the lawlike statement (normal conditions presupposed), error is possible in respect to the second premise (6) and in respect to the validity of the inference (1).

(8) Even an incorrect conscience binds in the sense that if one does not follow its statement the action is morally incorrect.

G. Zecha and P. Weingartner (eds.), Conscience: An Interdisciplinary View, 201–230.

1.2 *Thesis 2*

The conditions for the logical structure of Aquinas' theory of conscience satisfy the logical principles of reasoning in today`s science. The reason is this: Conditions (1) to (4) satisfy also the famous scheme of Hempel-Oppenheim for scientific explanation: The state of affairs described by the conclusion is explained by the states of affairs described by the premises if conditions (1) to (4) are satisfied.[2] The same holds for scientific predictions. And the same seems to hold for the derivation of the judgment (sentence) - done by a judge - by applying penal law to the facts of a case (which constitute an offence). Though in the latter case we have a norm as the law-like premise, conditions (1) to (4) are the same. This means that the logical structure of Aquinas' theory of conscience is a very general logical inference-form which is used in many other areas of scientific and practical reasoning.

There are, however, certain differences in respect to scientific explanations. It has been pointed out frequently that condition (2) is almost never really satisfied in scientific explanations (or predictions) because one cannot claim the law (or law-like statement) to be true. According to Popper most of our scientific theories, laws and hypotheses are false in the sense that they have some false consequences though they have a lot of true and interesting consequences. On the other hand there is high methodological security concerning the second premise in a scientific explanation or prediction, i. e., concerning the antecedent-instantiation (which may be an initial condition or another concrete condition). The reason is that this second premise is a kind of basic statement with space-time conditions describing the result of an experiment or of an exact observation. If this is so, then there is an important difference between such a scientific explanation and an argument of conscience according to Thomas Aquinas: In the former the law-premise can be false but the instantiation-premise is very likely to be true. Whereas in the latter the law-premise is true (cf. 2.21 and 2.22) - provided normal conditions obtain - but the instantiation-premise can be false. In fact, Thomas thinks that the main source of error in conscience is a false instantiation statement functioning as the second premise in the argument of conscience (cf. 3.41).

In the following chapters I will elaborate Aquinas' theory in more detail. In doing this I will not just describe Aquinas' theory, but I will try to interpret it in the light of investigations made about normative explanation, value-explanation and teleological explanation.

2. SYNDERESIS

2.1 *Synderesis as Habitual Knowledge of General Principles of Action*

Knowledge, St. Thomas says, is of two sorts: One can be found by research, investigation and comparison only, the other one is available for man without investigation and whenever needed. The second kind of knowledge is related like a principle to all other kinds of knowledge and it can be theoretical or practical.[3]

2.2 *Is there One Principle of Synderesis or Are there More than One?*

2.21 *Thesis 3*: If the description of the practical principle is given by the following properties, then there is more than one principle of synderesis: known without investigation, available when needed, known without error (under normal conditions).

Examples (of Thomas): "God must be obeyed", "Worship should be offered to God", "If God revealed that something should be believed, then it must be believed", "It is impossible that (unconditionally) something which is morally bad should be done".

2.22 *Thesis 4*: If the description of the practical principle is given by the above properties plus the following two then there is only one such principle of synderesis. (1) The principle is formal, i. e., it is invariant against any ethical or religious system, (2) the principle is not concerned with the existence or non-existence of the action, but with its moral obligation (cf. 3.3).

The first practical principle satisfying the conditions of 2.21 and the two of 2.22 is the following: The good should be done, the bad should be avoided.[4]

2.3 *Comparison with Principles in the Theoretical Area*

2.31 Principles in the theoretical area which satisfy the conditions of 2.21 for practical principles are simple principles of logic and mathematics.

Examples: Hypothetical Syllogism, Disjunctive Syllogism, Modus Ponens, some syllogistic modes like Barbara, etc. Simple principles of mathematics like the multiplication table etc.[5]

2.32 Other comparable principles in the practical area of values and norms are principles of natural law.

Examples: Man desires by nature to know. Living in peace is a high value for mankind. Preserving life is a high value. Life should be preserved. Control over natural forces should be improved. Living in a society is a high value for mankind etc.

2.33 First and more outstanding principles in the theoretical and practical area which have the properties stated in 2.22:

2.331 Theoretical area: Principle of non-contradiction (in a tolerant formulation: A statement and its negation cannot both be true), principle of logical consequence (an inference is valid if there is no substitution instance with true premises and a false conclusion), dictum de omni (what is true for all cases is true for any specified particular one) ... etc.

2.332 Area of values: Aristotle and Thomas: If something is desired by everybody (every human person), then it is (objectively) good. Examples of such goods are, according to both philosophers: preservation of life, increase of one's knowledge (according to interest and ability), living in a society etc.

2.333 Area of norms: Thomas: The good should be done, the bad should be avoided.[6]

3. CONSCIENCE

3.1 *Conscience as an Application of Knowledge*

According to St. Thomas Aquinas conscience is the application of knowledge to a special act (action). From the psychological and epistemological point of view, 'application' is here understood as an act (something actual), 'knowledge' is understood as something habitual and 'special act' is again understood as something actual. Concerned with the logical point of view I abstract from being actual and habitual, though these are important properties, which have also been mentioned in 2.21 and 2.22. What then is the logical structure of conscience?

Thesis 5: The logical structure of conscience is the application of a law-like statement or principle - (L) - known without investigation ... etc. (cf. 2.21) - to a more special (in the most special case a singular) (A) which results again in a more special (in the most special case a singular) statement as the conclusion (C). Here L is the principle of synderesis, A and C express states of affairs which are either types of an action or special concrete actions, or they express value-judgments or norms concerning such actions.

3.2 *An Example*

(1) What God has forbidden must not be done.
(2) Lying is forbidden by God.
(3) Therefore: Lying must not be done.

Here (2) is not singular but general and understood in a way which allows to derive: Also this special concrete lie is forbidden by God. And from this together with (1) also the special conclusion follows: This lie must not be committed. Observe that in this first example premises and conclusion are norms. If 'must not be done' is replaced by 'is bad' then (1) becomes a mixed statement consisting of a norm as antecedent and a value-judgment as a consequence and (3) becomes the value-judgment: Lying is bad.

The usual most general law-like premise, however, is: The good should be done, the bad should be avoided.

Accordingly, an argument of conscience has the following general form:

(1a) If something is good then it should be done.

(1b) If something is bad then it should be avoided.

(2a) Action h_1 is good.

(2a') Action h_1' committed by a in situation s (space-time conditions) is good.

(2b) Action h_2 is bad.

(2b') Action h_2' committed by b in situation s (space-time conditions) is bad.

(3a) Therefore: Action h_1 should be done.

(3b) Therefore: Action h_2 should be avoided.

Here (2a) is general and so h_1 in (2a) refers to an action-type, whereas (2a') is singular (special) and so h_1' in (2a') refers to a particular action committed by some particular person at a certain place and time. Therefore h_1 in (3a) has to be interpreted accordingly. What has been said for (2a) and (2a') holds analogously for (2b) and (2b'). Observe that here (1a) and (1b) are mixed statements consisting of a value-judgment in the antecedent and a norm in the consequent. Therefore also (2a), (2a'), (2b), (2b') are value-judgments and (3a) and (3b) are norms.

There is also the possibility that no value-judgments or norms occur in the premises or conclusion. This can be the case if (3) is only to say whether the action took place or not (cf. 3.31).

3.3 *Modes of Application in Conscience*

According to Aquinas there are two modes of application of knowledge to a special action: As to the first we are said to have conscience insofar as we know whether the special act (action) has taken place or not, as to the second whether it is correct or not. And this mode is twofold according to him: A process of taking counsel tells us (beforehand) whether the action should be done or should not be done and a process of discovery tells us (afterwards) whether the action was right or wrong.[7] In the following I will try a rough logical analysis of these three modes of application:

3.31 First mode of application

Thesis 6: The first mode of application, which tells us whether the action has taken place or not, can be analyzed in one of the following two ways 3.311 or 3.312:

3.311 One applies or uses a generally known (and accepted) principle - which is neither a value-judgment nor a norm - to find out or justify that a certain action took place (or didn't take place):

(1) If person a knows (of himself) that a (he) has acted (in such a way) that p occurred, then a has acted that p (occurs).

(2) a knows that a has acted that p (occurred) at time t.

(3) Therefore: a has acted that p at time t.

In this case a general principle of epistemic logic "$aKp \rightarrow p$" (if a knows that p occurs then p occurs) was used in (1) in respect to one's own actions whereas introspective knowledge based on memory was used in (2).

In the negative case - if it is established that the action didn't take place - there are two possibilities: (3) can have the form (a) it is not the case that a has acted that p occurred, or (b) it is the case that a has acted that non-p has occurred. (b) is of course stronger than (a) since acting in such a way as not to help (someone in some situation) - for instance by consciously avoiding to meet this person - is stronger than not-acting in such a way as to help.

3.312 The second way in which the first mode of application can be analyzed is this: In addition to the application of 3.311 one applies or uses a generally known (and accepted) principle which contains a value-judgment in the antecedent to justify or to explain teleologically that the action took place (or didn't take place):

(1) If p is (was) a high value (or an aim to be reached) for the person a and if a knows (knew) that acting that q (occurs) is (was) a necessary condition for obtaining p then - given

some further conditions - a acts (acted) in such a way that q occurs (occurred).

(2) p is (was) a high value (or an aim to be reached) for a.

(3) Therefore: a acts (acted) in such a way that q occurs (occurred).

This is a teleological argument which - expressed in a jargon - explains facts (i. e., (3)) with the help of values or motives (i. e., (2) and (1)).[8]

3.313 *Thesis 7*: Though the first mode of application is usually neglected in descriptions of Thomas' theory of conscience it is of great importance. That it is of great importance I want to substantiate by the following two conditions taken from legal proceedings:

(1) In the process of finding out whether the accused is guilty, the first thing is to find out whether the accused has acted (at time t and place l) in such a way as to bring about a certain state of affairs. Notice that no valuation or norm is claimed here: It is not yet the question whether these states of affairs (simply the facts of the case) are enough to constitute already an offence in the juridical sense. This is a later question and comes in only in the second mode of application.

(2) In the process of finding out whether the accused is guilty, a further important step is to find out the motives and goals for committing the action in question. Again, in a first consideration the action can (and should) be taken as a certain state of affairs not yet evaluated, i. e., not yet subordinated under the elements constituting an offence (as, for instance, "false testimony of a witness"). Therefore the teleological explanation described in 3.312 seems to be the adequate interpretation here, because it has no value-judgment in the conclusion.

3.32 Second mode of application

This mode is twofold according to Aquinas. Before the action has begun its result is whether the action should be carried out or should not be carried out. And after the action took place its result is whether the action was right or wrong. The first I will call the *normative mode*, the second the *evaluative mode*.

3.321 *Thesis 8*: The *normative mode* of application has the form of a normative explanation[9] in which a special norm is derived from a law-like statement (being a norm or at least containing a norm) together with a special statement (being a norm or a value-judgment or another descriptive statement). In the normative explanation the law-like statement is the principle of synderesis.

In general a normative explanation is a logically valid argument in which a norm is deduced from premises which contain at least one norm and satisfy the usual conditions of an explanation (cf. 1.1 and 1.2).

Examples of such normative explanations:

(1) If acting that *p* (occurs) is morally bad then acting that *p* (occurs) should be avoided.
(2) Acting that *p* (occurs) is morally bad.
(2') That a certain person *a* acts (at time *t* and place *l*) in such a way that *p* (occurs) is morally bad.
(3) Therefore: Acting that *p* (occurs) should be avoided.
(3') Therefore: That a certain person *a* acts (at time *t* and place *l*) that *p* should be avoided by *a*.

The expression "acting that *p* should be avoided" can be interpreted in a stronger sense saying that it should be acted in such a way that non-*p* obtains or in a weaker sense (which follows from the stronger) saying that it should not be acted in such a way that *p* occurs. There is still a weaker sense (which follows from the other two), but it is too weak for an adequate interpretation. It is this: It is not the case that it should be acted in such a way that *p* occurs. Writing these different forms in symbolic notation shows the differences which are caused by the position of the negation ('S' for 'should', 'A' for 'act that', 'SAp' for 'it should be acted in such a way that *p* (occurs)'): $SA\neg p, S\neg Ap, \neg SAp$. The second formula follows from the first one and the third one from the second one.

(2) or (2') can be obtained in different ways: either by presupposing that the person in question knows or is convinced himself that the action in question is morally bad. Or by a second explanation, in this case a value-explanation. For instance:

(1) If acting that p is forbidden by God (by the Ten Commandments, by a's own system of norms and values ... etc.),
then acting that p is morally bad
(2) Acting that p is forbidden by God (by the Ten Commandments, by a's own system of norms and values ... etc.).[10]

Since these three steps do not contain any special statement,
they have to be specialized (applied) to the action of a certain
person (as (2') and (3') in the first example are) in order to become a part of the normative mode of application.

A further example would be:

(1) If preservation of life is a high value, then any atomic war
should be avoided.

(1') If preservation of life is a high value for the politician a,
then any nuclear war should be avoided by the a.

(2) The preservation of life is a high value.

(2') The preservation of life is a high value for the politician a.

(3) Therefore: Any nuclear war should be avoided.

(3') Therefore: Any nuclear war should be avoided by the politician a.

It is of special importance that 'should be avoided' can be interpreted in a stronger and in a weaker sense when (3') is interpreted. In the stronger sense it means that the politician should
(positively) act in such a way as to avoid such a war whereas in
the weaker sense he just should not act in such a way as to bring
it about or to allow the war to occur.

3.322 *Thesis 9*: The *evaluative mode* of application has the form
of a value-explanation in which a special value-judgment is
derived from a law-like statement (being a value-judgment or a
norm or a descriptive statement). In this value-explanation the
law-like statement is the principle of synderesis.

In general a value-explanation is a logically valid argument in
which a value-judgment is deduced from premises which contain at least one value-judgment and satisfy the usual conditions
of explanation (cf. 1.1 and 1.2).

Examples of such value-explanations:

(1) If preservation of life is a high value, then pollution control
is a high value.

(2) Preservation of life is a high value.

(3) Therefore: Pollution control is a high value.

Premise (1) can be further grounded on something like this: If pollution is not controlled, life (for instance, of certain plants) cannot be preserved, i.e., a certain high value cannot be realized. However, it should be noted that the following very general principle is not valid: If Z is a high value in the sense of an aim (end) and M is a necessary means for Z then M is also a high value. The reason is that we sometimes have to put up with necessary means. Think of an operation (or poisoning drug) as a necessary means to preserve someone's life. Thus necessary means for an aim (end) get some relative value in respect to that aim (or are relative values in respect to that aim), but this does not mean that they are high values absolutely or in respect to any other aim (end).

(1) If God has revealed that men should not act in such a way that p (occurs) then acting (by men) that p (occurs) is morally bad.

(2) God has revealed that men should not act in such a way that p (occurs).

(2') p_1 is an instance (at time t and place l) of p.

(3) Therefore: Acting (by men) that p (occurs) is morally bad.

(3') Therefore: That a acts in such a way that p_1 occurs is morally bad.

3.4 *Error in Conscience*

St. Thomas' theory of error in conscience is also very simple. It confirms my thesis about the logical structure of conscience as an application of a law-statement to a more special statement in order to derive the factual, evaluative or normative conclusion. For he says at the beginning of the article[11] that error can occur in an application in a twofold way just like in a proof error can occur because some of the premises are not true (or valid) or because a fallacy in the deduction has been committed.

3.41 Concerning the premises there are two possibilities: The law-like premise, which is the principle of synderesis, and the special premise. Concerning the law-like premise (the principle of synderesis) Thomas seems to exclude error provided that normal conditions obtain: A case of abnormal conditions happens in "those who do not have the use of free choice or of reason because of an impediment due to an injury to the bodily organs from which our reason needs help".[12] However, the principle of synderesis is not fulfilled whenever one decides against it, i.e., when some force or passion "so absorbs the reason that in choice the universal judgment of synderesis is not applied to the particular act".[13]

In the specified premise Thomas sees the main source of error. This means that the main source of error is the premise number (2) or (2') in the given examples: Whether God has really revealed something (cf. 3.322) - a question where the heretics differ according to Thomas -, whether preservation of life (any life, a particular life) is a high value (cf. 3.321), whether a certain action is morally bad (cf. 3.321), whether a state of affairs is really a high value for the person a (cf. 3.312), whether a really knows whether a (he) has committed that action … etc.

I agree with Thomas that most of the errors and confusions concerning ethical and moral decisions lie in those specified premises. One of the main tasks of ethics is to offer here a rational method of judging evaluations and norms.

3.42 *Thesis 10*: Though not recognized, deductive fallacy is widespread in ethical and moral discourse. Specifically it is also used to justify decisions forbidden by the statement of conscience.

To defend my thesis I will just select one important case: The fatalistic justification of immoral decisions.

Assume that p is either an immoral action (forbidden by the judgment of conscience) or an action about which I cannot come to the conclusion that it is allowed. And further that p occurs (occurred). Then the widespread fallacious justification is the following:
(1) God wills (wanted) that p does not occur. (Assumption)
(2) Then: p does not occur (would not have been occurred).

Premise (2) is justified by correctly assuming that this is a consequence from omnipotence: whatever God wills occurs.

(3) But: p occurs (or: occurred already).

(4) Since (2) and (3) contradict each other, assumption (1) must be false, i.e., its negation must be true.

(5) Therefore: God wills (wanted) that p occurs (p to occur). And therefore: action p cannot be wrong.

In this derivation everything is logically correct except the last step: (5) is not the negation of (1). The (correct) negation of (1) is: It is not the case that God wills that p does not occur. But to derive (5) from this weaker statement is a logical fallacy by confusing different types of negation: Whereas from "wills that p" it follows "not wills that not p" (assuming rational willing), the other way is fallacious.

The "justification" of (5) is sometimes done also more directly (and consequently more clumsy) by the assumption of the fatalistic thesis: For any event p, if p occurs, then God wills (wanted) that p occurs (will occur).[14]

3.5 Comparison with Analogous Modes of Reasoning

3.51 *Thesis 11*: The *normative mode* of application is analogous (1) to the application of penal law in legal proceedings, and (2) to the application of laws of nature (scientific laws) in scientific predictions.

My justification of this claim is the following: First, the logical structure in the three cases is the same (cf. 1.1, 1.2, 3.32). Second, in both cases, that of penal law and that of scientific prediction, the law has already been established like the principle of synderesis. Third, the difficult task in all three cases is to apply the law to the special case. As regards conscience, recall what has been said in 3.41. In the case of the application of penal law (after it has been established whether the action took place or not) the important question is whether the pure facts (pure facts of the case) can be interpreted as constituting the elements of an offence. And in the case of applying a law of nature the important question is to find the restricting initial conditions which allow an application and so a prediction. Fourth, in all three cases the conclusion refers to an event in the future. In the case of conscience and in that of penal law it is a norm, in the case of prediction a descriptive statement.

3.52 *Thesis 12*: The *evaluative mode* of application is analogous - at least in some important aspects - to the application of laws of nature (scientific laws) in scientific explanations of past events.

My justification of this claim is similar to the one above: First, the logical structure is the same (cf. 1.1, 1.2, 3.321). Second, in both cases the law has already been established. Third, the difficult task in both cases is again to apply the general law to the special case (see above). Fourth, in both cases the conclusion refers to an event which occurs at present or has occurred in the past.

Institut für Wissenschaftstheorie,
International Research Center Salzburg
and
University of Salzburg

NOTES

1 Aquinas' theory of conscience is taken mainly from *De Veritate*, q 16 and 17 and from the *Summa Theologica* I q 79, 12 and 13; I-II, 1 94, 1 ad 2; q 96, 4; q 19, 5 and 6.

2 Though I have shown (in a forthcoming publication) with one of my colleagues that the addition of a relevance-condition (to the conditions for "scientific explanation") is necessary to rule out certain paradoxes, this is a special issue which does not need to concern us here since the relevance condition can always be added if needed. Cf. Weingartner and Schurz (1985).

3 *De Ver.*, q 16, 1; *S. Th.* I, q 79, 12; I-II q 94, 1 ad 2.

4 For a discussion of such an invariance principle cf. Weingartner (1983, p. 527f.) and Weingartner (1986).

5 I do not label them as 'analytic', because too much misuse and vagueness are accompanied with that term. Especially there is the danger that equivalences dependent on language-use enter, as Quine has pointed out correctly.

6 Cf. Thomas Aquinas, *De Ver.*, q 17, 1, and *S.Th.* I-II, q 94, 1 ad 2. Cf. the discussion whether such principles are scientifically testable in Weingartner (1983, p. 522f.).

7 Cf. Thomas Aquinas, *De Ver.*, q 17, 1, and *S.Th.* I, q 79, 13.

8 Whereas other authors (cf. Wright (1971) and Tuomela (1977)) have a wider concept of teleological argument, I have restricted this term to only those arguments which contain value-judgments in the premises but not in the conclusion, i.e., which - on the lines of Dilthey and Spranger - subordinate facts under a hierarchy of values ("Sinnzusammenhang"). Cf. Weingartner (1984).

The "further conditions" mentioned in (1) are at least the following two: a is able to bring about q, a prefers p to non-q. In the first premise (1) one can also replace 'knows' by 'believes', since in actual cases there isn't always knowledge (in a strong sense) available concerning the necessary conditions.

Thus I propose the following form as a general form of teleological arguments:

(1) If p is an aim (end) for person x within the field f and if x believes (knows) that q is a necessary condition for p in respect to f and if x prefers p to non-q within f, then: x acts in such a way as to bring about q.

(2) $p1$ is a certain aim (end) for the person $x1$ within the special field $f1$ and $x1$ believes (knows) that $q1$ is a necessary condition for $p1$ in respect to $f1$ and $x1$ is able to bring about $q1$ and $x1$ prefers $p1$ to non-$q1$ within $f1$.

(3) Therefore: $x1$ acts in such a way as to bring about $q1$.

This is a valid logical argument based on *modus ponens* and instantiation ($p1, x1, f1, q1$ are instantiations of p, x, f, q).

Von Wright's so-called "Practical Syllogism" differs from the argument given in 3.312 and from the more detailed one above in the following important point: The first premise in the Practical Syllogism consists only of the antecedent (or of the first part of the antecedent) of the premise (1); i.e., the Practical Syllogism reads like this (cf. v. Wright, 1971, p. 96):

(1) From now on A intends to bring about X at time t.

(2) From now on A considers that unless he does Y no later than at time t' he cannot bring about X at time t.

(3) Therefore, no later than when he thinks time t' has arrived, A sets himself to do X, unless he forgets about time or is prevented.

This Practical Syllogism is not logically valid, because there is no valid argument form of which it would be an instance. This is the reason why I have not chosen the Practical Syllogism as an interpretation of a teleological explanation. Cf. the discussion in Weingartner (1984) chapter 5.

9 The term 'explanation' is used here in a wider sense than is usual in works of philosophy of science, though it has the same formal properties. The German 'Begründung'would be more appropriate, but there is hardly an equivalent in English. 'Justification' seems to be too narrow.

10 What kind of authority is chosen here will depend very much on the maturity of the person. Prof. Kohlberg's theory of the different stages of maturity concerning ethical (moral) values and norms provides an interesting and detailed answer here.

11 Cf. *De Ver.* , q 17, 2.

12 *De Ver.*, q 16, 3.

13 Ibid

14 Cf. Weingartner (1974).

BIBLIOGRAPHY

Thomas Aquinas: 1964, *Quaestiones Disputatae De Veritate.* Marietti, Rome.

Thomas Aquinas: 1953, *The Disputed Question on Truth.* Translated by J. V. McGlynn S.J., Regnery, Chicago.

Thomas Aquinas: 1952, *Summa Theologiae.* Marietti, Rome.

Thomas Aquinas: 1963-73, *Summa Theologiae.* Latin text and English translation, Blackfriars, London.

Tuomela, R.: *Human Action and its Explanation.* Reidel, Dordrecht.

Weingartner, P.: 1974, 'Religiöser Fatalismus und das Problem des Übels', in E. Weinzierl (ed.), *Der Modernismus. Beiträge zu seiner Erforschung. Festschrift für Th. Michels.* Styria, Graz, pp. 369-409.

Weingartner, P.: 1983, 'Auf welchen Prinzipien beruht die Naturrechtslehre?', in D. Mayer-Maly and P. M. Simons (eds.), *Das Naturrechtsdenken heute und morgen.* Duncker & Humblot, Berlin, pp. 517-544.

Weingartner, P.: 1984, 'On the Introduction of Teleological Arguments into Scientific Discourse', in *Archives de l'Institut International des Sciences Théoretiques 26. Proceedings of the Conference of the Academie International de Philosophie des Sciences.* La Rabida, Sevilla, 1983, Office International de Librairie, pp. 196-217.

Weingartner, P.: 1986, 'Gibt es rechtssystem-invariante Normen?', forthcoming.

Weingartner, P. and G. Schurz: 1985, 'Paradoxes solved by Simple Relevance Criteria', in *Logique et Analyse.*

Von Wright, G. H.: 1971, *Explanation and Understanding.* Ithaca, New York.

DISCUSSION

Joseph Fuchs SJ, Ann Higgins, Georg Lind,
Heinrich Scholler, Werner Stark, Hans Strotzka,
Günter Virt, Paul Weingartner, Thomas E. Wren,
Gerhard Zecha

LIND: Do I understand your explanation rightly when I try to apply it to the process of psychological assessment or psychological diagnostics? I have found in Gordon Allport's treating psychometrics or psychological assessment a differentiation which is very similar to yours and in which he says: You first have to make sure that your measurement is according to the facts as really describing a behavior of the person you are assessing. Second, you have to describe it in terms of his intentions, motives, his inner motives and not just by the motives you assume. The third step which is unfortunately the only one in psychometrics so far, is judging that behavior on the basis of social norms that come from an external side. Do I understand that right if I try to liken Aquinas' theory to a psychological process like that?

WEINGARTNER: Yes. I see an analogy here. Your first step corresponds to Thomas' question about whether the act took place or not. A factual description answers this question (cf. 3.311). Your second step corresponds to the same question but in respect to the motive or intention. In this respect I said that the answer is given with a teleological explanation, i.e., explaining the action (the fact) with the help of values (motives, intentions (cf. 3.312)). The third step of judging the behavior corresponds to Thomas' judgment of the conscience whether the action should be done or avoided (before the action) and whether it was good or bad (after the action).

LIND: May I add another question: The conclusions, can they enter into new arguments? For instance, can the normative conclusion enter as an antecedent to the value-judgment?

WEINGARTNER: That can be the case, of course. An example is the justification of premise (2) in 3.321 (the second argument in chapter 3.321) of my article. Another case where some philosophers of law would speak of a normative antecedent is the application of penal law. They think that the reinterpretation of the states of affairs as a certain kind of offence means turning a descriptive factual statement into a norm. In my view this is not the case, i.e., they are both factual though to the state the offence in the juridical sense is different from the description of the state of affairs.

SCHOLLER: I would like to make three points: First: If somebody says, - according to the penal law - "He who steals will be punished, imprisoned", it's not a moral statement. If he would argue, "I shouldn't steal, because then I will be punished and imprisoned", then again it is not a moral judgment, because I don't see the cause of why "I will be imprisoned". Only if I say, "I ought not to steal because it's bad", then I think I have given a moral judgment. There is a theory saying: The state in acting penal law does limit itself to the sanction of imprisonment. The unwritten part of the imposed sentence of the penal law is: "You should not steal", but what is written down is just: "He who steals will be punished".

Second point: You know the problem is to pass from synderesis to conscience. There must be some kind of evidence, not just application of knowledge. Let's take the example, to honor the elders. To do good, to avoid the bad is part of the synderesis. To honor the elders might be also part of synderesis, but now when it comes to the application of knowledge, I have two systems of knowledge: One is to kill the hungry old father, the other not to kill him, and to serve him. So how shall I know which set of knowledge I have to apply? The *applicatio scientiae* cannot give me any evidence.

As a third point, I just would like to mention: That the system of Aquinas is now re-established by the penal law: Because you are not guilty and you cannot be punished if you err and if this error was unavoidable. To a certain extent our penal law system tried to implement this traditional concept of the erroneous conscience.

WEINGARTNER: Concerning the third point I agree that, as far as I understand, St. Thomas only says that if he does not know and has an erroneous conscience about it then he is excused for this case. Immediately afterwards he takes up the question: Is he excused in every respect? And he says: Not necessarily, because it could be the case that earlier he has omitted something important and relevant in respect to the avoidance of that error. So everybody has the obligation to keep himself informed and to avoid error and lack of available information in order to improve, correct and revise his knowledge. A similar view is taken into account in the penal law. To your second question, Thomas is of the opinion that there are certainly more such principles than only one. And I said only, if we take the most formal one then we'll only have *one*. But how far does it go? He also says that man is able to extend the set of the special principles of synderesis. Some more primitive people will have fewer evident principles, some more sophisticated will have more. But if we take a special principle like yours I have the same difficulty here. I just don't know whether I can subsume it under synderesis. An interesting question will be to find out whether he has criteria. Now to your first question: I agree completely that the penal law is different from a kind of moral law, or also from conscience. My comparison was more on the formal point. There are a lot of important differences: First, it would certainly not be the doctrine of Aquinas that everything we have in the modern penal law would be known as principles of synderesis. Second, there is this very important difference which you pointed out already: The structure of a law-statement in the penal law is a mixed norm or a mixed statement where the first part is factual and the second part is normative: If this and this is the case, this and this should be the case. On the other hand the structure of a law-statement belonging to the moral law is different. It has some evaluation in the antecedent: "If this is good, then that should be". Or: "If this is bad, then that should not be". In the penal law the evaluation is avoided. It says only, "If this and this has been committed, then..." (i.e., for instance, "If murder has been committed, then ..."). Of course you may say, it is always an evaluation because "murder" is negatively evaluated in our background. So, I think we have some kind of hidden evaluation here, but we have not an explicit evaluation with a value-predicate in the penal law. In the background of any penal law there seems to be some kind of moral law, perhaps based on some natural law. A sign for that may become apparent if one changes or revises penal law.

<u>VIRT</u>: Concerning the problem of erroneous conscience I think Thomas is in a theoretical dilemma: On the one hand he always says, "Morality means to act according to reason" (*secundum rationem vivere* is his formula). And there is the other axiom he also has in his tradition, *Bonum ex integra causa, malum ex quolibet defectu,* i.e., for a good action all the moments have to be good: the aims, the intention, the method etc. If just one of these moments is wrong, the action cannot be good. And that's the problem. Therefore he is in a dilemma which he cannot solve. But he tries to solve it by saying, "Erroneous conscience: conscience not *per se* can err, only *per accidens*". This, however, is not sufficient for us. He was not yet able to say, 'The erroneous conscience has its own dignity'. That was what Vatican Council II did.

<u>WEINGARTNER</u>: As far as I see Thomas would say: If there is some mistake somewhere, the action is not completely correct. But he wouldn't say, it's totally incorrect, because every action is done for some good reason according to him, that is: For all x: if x is an action then there is at least some good reason for which x is done. He does not claim that there is always the same good reason for every action done, but for any action as bad as it can be, there is always some (or other) good reason, for which it is done. Even he who commits suicide does it for some good reason, since he thinks to stop life is better than to continue. If an action is not completely good, it is - compared to the completely good action - a *privatio,* i.e., something bad, because it *could* be more complete, more perfect.

<u>FUCHS</u>: Well, I have several questions, but to this last one I think, Aquinas would say: If the action is lacking one point it is not totally good.

Point 8 of your first thesis says: "Even an incorrect conscience binds in the sense that if one does not follow its rule, the action is morally incorrect". But reading it in a different way, "The action is morally incorrect, if you do not follow an incorrect conscience" does not make sense to me. I think you used the

word 'incorrect' in two different senses: Once it means the opposite of rightness and once that of goodness. If you do not distinguish, sentence 8 is not clear. I would say, even an incorrect conscience in regard to rightness binds in the sense, "If one
does not follow its rule, the action is morally not good". I want
to continue along this line: I think the conclusions in these syl-
logisms are always the conscience-conclusions. What should I
decide in conscience? This conclusion - this is now my question - this conclusion is about moral goodness. I would formulate it this way: Moral goodness does not depend on the fact that
I'm doing the right thing; or that I do the wrong thing - this is
outside me. Moral goodness consists in regard to rightness,
i.e., that conscience tries to express itself in the right solution
and not in the wrong solution: it only tries.
Aquinas, going back to Aristotle, asked himself, "How do we
determine the moral truth (*veritas moralis*)? When do I have to
decide, to what act should I decide?" His answer is not: "Moral
truth consists in the correspondence of this norm to reality", but
his answer is quite different: "Moral truth consists in that your
decision is in accordance with your *appetitus rectus*." If you
have a tendency to go in the right way and try to act according to
this tendency then you are good. Not your correspondence to
the rightness within this world, but that you follow the moral
truth means you correspond to your *appetitus rectus* (the good
inclination to find out the right thing, not the actual correspondence to the right solution). This is Aquinas himself and
he has this from Aristotle. The respective text is in Thomas
Aquinas' *Commentary on the Nicomachean Ethics,* book VI,
Lecture 2 (1129 ff).
WEINGARTNER: First, to my point 8. It's perfectly in
agreement with my interpretation of the text in *De Veritate* (q.
17,4) if you say like Thomas: "For conscience is said to bind
insofar as one sins (acts morally bad) if one does not follow his
conscience." And he adds: "But not in the sense that he acts correctly if he does follow it". It's a very important point that
Thomas adds the second statement, since "if he follows his
conscience he acts correctly" does not logically follow from the

first and, moreover, it is not true according to him because his conscience may be in error.

A second point: You say: Moral goodness does not depend on whether I do the right or the wrong thing. In my view, it's at least a question whether you are not going one step too far here. Take the following example: The soldiers of Khomeini may work according to their conscience and their religious indoctrination which says that they should kill the others and they will go to heaven immediately, i.e., they act according to their appetitus or inclination to find the right thing (heaven) in your terminology. Though this is not a doctrine of the Koran, but in some Islamic traditions the actions of the soldiers would be morally good according to your opinion.

I would rather think that the view of Aquinas is that the soldiers are in some sense excused. Under the condition that their end is the heaven to which their appetitus is inclined they act accidentally good. But in respect to the means, where their erroneous reason tells them to kill others, they do not act morally good. Insofar and as long as they have no better knowledge and information they might be excused. But they are not excused in general since they might have been too superficial in investigating their case, in taking it too easy that their actions contradict the Fifth Commandment (viewed by Thomas as a natural law) etc. ...

FUCHS: Then you have to say, 'These soldiers are not morally good in their conscience and they are not morally bad in their conscience'. So they are morally neutral: and this is a concept Aquinas never would accept. He says explicitly: 'Every human act is a moral act, either good or bad'.

WEINGARTNER: Perhaps I can clear up the situation a little bit. Thomas clearly says: If he does not follow his conscience he sins (*"nisi conscientiam impleat peccatum incurret"*). From this follows logically: If he does not sin he follows his conscience. And then he says that it does not hold: If he follows his conscience he acts correctly (*"non autem hoc modo quod aliquis impleus recte faciat"*, *De Ver.* 17,4). Since the latter does not hold we *cannot* conclude (by hypothetical syllogism from the former): If he does not sin he acts correctly (although it certainly holds: If he acts correctly he does not sin). This means that "not to sin" leaves open two possibilities: acting correctly in the sense of morally good on the one hand and acting either indifferently (neither morally good nor morally bad) or in one respect good, in the other not good on the other hand. And in my view Thomas intends to leave these two possibilities open. Thus it holds for the case of the soldiers: Though they act according to their conscience, it does not follow that they act correctly or morally good.

(Note added after discussion: Thomas in fact accepts indifferent actions, see *De Ver.* 17,5.)

STARK: First a question: To what extent is your analysis of Aquinas' theory of conscience applicable to other parts of Aquinas' theorizing? The operation of conscience is part of life. Now it seems to me that in the so-called proofs for the existence of God there is a similar argumentation. God is part of life. And I think your analysis would be applicable to other parts of Aquinas' thought as well.

And then a second point on the universal applicability or validity of moral propositions. I think the answer lies in an entirely different part of Aquinas. He has these two concepts *multitudo* and *amicitia*. Man operates between these two poles. He starts with *multitudo,* living just side by side and ending up with a close and loving relationship to your fellowman. Now, anything that leads man from *multitudo* to *amicitia* is good and must be good in absolutely any society. Because the great problem of social life is the establishment of firmly integrated relationships. Now I think behind Aquinas there is not Aristotle, but Augustine with his *City of Man* and *City of God*. And in the further background, I think, there is really Plato.

WEINGARTNER: According to your first point, I would distinguish two questions: (1) whether he applies logic, i.e., logical argumentation to different problems; (2) whether there are certain structures of arguments applied. When we have (1) in mind, then I think he applies logic almost everywhere, but the arguments are different then. The whole structure of the *Summa Theologica* is a structure of logical argumentation: beginning with objections, giving the answer in general arguments and concluding with arguments which are corrections to the objections. In the proofs for the existence of God, however, the structure of the arguments is not the same as here. It is not that we have one law-statement and then an application. A few Polish logicians (J. Salamucha, E. Nieznanski) and Essler (in his *Introduction to Logic*) have tried to formulate some of the Five Ways in predicate logic. There are more law-like premises than just one, and the proof ends with an existence statement about an unique object, i.e., that there is at least one and at most one First Mover, for instance. Your second point, I understand as an interesting addition. I can only comment that love is for Thomas *the* cause of all the passions of the soul. It causes striving for something, because if love is extinguished one wouldn't have a goal. It causes also enjoyment when one has reached a goal. This central point certainly comes from Augustine.

ZECHA: The following question: It is new to me that conscience can produce a factual statement. I always had in mind that a conscience comes out with a norm which is an application of a law-like statement to a special situation or a value-judgment. The example you gave from the court of law was not quite convincing: It's just a type of memory statement, but has nothing to do with conscience. So, the excused person remembers a certain happening and says, 'Yes, that's true, *I* did that, *I* was it'. That's not a statement of conscience, but a recalling of what he did. So, I think conscience has to do with normative or evaluative judgments.

WEINGARTNER: I tried to find out the logical structure of the concept "conscience" in Thomas. I agree that nowadays a statement of conscience is understood as a normative or evaluative judgment. But, as I said, Thomas distinguishes three modes of application in conscience. And the first of the three is factual. He says, "According to the first mode of application we are said to have conscience of an act inasmuch as we know that the act has been placed or has not been placed as happens in the common manner of speaking when one says 'As far as my conscience is concerned, this has not taken place'. Of course, he mentions memory and also sensitive knowledge in this connection. And he seems to connect these two to the so-called *inspection* of a criminal case.

ZECHA: Thank you, I see. I also forgot that the Latin word *conscientia* actually means not only conscience in the traditional sense, but also memory and even consciousness.

Now to your condition 2 in your paper: Don't you think it is too strong? You said you were describing and interpreting Thomas Aquinas, but you were not criticizing him: 'The premises are true or valid' ... isn't that too strong? Because in the Hempel-Oppenheim-scheme it is too strong. Why is it not too strong here?

WEINGARTNER: Look at my thesis 1.1: "The statement of a *correct* conscience is the conclusion of an argument such that ...". If I would drop the word 'correct' here, then I would not need condition (2). An erroneous conscience might not have all the premises true; or it might use an inference which is invalid. But Thomas' view is 'If conscience is correct in every respect, i.e., if the statement of conscience (conclusion) is correctly justified, then the premises also have to be true.'

ZECHA: I am not yet quite convinced. Because he says, 'Conscience is the application'. He obviously has in mind that the application has to be done by someone. Is it not possible that instead of the premises' being true or valid, it should read, 'The premises are meant to be true or valid by the actor'? Because this would point to the subjectivity-factor of which we heard this morning in Prof. Fuchs' lecture.

WEINGARTNER: Of course, all a person can know is that he is convinced that his premises are true. And if they are in fact true and if the inference is valid, then his conscience is correct in every respect. But if one (especially the second) premise is false - though the person is convinced that it is true - we have an erroneous conscience. Although this erroneous conscience binds in the sense that if he does not follow its rule he sins, it does not bind in the sense that if he follows its rule he acts morally good.

STROTZKA: I am a complete outsider, but listening to the lecture and to the discussion something came in my mind. If the program committee had included a lecture about Aristotle's

Nicomachean Ethics which would have been possible, then I would expect that the speaker says, "This was a theory of that time, long ago, there were many interpretations and today we think about Aristotle in this or that way." If we would have had a lecture on Kant, I would expect the same.

In your lecture I had the feeling that Thomas is a contemporary of us. We look at his system as it were valid today exactly in the same way as it was 700 years ago. Does it make sense to speak about somebody in this way? Or should we put him in a historical perspective to some extent? Am I totally wrong?

WEINGARTNER: Not at all, this is an important question. My view about interpreting traditional philosophical problems is this: First, I find the problems in the history of philosophy very interesting but only if one tries to give a new interpretation in the light of our knowledge today. This I did also with Aquinas' theory of conscience, since I didn't hesitate to offer new theses, i.e., claims about the structure of his theory in the light of modern logic and the theory of explanation. I do not claim that this structure is explicitly appearing in the text. It's rather implicitly contained and explicitly only in some passages. Therefore, what I am doing is giving an *interpretation*.

Second, there is the question, "Is this method allowed or methodologically sound?" In my view it is the only method that leads to a progress of understanding traditional views. Let me give an example. According to the "Sinnkriterium" of the early Vienna Circle an important statement of Plato's cosmology was an example of meaningless metaphysics. The statement is from the *Timaios* saying that the essence of material things are geometrical figures. Of course, at first sight this seems meaningless. But if we know a little bit of the history of philosophy and of modern science the problem gets very interesting. The first point is this: Plato was attacking Democrit's theory that the mutual positions of atoms can be explained by an arithmetical theory. Plato's counter-example was: What would happen if we had four atoms in the corners of a square? Then the distances in the diagonals can only be represented by irrational numbers. So he saw: Arithmetic (then the "theory of the odd and the even") is not sufficient to explain nature. Plato was always striving for the aim of the Greek philosophers,i.e.,: to find invisible, abstract, universal and immaterial principles for explaining the visible, concrete, particular, and material things of the world. The second point is this: Since Plato could not dissolve irrational numbers (in the dialogues he tried different proofs to show that they cannot be reduced to rational ones) he offered as a solution to take simple geometrical figures which include some irrational distances as the "atoms of geometry", i.e., as atoms from which every geometrical figure and body (like a polyhydra) can be constructed. In fact he thought (wrongly) that all the geometrical figures and bodies can be built up by two triangles: 90, 45, 45, and 90, 60, 30, each with a hypothenuse, the length of which is an irrational number. And now you may understand better his view: If these two triangles are the atomic structure of the mutual distances of all atoms and all material things are built up of atoms then these two geometrical figures are the very structural essence of material things. The third point is now an interpretation in the light of modern science. Some connections suggest themselves, others are more hidden: Take a crystal structure and all what we know about it today, then Plato's idea sounds very modern. But what is more hidden is this: Newton's theory of gravitation and movement is impossible without Euclidean geometry. And this theory was his first great theory which offered an explanation of the universe. And then let's pass to Einstein's Theory of Relativity: Is it not also based on geometry, this time not Euclidean but non-Euclidean? We may now turn Plato's statement about the essence of material things into the broader statement: We need geometry to explain the material universe. And taken in this way the principle is a valid principle of modern science.

If, therefore, we interpret Plato's original metaphysical doctrine in this way, it gets very interesting and exciting. This is my view of how to interpret only metaphysical problems. And in a similar sense I tried to interpret the structure of Thomas Aquinas' theory of conscience with the help of modern logic and the theory of explanation.

STROTZKA: I must say this is an enlightening answer for me: thank you.

WREN: I would like to address my remarks as much to Prof. Strotzka as to our speaker, Prof. Weingartner. And that is about the worth of this kind of logico-structural inquiry. I think you can make intellectual coin out of doing this kind of non-historical analysis, logical analysis. But it depends on whether you have the right logical approach to the issues in question. I'm just suggesting that there might be an alternative approach. I would have liked not to treat normative and value-judgments as propositions of the sort that are envisioned in, say, Hempel's notion of reasoning. I would rather have preferred a totally different approach, one which regards the utterance of a normative or value-judgment as a kind of performative speech act in which one is actually making a commendation rather than uttering a scientific or factual proposition. This approach comes out of the Oxford analytical philosophers. The principal name here would be that of R.M. Hare, who himself made a lot of sense out of the notion of understanding 'good' and other value-loaden words as supervenient categories.

WEINGARTNER: You ask me whether I have *the* right logical approach when interpreting Aquinas. My first answer is: I do not know, I can only give you good reasons for my interpretation. But here we are all in the same boat: Nobody ultimately knows! My second answer is this: There might not be just one right approach. To assume this seems often to be a rather naive presupposition, i.e., there can be more ways than one and all of them can be very illuminating. If a thing is very complex and has a lot of aspects (like conscience) then - according to Thomas - only God can understand it in one action of understanding but concerning man we need two things:

(1) many scientists with different abilities to find out the different aspects and (2) more than one method to be applied in the investigations. Thus I gave a proposal for *one* interpretation. If you have another proposal then work it out carefully and tell us. Concerning the question whether norms are propositions which you attribute falsely to me I'd like to say: In my view norms are not true or false, they have different values (either two or more), e.g., valid or invalid. I have written an article against the usual method to change norms into their propositional counterpart by

taking out of them their so-called "propositional content". Finally, I have nothing against the speech act theory. Many things are still unclear about what exactly a speech act is. But I have nothing against an approach to interpret the theory of conscience from this point of view.

HIGGINS: I just would like you to give an example - maybe you can use the one about 'Honor the elderly' - and then the different norms of what it means to kill them or not to kill them. Now, what is the application of the modes here? How could it help in some problem that we face today?

WEINGARTNER: Concerning your example the first mode of application answers the question whether you (in a certain situation) have honored the elderly (for example have helped them to find a nice place to live, taken them into your house ... etc.) or did not do so. And this fact (whether you have honored them or not) can be explained in two ways: first by other facts (cf. 3.311 of my paper), i.e., by the knowledge of your memory, or second (cf. 3.312) teleologically, by giving some of your motives or aims.

The second mode of application is twofold according to Thomas: one is the normative mode before the action takes place and one is the evaluative mode after the action has been committed. The normative one answers the question whether a certain action (for instance, a special form of honoring the elderly) should be done or not. And it could have the following general form:

(1) If honoring the elderly is morally good (and you are in a situation in which the elderly need you and you are able to help) then you should do it.

(2) To honor the elderly is morally good and you are in such a situation.

(3) You should honor the elderly (in this specific situation). Here (1) is an instance of the general norm "The good should be done, the bad should be avoided" which is in the synderesis. (2) has to be judged with the help of human reason and by rational arguments and here conscience can err. (3) is the imperative (special norm) which tells us what we should do.

One could also think of another form of the normative mode concerning your example. First it is plain that the special norm "Honor the elderly" is not one which men have in the synderesis (i.e., as a habitual evident rule available all the time without investigation). But in the synderesis there could be the general norm (1') "Do as you would like to be done by" (or: "Do unto others as you want them to do unto you"). Then the second premise of the normative mode (normative explanation) would be something like: (2') I would like to be honored (to be taken care of) when I am old. Therefore: (3') I should honor (take care of) the elderly. In respect to the evaluative mode of application it can have the following form, when applied to your example: (1) To honor the elderly is morally good. (2) I have honored (taken care of) the elderly. Therefore (3) I have done something morally good. But the justification of (3) can be also more sophisticated or complex, for instance: (1') If our experience of living in a society shows us that to honor the elderly is good then all care for the elderly is good. (2') Our experience of living in a society shows us (now, in our society) that to honor the elderly is good. Therefore (3') all taking care of the elderly (now, in our society) is good. (4') I take care of the elderly (now, in our society). Therefore (5') I am doing something good.

End of discussion.

HEINRICH SCHOLLER

THE AMBIVALENT RELATIONSHIP OF LAW AND FREEDOM OF CONSCIENCE: INTENSIFICATION AND RELAXATION OF CONSCIENCE THROUGH THE LEGAL SYSTEM

1. INTRODUCTION

1.1 This article will deal with two concepts which deviate somewhat from the traditional problem of freedom of conscience and its relationship to law. These concepts assume a basic right to conscience, not only a right to freedom of conscience, and this article will address "intensification"[1] and "relaxation" of conscience with regard to the situation of the individual within the legal system. Constitutional law, in particular as it concerns basic rights, deals with relaxation of conscience, whereas criminal law is concerned with intensification of conscience which will be described in more detail. Thus, the legal system exhibits an ambivalence towards phenomena of conscience. On the one hand, it is reluctant to interfere with the individual conscience, indeed within certain sets of rules it elevates freedom of conscience to a systematic fundamental law[2]; on the other hand, it does not recognize the appeal to conscience as a viable defense and places all natural and civil liberties under the proviso of the law.[3] The legal system refers to immanent or extrinsic provisos also with regard to conscience.[4] The proviso of general law against conscience is exempted only in cases where the constitution or the law on a lower level grants conscience a sphere of freedom - be it a general sphere of freedom within the context of human and fundamental rights or a specific one within the context of a legal privilege. How can the same legal system, on a constitutional level, assume a basic right which has the systematic primacy[5] of all basic rights, namely that the individual in his conscience is exempt from the law, and at the same time let all moral behavior be judged according to the universal morality of the law and place this behavior under the proviso of the law?

231

G. Zecha and P. Weingartner (eds.), *Conscience: An Interdisciplinary View*, 231–261.
© 1987 by D. Reidel Publishing Company.

This ambivalence could simply be interpreted as a misunderstanding of the historical development. Originally the legislator, for constitutional reasons, wanted to grant a sphere of cultural freedom only for the religious conscience. Later, however, the concept of freedom or faith and conscience detached itself from its attributed rules, it rendered itself factually independent, to speak a new substrate as an abstract concept, namely moral consciousness.

1.2 As early as the 18th century the philosophical and natural law concept of conscience contrasted sharply with the positivistic concept as evidenced by the following comparison between Christian Wolff and J.J. Moser. Wolff perceives conscience as *"facultas iudicandi de moralitate actionum nostrarum utrum scilicet sint bonae, an malae; utrum committendae, an omittendae"*[6]. Wolff further states: *"Denique si iudicium de actione committenda, vel omittenda fertur, dum appetitu sensitivo vel aversatione sensitiva in contrarium partem trahimur, vel affectum impetu in eandem abripimur, conscientiam vocamus servam"*[7]. When Wolff wrote this in 1738 the concept of *"libera conscientia"*[8] had already been guaranteed 90 years earlier in the Peace Treaty of Westphalia. In contrast, a constitutional interpretation of freedom of conscience is provided by authors such as Moser or Boehmer (1732). Moser interprets freedom of conscience as legal norm on a purely deductive basis, although he is well aware of the history of the Westphalian Peace Treaty and its guarantee of *"libera conscientia"*[9]. According to Moser freedom of conscience is only a right to profess to one of the religions sanctioned in Germany. He characterizes the birth of freedom of conscience as a compromise between the contracting parties.[10] Boehmer also exhibits this same deductive legal thinking.[11] In his *dissertatio praeliminaris de iure circa libertatem conscientia* he deduces the right of freedom of conscience from the nature and meaning of conscience, without taking the actual law into consideration. To bridge this hiatus between the natural law concept and the constitutional concept of freedom of conscience and the constitutional guarantee of this right he was apparently the first to introduce the conceptual differentiation between *libertas conscientiae plena* and *minus plena*.

1.3 Protestant literature of the 19th century already had a very different concept of freedom of conscience and its importance in ethics and theology. In 1852 Baur wrote: "What is referred to as liberty of faith and conscience and the unalienable right that the Reformation bestowed upon mankind, is only a popular expression for an intellectual autonomy. It is identical to the principle of subjectivity, an absolute self-consciousness of human thinking liberated from an authoritarian faith. Protestantism is the principle of subjective freedom, of liberty of faith and conscience - of autonomy, in contrast to the heteronomy of the Catholic concept of Church".[12] Philosophy, Enlightenment and Protestantism have thus equated the principle of freedom of conscience with "autonomy against all heteronomy". This overburdening of the constitutionally guaranteed concept of freedom of conscience had to have an effect on the relation between protected fundamental laws and the constitutional proviso. Attempts to place freedom of conscience under the proviso of the state at the end of the 19th century and under the Weimar Constitution failed because of this overburdening.[13] At the constitutional level freedom of conscience became an absolute right, which is manifested in Art. 4 I of the *Grundgesetz*.

2. VARIOUS PHASES IN THE EXPANSION PROCESS OF THE CONCEPT OF FREEDOM OF CONSCIENCE

2.1 The tension between the philosophical and legal concept of conscience was further intensified by changes in the concept of conscience itself:
a) a change in the meaning; the concept of conscience loses all cultic-religious elements and develops into an ethical-moral, non-religious concept;
b) a functional change which I refer to as shift of subject and object ("Subjekt-Objekt-Verschiebung")[14]:

- freedom of conscience was originally a collective guarantee, i. e., of the religious community, and later developed into an individual right[15];
- this basic right is directed not only against the state but also against private social powers[16].

2.2 A further change can be seen in the development of the concept of freedom of conscience from a mere guarantee of the *forum internum*[17] to a guarantee of the *forum externum*.

2.3 Within the Anglo-American legal sphere a change akin to the German legal development cannot be found. There is no restriction to the *forum internum*, because freedom of conscience - a special guarantee of religious liberty was not required - was extended to the entire religious domain, therefore also to public worship. If it extended to a human rights guarantee (as, for example, in Rhode Island), then the baptist formula of "dictates of conscience"[18] was avoided and a formula according to natural law was chosen instead. In the Anglo-American sphere this form of freedom of conscience or faith has individualistic-legal character insofar as the holder is not the congregation but the individual.

3. "INTENSIFICATION" AND "RELAXATION" OF CONSCIENCE AND THE CONSCIENTIOUS OFFENDER

3.1 The classical spheres of conflict between law and conscience are dissident or minority religions[19] (i.e., religions outside the occidental religious tradition) and the conscientious offender.[20]

Equal rights for minority and dissident religions and freedom of ideology in general were established after the First World War, although problems remained, for example, regarding building permits for mosques or permits for kosher butchering. Apart from the classical problems of religious freedom are those cases in which members of religious minorities refuse to perform legal or civic duties, for example, to take an oath, render military service[21], or provide aid through blood transfusions.[22] These conflicts could not be solved by the extensions of a "spatial guarantee" of religious freedom through the expansion of legal norms. The conscientious offender, a religious or ideological dissident, expanded the areas of conflict described above from the merely religious into the ideological. The new areas of conflict can be divided into three groups:

- conscientious objection - based on religious or ethical reasons,
- conflicts within civil[23] or military service,
- conflicts in the context of demonstrations, including actual resistance.[24]

Dogmatically these groups differ considerably. The first group, the rejection of public duties, is a *status negativus*. The second group, the participation in state institutions, is a *status positivus*, and the third group, seemingly a *status negativus*, is in fact a *status activus*, i.e., the participation in the formation of state intent. Although the conflicts were traditionally in the *status negativus*, i. e., in the rejection of state demands, they can now be found not only in the *status positivus* but also in the *status activus*. The possibility of conflict has therefore extended to all areas of interaction between citizen and state or individual and state. Due to the expansion of the areas of conflicts and the simultaneous expansion of government sanctions and standardizations, especially through the instrument of criminal law, the courts are now faced with the question of what to do with offenders who either do not have the capacity, or do not want to understand the wrongfulness of an action. In the first case, the courts dismissed the imputation as wrong, parallel to a mistake as to the type of offence, if the offender was not capable of understanding the wrongfulness of his action, despite "intensification of his conscience"[25]. In the second case which is referred to as "hostility or blindness towards the law"[26], a plea of conscience against the law is not admitted. Both cases are based on a common idea: namely that through intensification the individual conscience can attune to objective values of society, indeed that conscience intends and aspires to this. "Enemies of the law" have the duty to give up this "hostility" and to join

other "friends of the law" in the sense of a conforming "affability with the law".[27] The postulate of "intensification of conscience" could oppose what was referred to in the constitutional
history of the past 100 years as "freedom of conscience", or
what was often perceived as negative state responsibility. If
freedom of conscience is to be understood, administratively as
well as legislatively, as negative state responsibility, then the
postulate of a previous "intensification of conscience" in order
to justify the use of freedom, is nonsensical. Why does the legal
system in this one traditional area not demand an "intensification
of conscience" and contend itself with a negative state responsibility, whenever the analysis of the legal norm shows that
conscience is concerned, and why does it demand an "intensification of conscience" from the individual in all other areas
and whenever an action is penalized?

3.2 The doctrine of the necessity of the intensification of conscience had its basis in a decision of the Senate for Criminal
Cases ("Großer Senat für Strafsachen") of March 18, 1952.[28]
This decision served to contradict the thesis of the Supreme
Court of the German Reich (*Reichsgericht*) according to which
the presence of "consciousness" on the offender's part, that by
fulfilling the terms and criteria of the criminal law he is violating
the penal norm, is not necessary. While paragraph 59 *Strafgesetzbuch* AF was applied regarding the offender's knowledge
of the acts constituting an offence, in case of denial on the offender's part, the proof that he had the necessary awareness of
the prohibited nature of an act at the time of committing the
offence, was furnished in a "normative manner". The court
must determine if the offender after interpolated, appropriate and
reasonable "intensification of conscience" could have had this
awareness.

This change in the judicature was later firmly established in
the revised text of the General Part of the Criminal Code in
paragraph 17.[29] What makes the judicature of the German
Federal High Court of Justice so interesting is not only the
changeover in the judicature to a complete system of criminal

law based on the requirement of personal guilt, but also the terminology used.

An expansive concept of conscience is employed, however, at the same time it is transgressed from within by the postulate of the "necessary intensification". Friedrich Manttil[30] was probably the first to describe the concept of "intensification of conscience". The judicature requires the exercise of conscience, of all "moral values", all "mental powers of perception", the "exertion of intellectual powers"[31], "reflection"[32], and "inquiries"[33].

According to its legal nature "intensification of conscience" can be regarded as "something different than the observance of care and diligence"[34], so that it "constitutes a higher requirement than the observance of care and diligence in cases of ordinary negligence". The circumstances of the case, the professional and social situation of the individual are considered, although there are no firmly established rules.[35] For knowledge of the prohibitive nature of an action, the moment before the decision to commit an action, or the time before the beginning of the execution of an offence is decisive.[36] It is of course noticeable that the postulate of the "exertion of intellectual powers" and the exercise of all mental powers of perception is opposed by the demand "of all moral values". Does criminal law demand a moral or an intellectual "intensification" in order to distinguish between what is prohibited and what is not? However, it is important to add that in the case of only negligent ignorance of the prohibition, despite knowledge of the factual circumstances, there can be no conviction on the grounds of knowingly committing an offence. The judicature and also the legislator have taken up a development which can already be seen outside of criminal law: The legal system is no longer evident in its totality, its rules and prohibitions are no longer self-evident - which is understandable because of its growing complexity, and in principle the offender's conscience is placed above the legal norm. As Manttil accurately notes: "The Federal High Court of Justice also places all those cases into this category in which the offender in full knowledge of the tenor of the legal prohibition and of the acts constituting an offence which fulfil the conditions laid down by the criminal law for a conviction, in regard to the special circumstances of his case, believes, rightfully from his viewpoint, wrongfully from the judge's point of view, that the judge will recognize in his case that his action is not covered by the legal prohibition[37], be it in the - unjustified - assumption that a higher legal norm supports his opinion."[38]

The fact that these circumstances are also included by the new judicature cannot be regarded as the inclusion of a marginal case, but as a fundamental decision. Naturally the growing complexity of the legal system must be considered, however, this growing complexity is again nothing other than the reverse of the importance of the individual voice of conscience, the norm of conscience as the higher norm, which can be voiced easier, clearer and faster than the complex public norm. The action of the conscientious offender is not just marginally included in the new understanding of *mens rea*, but forms a central point. Indeed, the questionableness of the judicature's formula of "intensification of conscience" becomes evident especially in the case of the conscientious offender. How can one demand from someone who acts out of an "over-intensified conscience" a stronger and higher "intensification of conscience" in another direction, namely for the benefit of the legal system and the public norm[39]? How can the public norm convert the offender who acts out of conviction to the opposite of his conviction? Is the inclusion of the conscientious offender in the sphere of modern criminal law possibly a mistake? Here most interpreters seek recourse in the interpretation of the concept of conscience, in that again an expansive or evasive interpretation provides the justification for the subordination of the legal norm, or the restrictive interpretation of conscience justifies the supremacy of the legal norm. This fear of the expansive power of the concept of conscience no doubt prompted the legislator not to include the judicature's formula of the "intensification of conscience" in the revised text of the criminal code of March 2, 1974 (*Strafgesetzbuch* für das *Deutsche Reich*)[40]. Paragraph 17 (error as to the prohibited nature of an act) reads as follows: "If the offender at the time of committing an act does not have the understanding of wrong-doing, he acts without guilt, if he could not avoid this error. If the offender was able to avoid the error, the sentence can be mitigated according to paragraph 49 I."The concepts "understanding of the wrongful character of one's doings" and "unavoidable error" are equivalent to the concept of the necessary "intensification of conscience". The law does not say in which way the offender can or could have avoided the error. Actually the legislator sanctioned the judicature's view as criterion for the ability to avoid an error, although the postulate of the "necessary intensification of conscience" cannot be regarded as the sole criterion for the provableness or non-provableness of the ability to avoid an error.

3.3 The short discussion of the problem of "intensification of conscience" in criminal law showed a similar relation between criminal law and Article 4, paragraph 1 of the Basic Law (*Grundgesetz*) - the guarantee of freedom of conscience - as the relation of Article 4, paragraph 1 *Grundgesetz* to Article 4, paragraph 3 *Grundgesetz*. The two norm spheres of the constitution cannot be juxtaposed unconnected, as the relation between the constitutional right of freedom of conscience and criminal law is similar to the relation between this constitutional right and the right to conscientious objection. This general relation can be characterized by several elements[41] which can be ascribed to Article 4, paragraph 1 *Grundgesetz* or freedom of conscience in general: a quasi institutional element (in order to guarantee a neutral state or the principle of non-identification [Herbert Kruger]) and a directing element which binds the legislator to appropriate regulations and the creating of alternatives. The duty of the legislator to create alternatives or to derive "goodwill rules" from the constitutional right of freedom of conscience against legal frictions would signify a continuous principle. The inclusion of the right to conscientious objection on a constitutional level would have to be regarded as its most important establishment. In a different context I have referred to the establishment of such "goodwill rules"[42] or the realization of "emanations"[43] of freedom of conscience as "proviso constitutional rights"[44]. The "proviso constitutional right" is not merely the *lex specialis* in relation to the *lex generalis*; it takes into account the special conscience situation in a concrete case by suspending the general legal norm or by creating alternatives. The Federal Constitutional Court (*Bundesverfassungsgericht*) has repeatedly spoken of deducing "goodwill rules" or alternatives from Article 4, paragraph 1 *Grundgesetz* with regard to conscientious offenders.[45] This realization of a "goodwill rule" manifested itself especially in criminal or criminal procedure law.[46] The creation of paragraph 17 revised text of the criminal code (*Strafgesetzbuch*) can therefore be regarded as an emanation effect of Article 4, paragraph 1 *Grundgesetz*, although concrete evidence for this from the motives of the legislative procedure cannot be furnished. As this is more or less the codification of the doctrine of necessary "intensification of conscience" with regard to avoiding errors, it is obvious that the doctrine of conscience which has gained importance through Article 4, paragraph 1 *Grundgesetz*, also had its emanation effect here. Furthermore, within the sphere of conscientious objection the same restringency against the expansion of conscience, which we also know in criminal law under the aspect of the necessary "intensification of conscience", can be found.

Here also a distinction is made partly between genuine and not genuine, legitimate and illegitimate, exercise of conscience[47], although conscience is not open to scrutiny by others. Restringency as criterion of a genuine exercise of conscience can also be seen in the introduction and realization of the now modified proceedings for the introduction of evidence with regard to conscientious objection.[48] With regard to the reform of proof regulations, the lawgiver was accused to have suspended freedom of conscience.[49]

The concept of conscience in the judicature of the Federal Administrative Court is based on the decision of October 3, 1958[50], which perceives conscience as the individual understanding of what is permitted and what is not, and the duty to act according to this understanding.[51] In addition to this characteristic of a compulsion from within, the judicature also perceives conscience as something which can be "wakened" from the outside, that it can therefore not only be subjected to an inner but also to an outer intensification.

3.4 The question examined here is whether the concept of "intensification of conscience" in criminal law in the assessment of the ability to avoid an error is the same for the conscientious offender as for the conscientious objector. Under certain conditions this can be affirmed, although there can be different viewpoints. Whereas the viewpoint of criminal law is based on the citizen who has fulfilled the statutory definition of an offence, but did not recognize the prohibitive nature of his act, the viewpoint of the law of conscientious objection is based on a citizen who clearly recognizes the necessity of an act but resists this act, pleading conscientious objection. This legal concept presupposes that the citizen who is liable for military service only then refrains from doing his legal duty if he has seriously and persistently examined, if not "intensified", his conscience. From this point on, the concept of conscience changes. Whereas criminal law employs the possibilities of information and the duty to inquire, to prove to the offender that had he tried this he would be differently informed and thus morally structured, conscientious objection to military service only applies if there is an underlying examination of conscience which cannot be restructured or changed through information. The premise of criminal law is that the complexity of modern society, the inadequate comparative valuation between criminal law and laity are the cause of this.[52] The premise of conscientious objection on the other hand is the irreconcilability between conscience and public norm in a determinable group of people. The intensification of conscience by the conscientious objector is not an instrument for probing introduced by the judge, but a *de facto* physical procedure which is recognized by the law when it reaches a certain threshold. That this threshold is different in criminal law and in the law of conscientious objection is a result of the necessity of the legitimacy of the state's actions in punishment or defence. However, there is no fundamental difference. The difference between "action" and "negligence" which is generally of importance in law, is not of great sign-

ificance here. Both spheres are connected by the concept of the
conscientious offender, who is a borderline figure perhaps in
criminal law, but in the law of conscientious objection he is the
prototype of the addressee referred to by the legal norm.

4. "CONSCIENCE" AS NORMATIVE AND FUNCTIONAL AMBIGUITY

According to Luhmann's functional concepts[53] of conscience
and freedom, thinking in alternatives is not for the lawyer, "da
es das Entscheiden erschwere" (as it impedes decision-making).
The lawyer tends to approach reality and justice with the idea of
rules and exceptions and not through a search for functional
equivalence. Luhmann stated in one of his early articles on conscience and freedom of conscience: "The purpose of freedom of
conscience is only to protect the individual and his various roles
from the crises of conscience. Maintaining the continuity of self-
realization and of role relations, the true function of conscience
is more important than freedom of conscience and becomes the
criterion for the evaluation of conflicts between law and conscience."[54] He further states that it is not the purpose of conscience and freedom of conscience to enable the individual to avoid
the consequences of his actions. He also introduces the distinction between "ascribed roles" and "achieved roles" with regard to
a possible conflict of conscience.[55] According to Luhmann, in
an ascribed role negligence based on a crisis of conscience
would be the least violation of the legal and social order. On the
other hand in an achieved role, action would constitute the
strongest violation, because in this case the social order would
not have enough "funktionale Äquivalenzen" (functional
equivalences).[56] Luhmann then raises the question of the kind of
sacrifice (in the form of an alternative action which is in
agreement with one's conscience) that can be expected from the
individual for his conscience.[57] The "voice of conscience" has
changed into a function for the solution of social conflicts.[58]

However, two objections must be raised against this concept: 1. It is becoming increasingly difficult to differentiate between achieved and ascribed roles, as nobody can say of a

certain role that it is only achieved or only ascribed. Within public professions there is a broad spectrum between the publicly instituted, civil service professions and professions based on private initiative. This spectrum is comprised of professions which are publicly bound and controlled. Even the freest self-achieved professional roles can only be achieved if other ascribed roles (i.e., grade school and intermediate school education, university examinations) have previously been realized. The ascribed role of the conscript seems to be straightforward, however, this is not the case when one thinks of the role of the taxpayer. According to a widespread opinion the social state, i.e., the supply of achievement, realizes itself within the "tax state". Instead of differentiating between achieved and ascribed roles it would be better to speak of the different forms and degrees of state control. 2. The second objection concerns Luhmann's shift of the problem. A solution which "spares individuals from conflicts of conscience" presupposes that the social or legal norms become incorporated in order to eliminate conflicts of conscience. The individual identifies himself with his profession, or he achieves the elimination of conflicts of conscience through a second group of institutions, which allow him to present aspects of his behavior which he cannot choose, as impersonal. Conscience is thereby eliminated, conflicts do not even arise. In this sphere of relief mechanisms Luhmann places freedom of conscience, which should supplement the existing alternative abundance of the institutions and the possibility of impersonal behavior in case the state reduces, directly or indirectly, alternatives of action, thereby creating conflict situations for the individual. For Luhmann, as for Comte,[59] there is no freedom of conscience with regard to mathematics or physics, as freedom of conscience only serves to protect the individual and his manifold roles from conflicts of conscience. The limitation of conflicts of conscience through inherent barriers, and not freedom of conscience, must resolve the conflict, in order to avoid conflicts of conscience or to replace them from the beginning with alternatives or functional equivalences ("funktionale Äquivalenzen").

Luhmann emphasizes in a very dialectic manner that not the "freedom of conscience" is protected but the "conscience of freedom", a phrase from the time of the Reformation with which Luther aptly characterized the problem. The principle that the law is the guarantor of freedom and not the individual decision which is directed against the law, also applies to conscience. Luhmann's theories have been dealt with in such detail here, because they show the difference between the functional system theory and the normative theory of law, and because this theory of conscience as functional equivalence is incompatible with a central element of modern criminal law. According to Luhmann the judge may not inquire as to the intensification of conscience which would be possible for the defendant, as it is the duty of the law to prevent the conflict of conscience altogether und thereby any conflict situations.

5. SUMMARY

The concept of freedom of conscience set a process in motion which expanded the sphere of this fundamental right with regard to religious freedom in such a manner that a diverse system of religious institutions and church law, on the one hand, and civil legal institutions, on the other hand, developed. This was generally referred to as the separation of temporal and ecclesiastic power. The expansive process of individualization also changed the content of this right; it became relevant in all those areas of law and the social order which dealt with the ethical solution of conflicts between state, state law and the individual. Eventually even criminal law, the last bastion of the legitimate barrier of freedom of conscience, was influenced by its principles. The postulate of "intensification" of conscience in criminal law and the privilege of "relaxation" of conscience in administrative law (criminal law) - especially with regard to the right to conscientious objection - are therefore not real contradictions.

The expansive process of the guarantee of freedom of conscience cannot merely be controlled by laws or a sophisticated social order which has an abundance of functional equivalences at its disposal. We are dealing here with a continuous process of equalization between two diametrically opposed principles, namely that of freedom of conscience and that of the state legal authority - or to paraphrase this - the contrast between "relaxation" and "intensification" of conscience within the legal system in order to avoid legal conflicts with the rights of others. Within this continuous process it is the lawyer's noble duty to assume a neutral role of understanding, judging and helping.

University of Munich

NOTES

1 This is the socio-ethical formulation of the philosophical postulate of the "call of conscience". See: Ebeling, G., Theologische Erwägungen über das Gewissen. Grußwort und Glaube, Tübingen 1962, in: *Das Gewissen in der Diskussion*, Darmstadt 1976, p. 142 (pp. 156-160). Kuhn, H., Begegnung mit dem Sein - Meditationen zur Metaphysik des Gewissens, Tübingen 1954, in: Blühdorn, J., *Das Gewissen in der Diskussion*, Darmstadt 1976, p. 162 (pp. 171-196). Welzel, H., Vom irrenden Gewissen. Recht und Staat in Geschichte und Gegenwart, Tübingen 1949, in: *Das Gewissen in der Diskussion*, Darmstadt 1976, p. 384 (p. 401). Kümmel, F., Zum Problem des Gewissens, in: Bollnow, F., *Erziehung in anthropologischer Sicht*, Zürich 1969, pp. 168-192, in: *Das Gewissen in der Diskussion*, Darmstadt 1976, p. 441 (pp. 447 and 454).
2 Whereas Georg Jellinek emphasizes the historical and Carl Schmitt the systematic primacy of freedom of conscience, Anschütz places freedom of conscience under the proviso of the law. Anschütz, E., Religionsfreiheit, in: Anschütz/Thoma, *HBdDStR XX*, Vol. 32, p. 675. Anschütz, E., *Die Verfassung des Deutschen Reiches*, 1929, Note 3 to Article 135. See: Scholler, H., *Die Freiheit des Gewissens*, Berlin 1958, p. 88. Brinkmann, K., *Grundrecht und Gewissen im Grundgesetz*, Köln 1965, p. 107.
3 Anschütz, E., Religionsfreiheit, in: Anschütz/Thoma, *HBdDStR XX*, Vol. 32, p. 675.
4 See: Herzog, R., in: Maunz/Durin/Herzog/Scholz, Article 6.
5 Schmitt, C., *Verfassungslehre*, 1928, p. 158. See also: Scholler, H., Rechtsverstehen in den Gegenwartsströmungen der Philosophie, in: *Revista Internationale di Filosofia del Diritto*, 1973, pp. 498-518, with the title: Interpretatione del Diritto nelle Correnti contemporane de la Filosofia.

246HEINRICH SCHOLLER

Bäumling, R. and Böckenförde, E.W., Das Grundrecht der Gewissensfreiheit, in: *VVDStRL* 28, Berlin 1970. Scholler, H., Zum Verhältnis von (innerer) Gewissensfreiheit zur (äußeren) religiösen Bekenntnis- und Kultusfreiheit, in: *Grund- und Freiheitsrechte im Wandel von Gesellschaft und Geschichte, Beiträge zur Geschichte der Grund- und Freiheitsrechte vom Ausgang des Mittelalters bis zur Revolution von 1848,* Tübingen 1981, p. 184. Mock, E., Souveränität, Gewissen und Widerstand. Zur Entstehung dreier Erklärungskategorien des demokratischen Verfassungsstaates, in: *Österreichische Zeitschrift für Öffentliches Recht,* Vol. 27, p. 176 (p. 287). Mock, E., *Gewissen und Gewissensfreiheit,* Berlin 1983. Mieth, D., Gewissen, in: *Christlicher Glaube in moderner Gesellschaft,* - Freiburg, Basel, Wien 1983.

6 Wolff, Ch., *Philos. Practica Universalis,* 1783, p. 318, paragraph 417. Wolff provided a philosophical definition of the concept of conscience and not a definition in terms of human rights, p. 318.

7 Wolff, Ch., *Philos. Practica Universalis,* 1783.

8 Scholler, H., Zum Verhältnis von (innerer) Gewissensfreiheit zur (äußeren) religiösen Bekenntnis- und Kultusfreiheit, in: *Grund- und Freiheitsrechte im Wandel von Gesellschaft und Geschichte,* Tübingen 1981, pp. 185. Scholler, H., *Die Freiheit des Gewissens,* Berlin 1958, p. 83. Scholler, H., *Das Gewissen als Gestalt der Freiheit,* München 1962, p. 24.

9 Moser provides the following definition: "Die Gewissensfreyheit bestehet überhaupt darinn, wann der Mensch in Religionssachen denken und handeln darf, wie er will, ohne von der geistlich oder weltlichen Obrigkeit darinn verhindert oder deswegen bestraft zu werden. Eine solche unumschränkte Gewissensfreyheit aber ist unserer Teutschen Reichsverfassung nicht gemäss."(Freedom of conscience means that in religious matters the individual can think and do as he pleases; without being hindered or punished by ecclesiastical or secular authorities.
Such a limitless freedom as conscience is, however, not in conformity with the German Constitution). Moser, J.J., *Von der teutschen Religionsverfassung,* Book I, Chpt. 4, 1774, p. 36. Moser, J.J., *De exercitione religionis domestica,* Chpt. 5, 1736, p. 7: "Sie könnten sie, Evangelische, jedoch davon nicht abstehen, dass den Unterthanen die Libertas Conscientiae verstattet, Sie zur Emigration nicht gedrungen, sondern ihnen freygelassen werde, zu bleibe, und das Exercitium ihrer Religion in der Nachbarschaft zu suchen, auch in ihren Häusern Gott mit Lesen, Singen und Beten zu dienen."

10 "*Necessitate, matre novarum inventionum admodum faecunda.*" Moser, J.J., *De exercitione religionis domestica,* Chpt. 15, 1736, p. 12. Scholler, H., *Das Gewissen als Gestalt der Freiheit,* München 1962, p. 24.

11 Boehmer, *Dissertatio Praeliminaris de Iure Circa Libertatem Conscientia Ius Ecclesiasticum Protestant.*, lib. II, 1732, Chpts. 37 and 40.
12 Baur, F., *Die Epochen der kirchlichen Geschichtsschreibung*, 1852, p. 257. Baur, F., *Der Gegensatz des Katholizismus und Protestantismus nach den Prinzipien und Hauptdogmen der beiden Lehrbegriffe*, 1834, p. 401.
13 Anschütz, E., loc. cit. See also: Scholler, H., Gewissen, Gesetz und Rechtsstaat, in: *DÖV*, 1969, pp. 526-535. A more detailed version of this article by the same author appeared in: *Das Gewissen in der Diskussion*, Darmstadt 1976, pp. 407 - 440.
14 "Die im Grunde genommen unrettbare Freiheit des Individuums tritt allmählich in den Hintergrund und die Freiheit des sozialen Kollektivismus in den Vordergrund." Kelsen, H., *Allgemeine Staatslehre*, Berlin 1925, p. 325. Regarding freedom of opinion and the press, see: Scholler, H., *Person und Öffentlichkeit*, München 1967, pp. 319-320. Regarding freedom of conscience, see: Scholler, H., Zum Verhältnis von (innerer) Gewissensfreiheit zur (äußeren) religiösen Bekenntnis- und Kultusfreiheit, in: *Grund- und Freiheitsrechte im Wandel von Gesellschaft und Geschichte*, Tübingen 1981, p. 199.
15 Brinkmann, K., *Grundrecht und Gewissen im Grundgesetz*, Köln 1965, p. 132. Zippelius, in: *Bonner Kommentar*, Article 4.
16 Scholler, H., *Person und Öffentlichkeit*, München 1967, pp. 321, 325 and 329.
17 Scholler, H., Zum Verhältnis von (innerer) Gewissensfreiheit zur (äußeren) religiösen Bekenntnis- und Kultusfreiheit, in: *Grund- und Freiheitsrechte im Wandel von Gesellschaft und Geschichte*, Tübingen 1981, p. 199. Kümmel, F., Zum Problem des Gewissens, in: Blühdorn, J., *Das Gewissen in der Diskussion*, Darmstadt 1976, p. 454. Klier, G., *Gewissensfreiheit und Psychologie*, Berlin 1978, pp. 37 and 50. Matros, N., Das Selbst in seiner Funktion als Gewissen, in: *Salzburger Jahrbuch für Philosophie* 10/11, 1966/67, pp. 169-213 (also in: *Das Gewissen in der Diskussion*, Darmstadt 1976, p. 187 (pp. 200 and 201). Reiner, H., Die Funktionen des Gewissens, in: *Kantstudien* 62, 1971, pp. 467-488 (also in: *Das Gewissen in der Diskussion*, Darmstadt 1976, p. 285 (pp. 292 and 308). For the differentiation between *forum internum* and *forum externum* regarding error, see: Welzel, H., Vom irrenden Gewissen. Eine rechtsphilosophische Studie, 1949, in: *Das Gewissen in der Diskussion*, Darmstadt 1976, p. 384 (p. 389). Scholler, H., Gewissen, Gesetz und Rechtsstaat, in: *Das Gewissen in der Diskussion*, Darmstadt 1976. p. 412.
18 The concept of a dictate of conscience first appeared in the draft of the Constitution of the English Levellers in 1647: "...because therein we cannot remit or exceed a title of what our conscience dictates to be the mind of God." The Agreement of the People, 28 October 1647, reprinted in:

Jellinek, G., *Die Erklärung der Menschen- und Bürgerrechte. Völker-rchtliche Beiträge*, Vol. 1, 3, 1919, p. 78. Asalander, G., Vom Werden der Menschenrechte, in: *Leipziger rechtswissenschaftliche Studien*, Vol. 19, Leipzig 1926, pp. 72-74.

19 Lanares, P., Sekten und neue Religionen, and Flasche, R., Jugend-religionen zwischen Verunglimpfung und Verfolgung, and v. Campen-hausen, A. Frhr., Verfassungsrechtliche Gesichtspunkte zur Rechtslage der neuen Religionen, in: *Gewissen und Freiheit*, 1982, pp. 28, 50 and 68. Welzel, H., Vom irrenden Gewissen. Eine rechtsphilosophische Studie, 1949, in: *Das Gewissen in der Diskussion*, Darmstadt 1976, p. 384. Mo-krosch, R., *Das religiöse Gewissen*, Kohlhammer WK, Vol. 637, Stuttgart 1979.

20 BayVGH BayVBl. 1981, p. 87, with dissenting opinion. Scholler, H., in: BayVBl. 1981, p. 305. See also: Scholler, H., Gewissensfreiheit des einzelnen - Anspruch der Gesellschaft, Gewissen und Gewissensprüfung im Rechtssystem der Bundesrepublik Deutschland, in: *Gewissen. Aspekte eines vieldiskutierten Sachverhalts*, Katholische Akademie Schwerte, Dokumen-tationen 7, 1983, p. 77.

21 Krölls, A., *Kriegsdienstverweigerung - das unbequeme Grundrecht*, 2nd edition, 1983. Eckertz, R., Die Kriegsdienstverweigerung aus Gewis-sensgründen. Eine Kritik des Urteils des Bundesverfassungsgerichts vom 13. April 1978, in: *FiSt, Texte und Materialien der Forschungsstätte der evan-gelischen Studiengemeinschaft*, No 13, 1971. Eckertz, R., Maßstab und Verfahren der "Gewissensprüfung" im neuen Kriegsdienstverweige-rungsrecht, in: *NVwZ* 1984, p. 563. The decision of the Bundes- verwal-tungsgericht from May 27, 1984, in: *NVwZ* 1984, p. 446. The reform of the "Kriegsdienstverweigerungsrecht" has been criticized. Eckertz, R., in *KretJ* 1982, p. 2522; Günther, H., in: *DVBl.* 1983, p. 1084; Becker, J.J., in: *RiA* 1984, p. 97. Becker, J.J., in: *RiA* 1985, p. 49. See also: Schumacher, F.J., in: *DÖV* 1983, p. 918; Berg, W., in: *JA* 1983, p. 632; Schultz, G., in: *MDR* 1983, p. 991; Franz W., in: *MDR* 1984, p. 1.

22 *BVerfGE* 32, p. 98.

23 See: Podlech, A., Das Grundrecht der Gewissensfreiheit und das beson-dere Gewaltverhältnis, in: *Schriften zum öffentlichen Recht*, Vol. 92, Berlin 1969. Hirsch, E., Zur juristischen Dimension des Gewissens und der Unverletzlichkeit der Gewissensfreiheit des Richters, in: *Schriftenreihe zur Rechtssoziologie und zur Rechtstatsachenforschung*, Vol. 43, Berlin 1979. For a review see: Scholler, H., in: *DÖV* 1969, p. 583; see also the judgment of the *BayVGH*, 21.12.1984.

24 Ahrend, K., Bürger oder Rebell? Juros, H., Das Recht auf Widerstand als Gewissensproblem. Kewenig, W., Widerstand zwischen Theorie und Praxis. All in: *Widerstand in der Demokratie* (Veröffentlichungen der Landeszentrale

für politische Bildung in Hamburg und der Katholischen Akademie Hamburg, 1983), Landeszentrale für politische Bildung Hamburg - Katholische Akademie Hamburg, Vol. 83, pp. 7, 36 and 54.

25 See footnote 1; the jurisdiction however discontinued to use the term "intensification of conscience" (Gewissensanspannung).

26 The German terminology differentiates between "hostility" (Rechtsfeindschaft) and "blindness" (Rechtsblindheit) towards the law; compare Carl Schmitt's theory of the "Freund - Feind - Verhältnis" and see the more modern concept of "Streitbare Demokratie": Lameyer, J., Streitbare Demokratie, in: JöR, Vol. 30, Tübingen 1981, p. 147.

27 In contrast to "hostility or blindness towards the law" the author uses the complementary terminology of "affability with the law" (Rechtsfreundschaft und Rechtssichtigkeit).

28 Beschluß des Großen Strafsenates (March 18, 1952), BGHSt 2, p. 194.

29 See: Schönke/Schräder, Strafgesetzbuch, paragraph 17. For the constitutionality of paragraph 17 see: BVerfGE 41, p. 122 (p. 124). Kramer, M. and Trittel, M., Zur Bindungswirkung der Entscheidung des Bundesverfassungsgerichts über die Verfassungsmäßigkeit des Paragraphen 17 StGB, in: JZ 1980, p. 392.

30 Manttil, F., Gewissensanspannung, in: AöR 1977, p. 201.

31 BGHSt 4, p. 5 (p. 243); BGHSt 9, p. 172; BGHSt, JR 1954, p. 188.

32 BGHSt 9, p. 42.

33 BGHSt 2, p. 201; BGHSt 9, p. 172.

34 BGHSt 2, p. 202; BGHSt 9, p. 42 (p. 172).

35 BGHSt 4, p. 243.

36 BGHSt 2, p. 201; BGHSt, JR 1954, p. 188.

37 BGHSt 2, p. 206.

38 BGHSt 4, p. 1.

39 The concept of the public norm is a topic of Heidegger's existential philosophy, but is not used in a derogatory sense here.

40 BGBl.I, p. 469.

41 See: Scholler, H., Gewissen, Gesetz und Rechtsstaat, in: Das Gewissen in der Diskussion, Darmstadt 1976, p. 407 (p. 412).

42 Kriegsdienstverweigerungsrecht, legal principals, Scholler, H., Gewissen - Gewissensfreiheit - Kriegsdienst - Kriegsdienstverweigerung, in: Zeitschrift für evangelisches Kirchenrecht,Vol. 27, 1982, p. 20; Scholler, H., Rules, Principles and Judicial Policy. Essays on Third World Perspectives in Jurisprudence, Singapore1984, p. 327.

43 The Federal Constitutional Court uses the word "Ausstrahlung" (emanations of fundamental rights).

44 See footnote 42.

45 Bopp, U., Der Gewissenstäter und das Grundrecht der Gewissens-freiheit, in: *Freiburger rechts- und staatswissenschaftliche Abhandlungen*, Vol. 38, 1974, especially pp. 23 and 24. Regarding civil disobedience see: Ahrend, K., Bürger oder Rebell? and Kewenig, W., Widerstand zwischen Theorie und Praxis. All in: *Widerstand in der Demokratie* (Veröf-fentlichungen der Landeszentrale für politische Bildung in Hamburg und der Katholischen Akademie Hamburg, 1983). Landeszentrale für politische Bildung Hamburg - Katholische Akademie Hamburg, Vol. 83, pp. 36 and 54.

46 See Herzog, R., in: Maunz/Dürig/Herzog,*Grundgesetz-Kommentar*, art-icle 4, Rdnr. 147.

47 *BVerfGE* 32, pp. 23, 33 and 98.

48 Eckertz, R., in: *NVwZ* 1984, p. 563. See also the literature in footnote 21 of this article; see *SZ*, No 39, 14.2.1985, p. 10.

49 Podlech, A., Das Grundrecht der Gewissensfreiheit und die besonderen Gewaltverhältnisse, in: *Schriften zum öffentlichen Recht*, Vol. 92, Berlin 1969. Westermann, Ch., Argumentationen und Begründungen in der Ethik und Rechtslehre, in: *Schriften zur Rechtstheorie*, Vol. 61, Berlin 1977. Klier, G., Gewissensfreiheit und Psychologie, in: *Schriften zum öffent-lichen Recht*, Vol. 335, Berlin 1978, Fuchs, J. (ed.), *Das Gewissen*, Düs-seldorf 1979 (zur Fristenlösung p. 71). Mokrosch, R., *Das religiöse Ge-wissen*, Stuttgart 1979. *Gewissen im Dialog*, hrsg. von dem Ev. Kir-chenamt für die Bundeswehr, Gütersloh 1980; there also Lehming, S., Gewissen als Thema theologischer Arbeit, p. 13; Claß, H., Gewissen und Glaube, ibid., p. 17. Siemers, H., Ein Podiumsgespräch über das Gewissen - Das Gewissen aus der Sicht des Verhaltensforschers, p. 30. Pannenberg, W., *Anthropologie in theologischer Perspektive*, Göttingen 1983. Mock, E., Gewissen und Gewissensfreiheit. Zur Theorie der Normativität im demokratischen Verfassungsstaat, in: *Schriften zur Rechtstheorie*, Vol. 104, Berlin 1983.

50 *BVerwGE*7, p. 242. A compilation of the decisions of the Bundesver-waltungsgericht can be found in: Buchholz, U., *BVerwG zur Gewissens-entscheidung bei der Wehrdienstverweigerung*, No. 448. 0 to paragraph 25 WPflG Nr. 1-137. Lisken, H., in: *NVwZ* 1982, p. 664. Tiedemann, P., Der Gewissensbegriff in der höchstrichterlichen Rechtsprechung, in: *DÖV* 1984, p. 61 (p. 67).

51 Pitschas, R. Mittelbare Wehrdienstverweigerung und Arbeitsförderungs-recht, in: *NJW* 1984, p. 889. Eiselstein, C., Das "Forum Externum" der Gewissensfreiheit - ein Weg in die Sackgasse, in: *DÖV*1984, p. 794. Steiner, U., Der Grundrechtsschutz der Glaubens- und Gewissensfreiheit, in: *JuS* 1982, p. 157. Regarding the revised text of the law of conscientious objection and the oral examination of conscience, see: BVerwG, DÖV

1984, p. 676; see also SZ, No. 120, May 25-27, 1985, concerning medical training.

52 Kaufmann, A., *Die Parallelwertung in der Laiensphäre. Ein sprach-philosophischer Beitrag zur allgemeinen Verbrechenslehre* , München 1982, p. 29.

53 Luhmann, N., Gewissensfreiheit und das Gewissen, in: *AöR*, Vol. 90, 1965, p. 257 (p. 283). Luhmann, N., *Grundrechte als Institution. Ein Beitrag zur politischen Soziologie*, Berlin 1965. Commentary of the author, in: *BayVBl.* 1965, p. 434.

54 Luhmann, N., Gewissensfreiheit und das Gewissen, in: *AöR*, Vol. 90, 1965, p. 284.

55 Luhmann, N., *Funktionen und Folgen formaler Organisation*, Berlin 1964, p. 372.

56 Luhmann, N., loc. cit., p. 282, footnote 66.

57 Indirect conscientious objection has recently been the subject of various labor court decisions. The same problem was involved in a decision where the court had to decide if the conscience of a member of an insurance company was violated because abortions were being paid for by the contributions of all members, including the plaintiff's, who is strictly against abortion. Decision by the First Senate of April 18, 1984, *EuGRZ* 1984, p. 433 and the critical commentary by Geiger, W., Das Verhältnis von Bundesverfassungsgericht und vorlegendem Gericht im Falle der konkreten Normenkontrolle. Eine Kritik an der Entscheidung des BVerfG vom 18. April 1984, in: *EuGRZ* 1984, p. 409.

58 Of a different opinion is Helmut Kuhn, who refers to his analysis of conscience as a "Begegnung mit dem Sein". See in extracts: Kuhn, H., in: *Das Gewissen in der Diskussion*, Darmstadt 1976, p. 162.

59 Luhmann's definition of conscience as a mere function is the same as Comte's well-known theory. See: Scholler, H., Das Gewissen als Gestalt der *Freiheit*, München 1962. Scholler, H., Martin Luther on Jurisprudence: Freedom, Conscience, Law, in: *Valparaiso University Law Review*, Vol. 15, 1981, p. 265.

DISCUSSION

Josef Fuchs SJ, Ann Higgins, Lawrence Kohlberg,
Georg Lind, Heinrich Scholler, Hans Strotzka,
Paul Weingartner, Thomas E.Wren

WREN: My question concerns your expression 'relaxation of conscience'. Would it be correct to read it as referring to the loosening of the connection between conscience and law, such that the so-called relaxation that we have is a duty-free zone of moral consciousness? This would mean you have little pockets of pure conscience, such as what the conscientious objector feels, which are allowed by the legal system. Or would it be correct to read it as including a converse notion, that of a tightening of the relationship of conscience with the law, such that the law actually operates to inform, to shape the conscience?

SCHOLLER: I think this is quite correct. I don't know if you can call it 'relaxation' or not, but I will give you an example. If you, being a Catholic, decide on a Sunday to go to a Protestant church you can do this by law; there is no limitation. By state law you are free to go to any service you want. So the system gives you some pockets, especially within the field of religion. This was not so some one hundred, two hundred years ago, when in Munich we had different shops for Catholics and Protestants. There was no relaxation, you had to decide by law.

WREN: Instead of the tightening of conscience, you mean a relationship between the law and conscience. So it's not so much conscience that is tense, but it is a relationship which is tense - or shall I say 'tight'?

SCHOLLER: I might call it 'tightening', actually it's tightened by the law, but basically, you know, we are educated in a system. We are born in a system and we are educated in a system and this tightening starts just from the beginning.

LIND: You mentioned as an example a conscientious objector. But this is actually a third type of relation between law and conscience. It is not exactly a free pocket for law, a free pocket where you can decide what to do. But it is the law in the way that it invokes the conscience and puts up some criteria for evaluating your conscientious objection. So it is in a way different from the real tight relation where the law says, 'You must not murder'. On the other hand, you have that example of what church you want to go to: The law says, 'I do not bother about it whatever you do'. But with this example of conscientious objectors you have a mixture of some value; it says, 'Within certain limits you are allowed to make the conscientious decision'. So it's a third type.

SCHOLLER: May I answer? I detected three different fields: First, there's the traditionally granted freedom of conscience, referring originally to religion and later to any kind of ideology (*Weltanschauung*) where you are free to believe. Second, there is another field which developed from the first one, I agree. There is a category of conscientious objectors, about which criteria are demanded by law. I have to prove before a court that my conscience doesn't at all allow such a thing. And the third category, which I mentioned at the beginning, is, let's say, typically shown by criminal law, in which generally I cannot say, "I'm acting on behalf of my conscience".

I'm still puzzled about why in a legal system we have so many, that is, three very different approaches to the rule of conscience. I tried to show how to reduce the three different approaches to two.

WEINGARTNER: One very important point is the following question: What is the cause for the change of norms? Is it because new facts are coming up in history, which were not the case earlier? Is it the case that we learn more about facts that were already there, but we know more? One important third possibility is: Do we sometimes say that some norms are not just and so they have to be changed or replaced? In this case we would judge a norm by some higher kind of meta-norm. One example are the methodological norms in natural science. There was a norm through some centuries: "Look for effects that have a continuous dependency upon their causes, 'continuous' in the sense of 'describable by differential equations'." Now, this norm was held for centuries and then quantum physics came and one saw that in the area of microphysics this methodological norm had to be changed because there was not always a continuous dependency here. I have also been convinced by a little booklet by Savigny *Die Uberprüfbarkeit der Strafrechtssätze* that there is a very similar situation in the history of penal law which shows that certain norms have been revised and the revision in most cases is that some content is changed.

SCHOLLER: Yes, there are three elements or reasons for change - new facts, new learning, and the problem "idea of justice". An example for new facts: These differentiations of religion between Catholic and Protestant believers in churches and so on were based on the assumption that you have to have one religion in one country; you cannot rule as a monarch in a country with two religions. After the Thirty Years' War people learned that you can easily live with different religions in one society. Secondly, there is a learning process. People really came to know each other better and came to realize that these people have the same basic ideas and basic needs. So there was a learning process and people realized, "Why should we exclude the Jews from participating in society?" So, the effect was the experience, I guess, of living together happily with Jews and atheists.

And finally there is one more reason for the changing of content: This is a process of individualization which became stronger and stronger during the last 150 years.

STROTZKA: If I understand you correctly, you are referring to a court decision of October 1958 where, apparently, to abstain from military service is only allowed if you get into danger of mental illness.

SCHOLLER: Yes, that is correct. The constitution grants freedom of conscience for conscientious objectors only if there is a serious conflict within the person which would lead to the destruction of the personality if he is forced to obey and fulfil the military service by killing other people. It is a tightening of conscience.

STROTZKA: Are the people aware that this forces somebody who is applying for conscientious objector status to dissimulate?

SCHOLLER: Yes, naturally. There is a jurisdiction which did not continue on the same strict level but accepted a kind of milder approach. And then we had up to 7O,OOO applications a year. The most recent change was to extend the civil service by three months which is a substitute for the military service. By this extension you get a certain criterion for judging the objecting person. This shows that the law demands a high degree of conscious judging.

STROTZKA: For me it's a good example that every use of psychiatry is also a danger in democracies.

FUCHS: First an observation about the question of changes in law. In Christian churches it was always tought, "Everybody has religious freedom". This was the principle. But through centuries they made a distinction: A non-Christian is not obliged to become a Christian. He is free. But if you are a Christian, you are not free any more to leave or to contradict truth, etc. They could kill you by fire, and they did! There was one Christianity. What happened that we have changed? It's not simply new facts, but also changes of insights and evaluations. For instance, there is a famous saying, *"Error non habet ius"* which is "Error does not have rights". This was accepted. If you have the wrong religion, please leave! You have no right because you are living in error! This was so until Vatican II, still in Vatican II, also in the discussions. Finally they decided, "Very well, this was a new evaluation: Error has no rights. But persons have rights in regard to what they think in their 'conscience'".

This was a new excellent formulation, known before, but not accepted, and then finally also accepted. So there are new insights, new evaluations and they will also change the law-systems, both in state and church.

But I have another question: Very often you used the formulation "conscience as norm". I think it is a very ambiguous formulation. If I understand, for instance, that conscience is a norm for my own decisions and acting, then I have no difficulty. But if somebody will say, "Conscience of somebody becomes also a norm of applying to state-law", I would have difficulties. How do we understand "conscience as norm" in this two different cases? Take this example: Does the conscientious objector have a right for himself against this law? I think behind these discussions is the idea of the difference of laws. If they force him to work against his moral conscience, they would offend his moral goodness. And nobody is allowed to do this! It's the personal right to follow my conscience, not the right to be exempted from military service. There is a difficulty between the rights of what we have to do within this world, and the right to follow one's convictions.

SCHOLLER: I think it's difficult here for law to answer your question because the construction of the law is simpler. A law contains an obligation to military service, but it grants exceptions. An exception applies if a certain factual situation is proved. He can demand to be set free from the duty. I suppose what you have in mind is the motivation of law, and this is more important for our argument than the technicality of how we proceed to get rights. The motivation of the law, I agree, is a value, a kind of morality or goodness which must be respected by the community as a personal value.

FUCHS: I think you are right. The law we are given is much simpler, and we are not entering the whole question of morality. My question is if behind all this is maybe something different? Maybe those who enacted the law did not reflect on this?

SCHOLLER: Maybe not the lawgiver, but when it comes to the law, this is a big process in a society. The lawgiver is but a part of the technical process.

FUCHS: An example: In the United Nations we have a Declaration of Freedom. We have also Religious Liberty and Freedom of Conscience. What is the motivation behind this Declaration? I would say nothing but practical national or international political utilitarianism. We have to agree on this; otherwise how can we live with other nations? What's behind this agreement: ideas, motivations, values, moral goodness, morality? All the states signed the Declaration. What they have *really* signed is the *deeper contents* of these affirmations whose roots they have not told us. So, this is my explanation.

WREN: The fact remains that there's something paradoxical about a society developing a set of conventions that are themselves postconventional, where I use "postconventional" in the sense of your example of the Vatican II shift from the idea of error, not having rights, to the idea of persons having rights. What we see then is some kind of a transformation. Such transformations on the individual level have been studied by cognitive development psychology, which considers the subject's shift from a conventional to a postconventional way of understanding the meaning of social rules. One wonders how such a shift is also possible for a society, especially a society like the Roman Catholic Church which is also not just a set of conventions but a network of doctrinal metaphysical tenets.

KOHLBERG: I'm really very puzzled because of the difference between the American and European legal tradition. In America during the Vietnam war one was allowed to be a conscientious objector only to accept alternative service, only if one belonged to a religious group that was pacifistic by nature. This was the only thing that was recognized directly by the American law. They didn't know what conscience was. I am puzzled that the American legal system doesn't have any way of defining "conscience". If it did it would be able to find some criteria other than strict membership in a pacifistic group to justify conscientious objection. I'm not prepared to say I have any advice to offer to the laws how to define "conscience" in the sense of conscientious objection. If the moral psychologist can really help with this is a complicated question.

SCHOLLER: First, I think we have the same problem in Germany or even a bigger problem because we accept the conscientious objector who does not belong to a specific religious group or orientation. But then by what criteria could the courts accept the objections? If the conscience would be violated, then you can apply for the civil service. The latest development is that they prolonged the alternative service by three months as one criterion for the serious decision based on conscience. So the problem is not yet solved, but we would have a system of criteria.

LIND: Do I see correctly that we actually had two types of problems involved? One is, where there are more types but one which could be very crucial to the recent discussion: You have exemptions from the law when the individual is in a way lacking capabilities, not being really able to comply with the law, and the law in a way accounts for these deficiencies that it lowers the penal ties for certain cases.

Then you have the other case where not the individual is deficient but the state; the law is deficient and in a way these conscientious objection issues and also the issue of the right to head a demonstration against nuclear war is a new theme which is not related to that of freedom of church practices. I think it is a new theme which comes out of a conviction of a democratic society that laws are always fallible, not perfect enough, and the majority may enact unjust and wrong laws; so the individual should have some rights to object against unjust regulations or state norms. When a conscientious objector says, "It is not good to kill people in war", what means can he take? Can he break a law to object against armament? This has been a very hot discussion the last years, at least in Germany. I wonder whether you can still handle this problem within your conception of tension and relaxation of laws or whether this is a new quality.

SCHOLLER: When I finished my paper, I became aware that I should go back again and include the problem of civil disobedience to a large extent; maybe I shall do it later. I read Rawls again in order to gain some ideas on civil disobedience from his book, but it's very difficult because it's a violation of the law based on, let's say, our higher morality of the interpretation of the whole legal order.

LIND: I just want to emphasize my point again. I think it's important in the context of moral developmental theory and as to the question of whether you should educate people beyond, so to say, the moral development of your state laws. What should you advise someone to do if he finds out that some of the laws are unjust or morally defective?

What I intended with my question was: Is your way of historical accounts, which I find very interesting, a fruitful way for dealing with problems that only arise in modern societies? I think of problems between an existing social system and the opposing individual who claims to have more insight into the morality of a law or of a regulation of a state act than the state itself has?

SCHOLLER: Since people are using this freedom of conscience as a basic stronghold for their position, we have to look into it; we cannot just throw history away. But it's true that you can always debate history.

HIGGINS: I do want to ask you to elaborate one part of your paper where you make the comment that the "differentiation between doing and not doing is not very helpful in a modern legal system". You end with saying that "participation is becoming more important and non-participation becomes the essential crime". I would like you to elaborate on this idea that "non-participation becomes the essential crime".

SCHOLLER: The classical answer is: If you violate a law by omission, it's a very slight violation, yes? Your crime hurts much more the protected good things if you violate by doing. I think this is wrong because we are now changing into a society in which not-doing, non-participating, is crucial, is more essential. You cannot say, "He can do it relying on his conscience" because he is only neglecting a duty. Maybe it's more important to neglect a duty to vote than to destroy a window. But we agree that participating is essential. I have a comment for Mr. Lind: You know, we have a sort of field of force concerning the relation between law and conscience which I didn't mention and that's the educational system. In this field, a conscience is shaped, enforced in youngsters and children. For example, the new law on protection of the environment which is now a goal of education is based on the constitution; it is enforced by education. The state enforces the shaping of conscience.

FUCHS: I have the conscientious objector in mind. I think in conscience he is convinced, "It is not allowed, so I cannot do what they ask me to do". And now, should the state, could the state as the authority in an extreme case eventually insist in leaving the consequences to the conscientious objector? This means that he ought to be faithful to his conscience and accept all the consequences of his being faithful.

SCHOLLER: Let me answer the question according to the positive German law. I would have to say if he is really deciding
within the Guarantee of Article 4, Section 3, he can refuse to
join the military service. If he refuses, the conscientious objector is then ordered to serve in a factory where military weapons
are produced or the bakery where bread is produced for the
army. He refuses this alternative service too because he says,
"This will help the army because I am producing guns or I'm
producing bread, and this bread is feeding the army". So now
we have the problem of whether we can again apply Article 4 or
not. Up to now the courts in Germany had decided that the man
who refuses the work in the factory doesn't get his unemployment benefit. He is not forced to work. In our society we
have many subtle possibilities of enforcement. He doesn't get
his compensation. He is offered a second time, by another factory, which now does not produce bread, but sausages. He refuses again, and finally he will get no benefit at all: a kind of enforcement...

HIGGINS: I just have one thought to tie together Georg's and
my paper on education and the discussion about the law that
we've just been having. That is to talk about what we call in
America "the spirit of the law". I mean we talk about the letter of
the law and the spirit. The spirit is not just goodwill but the full
intent of the law. What's the real intention, the point of having
this law? To what end? I just want to make the analogy with the
work we've done in the school where I think one of the essential characteristics of the moral discussion we had with the
students was really their creation of rules and laws in their own
school: the letter of the law, "do this, do that", but also to
understand the spirit of the law and the connection between the
two. It's that kind of parallelism that I'll just make.

LIND: Things are not as simple anymore as they have been in
Kant's time. Obviously he said, "Reason about things, but
obey". Nowadays our circumstances are sometimes to break the
law as a course of reasoning or by breaking the law you are able
to reason. I think of cases like someone betraying his country
who gives the blueprints of the atomic bomb to the Soviet
Union because he thought it would help keep peace and give

balance in the world. Or take somebody who betrays his factory, giving away blueprints or plans to the public in order to show that some very dangerous chemicals are being produced that are extremely harmful for many people. In many instances this may be causing problems for the conscience. Education, that was the point of my paper in a way, seems really to foster cognitive moral sensibility for such problems. If it is enough, we don't know, but there is a growing moral sensibility in students, both high school and university students. The suggestion I would like to make at that point is: These problems should not be looked at as threatening the existence of society, but rather as a source of disequilibrium which could be a starting point again to foster the cognitive moral development of society, which is a different unit than the cognitive moral development of an individual. Hopefully, these problems are creative rather than destructive.

End of discussion.

HANS STROTZKA

PSYCHOANALYSIS AND ETHICS

This brief essay is to give a twofold answer to the problem referred to in the title:

1. the contribution of psychoanalysis to ethics and moral theory;

2. the moral aspects of psychotherapy (and psychoanalytic psychotherapy in particular).

When considering the first point, we find that Freud commented rather unwillingly and sparsely on philosophy and ethics. "That which is moral is self-evident", and "I feel that as long as virtue does not pay on this earth, ethics will preach in vain" (1948) are typical statements in this context. Freud's negative and pessimistic view of man and the world, ranging from the "savage" who has to be tamed, the need of instinctual renunciation for the sake of social and cultural activity, to the conception of the death instinct, finds its confirmation in our everyday experience of unlimited egoism, social indifference and brutality. And there is no denying that "filling your guts comes before morality" (Brecht), that power can hardly be acquired or maintained without cunning and force (Macchiavelli) and that - probably as a result of growing alienation - narcissism (in terms of detachment, disengagement, self-value crises as well as narcissistic rage) increasing (Lasch).

Nevertheless, surprising examples of the victory of "eros" over "thanatos" can be found both in everyday life and in clinical experience (e.g., necrophilia with E. Fromm), and the single observation that firemen commit arson in order to be able to extinguish the fire does not disprove the (moral) value of the firebrigade.

Now there is general agreement that social and technological developments on the one hand and the loosening of religious-moral ties on the other hand have caused an ethical defect, which is above all reflected in uncertainty with regard to educational principles. Scientific advances, such as nuclear

G. Zecha and P. Weingartner (eds.), Conscience: An Interdisciplinary View, 263–293.
© 1987 by D. Reidel Publishing Company.

power for peaceful uses and armament, biology, transplant-
ation and intensive-care medicine, automation, microelectron-
ics, etc., force us to take unprecedented ethical decisions which
frequently have global effects and affect future generations as
well. By contrast, traditional ethical concepts frequently apply
only to individuals or their more immediate reference groups. A
deontological ethics with its everlasting, universal norms of a
transcendental origin can no longer cope with the complex
nature of a pluralistic, rapidly changing society.

A pluralistic and consequentialistic responsibility ethics
seems to be best suited for this situation.

I have tried to outline such a concept (Strotzka, 1983) on the
basis of John Rawls' principles of "social justice as fairness" by
referring to psychoanalysis as a comprehensive theory of behavior. Despite the general reticence on the part of psychoanalysts, who generally share Michel Foucault's view that no
ethics can be developed on the basis of psychoanalysis, it was
possible to draw on Heinz Hartmann, E. H. Erikson, J. C. Flü-
gel, A. and M. Mitscherlich, H. E. Richter and, more recently,
Nedelmann and Becker.

There are two main points of reference:
1. Our knowledge of the *Super-Ego* which - by identification
   with (or in opposition to) environmental values - develops
   into our "conscience", attributing values to our thoughts and
   feelings and determining the ethical system on the one hand
   and the moral actions of the individual on the other hand.
2. The role of the *affect of shame*, which has received increasing attention recently and which I would like to discuss first. In this context I draw on Helen Bloch-Lewis
   (1971), Gerhart Piers and Milton B. Singer (1971), Leon
   Wurmser (1981), and in particular James Gilligan (from
   Lickona, 1976).

With psychoanalysis the study of moral experience became
an empirical psychological discipline. Initially, interest centered
almost exclusively on "guilt" as the endpoint or highest stage of
moral development. The precursor of guilt, the affect of shame,
which is even more important for moral experience, has mostly
been ignored.

By *shame* Gilligan means "narcissistic wounds", such as feelings of humiliation, incompetence, weakness, dishonor, disgrace, contempt, rejection, and the feeling of not being able to "take care of" oneself. It is thus a (suspected or real) defect to which we react.

By *guilt*, on the other hand, we mean the feeling of having committed a sin, a crime, an evil, or an injustice, of having been harmful to others and of deserving punishment. It is a matter of an action or its omission. Gilligan interprets morality as a force antagonistic to life and to love, causing illness, death, murder and suicide. It is a necessary but immature stage of affective and cognitive development; regression to this stage represents neurosis or even more massive psychopathology.

Moral beliefs and value-judgments correspond to affects of shame and guilt. They clearly have their adaptive utility, as does physical pain. Like other syndromes, however, they can easily be maladaptive.

'Maturation' then means the development of shame and guilt into the capacity for active love of oneself and others. 'Morality' is thus interpreted as the motivation of behavior, as the cognitive structuring of social relations in terms of moral ideals ("ought" and "should") rather than in terms of scientific ideas (psychological understanding).

Psychoanalysis provides an intellectual framework that enables one to make decisions on how to live and what to do; unlike ethics, it is not *perspective* (i. e., telling people what they should do) but *interrogative*, asking them what they want to do. This is the only way of ensuring people to act out of love rather than out of compulsion or constraint. Contrary to philosophical ethics, psychoanalysis refers above all to the conscious or unconscious motivations underlying our actions. The first and universal answer to the question of what one has to do is simply, "To live".

Anthropologists distinguish between *shame cultures* to refer to societies in which the source of moral sanctions is perceived to reside in other people, in their criticism, ridicule or contempt, and *guilt cultures*, which rely on an internalized conscience and its resultant absolute standards of morality and the feeling of sinfulness. Piers and Singer, however, question this strict distinction.

Shame cultures are predominantly found in so-called primitive societies (e. g., the Kwakiutl Indians, Benedict), while guilt cultures are mostly found in Judeo-Christian societies (e. g., the Hutterites, Kaplan and Plant). Shame cultures place a positive value on aggressiveness toward others, guilt cultures place a positive value on aggression directed toward the self. What Nietzsche called the "transvaluation of values" is the reversal of moral values held by a shame culture to those held by a guilt culture (the transformation of master morality into slave morality).

With the emperor Constantine's conversion in 313 A. D. Christianity changed to a mixed shame-and-guilt culture. Freud (in: *Civilization and its Discontents*, 1930) saw guilt feelings as the cause of ethics. He did not have yet a theory of shame. According to present-day theory shaming is one of the most important triggers that release our pre-existing potential for aggression. While Freud sees shame and guilt as more or less parallel, Gilligan (like Piers, 1953) sees them as antagonists.

The development of the capacity to experience shame precedes that of the capacity to experience guilt in all stages of libidinous development.

In schizophrenia the Ego is overwhelmed by oral shame, in psychotic depressions by oral guilt, in paranoia by anal shame; compulsive-obsessive disorders result from feelings of guilt over anal-sadistic impulses. Hysteria, sociopathy, sexual sadism, phallic narcissism and pseudo-hypersexuality (the "Don Juan" syndrome, nymphomania) are caused by phallic shame resulting from an underlying early phallic-urethral wish to be passively loved but not to love others in return. Masochism, finally, is caused by feelings of guilt over phallic-sadistic-competitive impulses.

By a shame ethics we mean a value system in which the most negatively valued experience is humiliation, and in which the highest good is pride. A guilt ethic pride is unconscious, while in the shame ethics shame is unconscious.

shame ethics	guilt ethics	
pos.	neg.	love of self, pride, egoism, narcissism
pos.	pos.	love of others, sympathy
neg.	neg.	hate and aggression toward others, sadism, murder, war
neg.	pos.	hate and aggression toward the self, masochism, suicide, martyrdom

Gilligan's view is above all based on similar findings by Piaget and Kohlberg.

Intensive shame always lies behind intensive guilt - shame feeds the anger that feeds the guilt.

If shame, like guilt and unfulfilled narcissistic wishes can be openly and honestly acknowledged, the need for both morality and immorality will disappear.

Moral dilemmas generally constitute exclusive choice situations in which one person can be helped only if another is hurt, whereas psychoanalysis works constantly to transcend the dichotomy between egoism and altruism. By way of example Gilligan mentions the situation of Socrates, who could easily have saved himself without destroying either his identity or the state.

In other words, morality creates the very dilemma it claims to be able to resolve.

Guilt ethics holds that one must hurt oneself in order to help others, shame ethics holds that one must hurt others in order to help oneself. A psychotherapeutic approach, on the other hand, is always directed toward the solution of conflicts. It boils down to a love relationship in which through meeting one's own needs one meets another's. Both sexual love and parent-child love are classical examples.

So much on Gilligan's view. Even a cursory look at this theory shows that it can solve only a part of the ethical problems. It applies almost exclusively to interhuman relations, a field in which it is, no doubt, extremely helpful as it can, above all, solve the unbelievably frequent problems resulting from neurotic (and probably psychotic) morality.

It will have to fail in those cases, however, where problems are brought about by new technologies. In those cases one will have to fall back on the concepts of justice, fairness, and responsibility for mankind and future generations, as I have tried to do in my previously mentioned book.

While Gilligan concentrates on the relation between shame and ethics, Wurmser emphasizes the clinical aspect in relation to the Super-Ego.

This book, too, tries to provide a theoretical and clinical proof of the fact that the concept of shame, despite its enormous significance, has been ignored in psychoanalytical theory. Ample references to the literature and numerous vignettes of case studies illustrate this point. Democritus already recognized shame as one of the essential roots of ethical consciousness. Curiosity is subject to shame just as is self-exposure. The Super-Ego is a large defense structure and shame must be viewed as resistance, as being related to "loss of face". The "object pole" is the factor in front of which one is ashamed, the "subject pole" is the self-aspect. The former can be broken down into expectations, criticism, and punishment; it is originally always a person; later it is an inner representative of such a person in the Super-Ego. The latter can be subdivided in the action itself, its results, and its reflection on the whole acting person. Sandler states that shame might be related to "I cannot see myself as I want others to see me" (p. 45). The passive experience of humiliating others, thus making everyone appear ridiculous (sarcasm and cynicism). Integrity and related shame refer to a highly sublimated form of narcissism (Rangell, the "syndrome of the compromise of integrity". Ambition, power, and opportunism grow wild and proliferate.).

Shame is a special form of anxiety but also a character trait, a symptom and a distinctly differentiated form of inner tension. Ultimately, it is also an external situation. Pride, honor and dignity are directly opposite to the reaction pattern of shame. Vanity is synonymous with conceit. Jacobson: Shame refers to visual exposure, guilt predominantly to verbal demands, prohibitions and criticism (p. 52). The feeling of unexpectedness plays a major role in connection with shame. Shame anxiety is the type of anxiety evoked by sudden exposure and signalling the danger of contemptuous rejection. It is specifically self-potentiating and thus especially prone to loss of control. The triad of *weakness, defectiveness* and *dirtiness* is feared most.

One boundary which should not be transgressed is the boundary of privacy, the boundary of power expansion ("Geltung") the other one. *Guilt limits strength, shame covers weakness (or reveals it by blushing, e. g.).* The roots are to be found in the family.

Self-observation for the sake of moral evaluation is one of the cardinal functions of the Ego and the Super-Ego. It is a kind of scopophilic activity focussed on the self, which can be projected: "They observe me; what do they think of me?" The major anxiety in shame is loss of object and loss of self. The other person turns away in contempt. He who is not loved stops loving himself. In comparison, the major anxiety in guilt is that one will be castrated, mutilated, killed. *In shame, death is due to isolation rather than to physical attack.* In shame-proneness there is invariably the sense of unlovability. Shame serves as a defensive attitude and reaction formation against two partial drives: the drive toward exhibitionism and the drive toward voyeurism (or scopophilia).

As a consequence of conflicts of the oral phase, shame has the content: "I am ashamed in front of an ideal of absolute perfection", and "I am ashamed for my object-creating and object-destroying wishes". The fear is: annihilation by total isolation, rejection, and fragmentation.

In the anal phase I am ashamed in front of an ideal of self-sufficiency (autarchy), autonomy, of self-control and cleanliness and I am ashamed for my wishes to remain dependent and weak, and for my desires to surrender masochistically to humiliation.

As a consequence of phallic-oedipal conflicts, we are ashamed in front of an ideal of being of hermaphroditic completeness and for showing that we are castrated. The fear is not to be loved or respected but to be ridiculed for being castrated. Severe early traumatization in object relations leads to a massive overcathexis of the wish to create attachment and to exert power by magical looking, thus creating and changing reality, an attempt that always fails. This entails a severe state of helplessness and despair about ever being able to love and be loved. Emotional object-constancy and self-constancy, developing in the third year of life, are menaced by the conflicts described.

Shame is one of the major motive forces for repression, in addition to pain and self-reproach. Paranoid delusions of being watched and of watching others (naked) can be a severe lifelong burden. Freud in 1905 considered the eye as a specific erotically stimulating zone (for exhibitionism and scopophilia). Scopophilia itself plays a central role in self- and nonself-differentiation and in the processes of identification, introjection and Super-Ego formation. Both scopophilia and exhibitionism use libidinous as well as aggressive energies. Visual perception as an active, explorative process starts with the first days of life.

However, shame is also rooted in anal-muscular and urethral eroticism, and is opposed to self-control, autonomy and self-reliance. Wurmser distinguishes between two major partial drives: *theatrophilia* as the desire to watch and observe, to admire and to be fascinated, to merge and master through attentive looking. *Delophilia* is defined as the desire to express oneself and to fascinate others by one's self-exposure. Both originate in archaic times.

Shame first appears in the rapprochement phase at the age of 18 months.

Unconscious shame contents are castration shame, a masochistic orientation in women, a homosexual-masochistic orientation in men, weakness of anal and urethral control (dirtiness, shame for general weakness and dependence, showing one's feelings, especially love, tenderness, needing).

In "borderline" neurotic and psychotic patients the shame syndrome shows the following characteristic features: depersonalization, depression, eating disturbances and thought disturbances, abrupt switches in affect, concretization, over-generalization or over-inclusion, disturbance of focal attention.

Shame protects against the physical exposure used as a means of power within the family and against the exhibitionistic misuse of the child in society. Shame can be masked by depression, anxiety, homosexuality, drug addiction, imposture and lying, paranoid symptoms and writing inhibition. In addition, there may be contempt, spite, rage, and "numbness". Narcissistic defense mechanisms are: arrogation of power, grandiosity and idealization. Three symptoms are seen as particularly important in the fight against shame: depersonalization, lack of understandability and shamelessness.

Depersonalization reflects a denial of loss of the self, paralleled by a loss of part of the object world.

Thought disturbances may be simple regression, faulty learning or symbolically meaningful compromise formations between wish and defense. Frequently there may be mystifications.

Shamelessness often constitutes a reaction formation against severe traumatic humiliation. The cynical, arrogant, opportunistic shameless person with Rangell's "syndrome of the compromise of integrity" will show defense against the conscience as well as defense against ideals and values and their replacement by narcissistic power, ambition, and revenge (the return of the repressed).

In terms of therapy, shame poses many technical difficulties that, if not recognized and analyzed, stymie progress and even continuation. Shame resistance may take the form of silence and acting out.

Heroically transcending shame is the search for personal integrity and self-loyalty or authenticity. Masking, understood as a defense against the fear of death, shames death by ridicule, but it also impersonates the uncanny force of the dead ancestors - the heroes - and vanquishes the fear by identification.

The myth of original sin is the beginning of shame, morality and ethics. Nakedness and sexuality, fratricide (Cain and Abel), child sacrifice (Abraham) are a continuation of this development. Guilt is linked with action (penetration) and masculinity, shame is linked with weakness and femininity.

Ethics and morality are socially structured attitudes to cope with shame and guilt.

The significance of shame for the origin of values, which are of course, represented in the Super-Ego, also emerges from an everyday observation: Adults keep telling children, "You are too young for this, too stupid, etc., this is something you do not yet understand; this is nothing for you, etc.", thus shaming them, exposing them and frustrating them. Just because we have become so used to this we tend to overlook the extent of narcissistic woundedness, despair, and rage caused by such remarks and consequently tend to neglect them in therapy.

However, all this has a decisive influence on self-esteem as well as personal ethics and morality.

Helen Bloch shows that individuals with predominantly field-dependent perception (in keeping with Wilkins' "conceptual analysis") tend to feel shame, whereas those with field-independent perception tend to feel guilt. Non-analyzed shame in transference is an essential factor in a negative therapeutic reaction. Guilt arises from the identification with threatening parents, shame arises from the failure of identification with loving parents or other "models". The feeling of responsibility is a function of guilt; shame is more strongly body-related than guilt.

Similarly, Piers differentiates unconscious shame as anxiety arising from the failure vis-à-vis the internalized parental ideals. The threat implied is rejection (abandonment). Unconscious guilt, on the other hand, is the anxiety that is generated whenever a boundary set by the parents is transgressed, and the unconscious threat in this case is castration (mutilation).

I have discussed shame at considerable length because there is hardly any reference to it in my book. However, I will be very brief in discussing the Super-Ego. Piaget and Kohlberg investigated the development of values and morality from the viewpoint of developmental psychology, and there is no contradiction to the psychoanalytic concepts. Let me quote from my book (1983):

"The relation between Freud's and Piaget's views can best be seen from the most recent survey by André Haynal (1975). Piaget finds evidence of a heteronomous morality in the child below the age of seven years, reflecting the child's egocentric point of view. Its elements are: objective responsibility, rigid rules, absolute values, breaking of rules backed by punishment, duty as obedience vis-à-vis authority, mutuality, reconciliatory and immanent justice, collective responsibility.

By interaction with the peer group, the older child develops a morality of co-operation, which is characterized by autonomy and mutual respect. Its elements are: responsibility depending on intentionality, flexibility of rules, relativity of values, moral values independent of sanctions, restitutional justice, naturalistic causality, and individual responsibility.

As early as 1932 de Saussure held that the Super-Ego could be defined as a residue of realistic and egocentric thinking. To the three stages in the development postulated by Freud - primary identification, secondary identification through anxiety and tertiary identification through neutralization of aggressiveness - correspond Piaget's three stages of moral development, non-differentiation and participation, heteronomous morality based on unilateral respect (moral realism), and co-operative morality on the basis of fair exchange.

In this highly simplified description of the development of the Super-Ego as a representative of the value concepts of an individual within the framework of psychoanalytic theory we follow the summary given by Dieter Eicke: "The Super-Ego influences instinctual life as well as the ego-functions. It is linked with education through parents, teachers and society. It is composed of wishes, ideals, inculcated behavioral norms and value-judgments, and affects. It punishes, it lives, it gives rise to qualms of conscience and self-observation, it regulates self-confidence as well as many actions. It produces the habits, attitudes and behavior pattern of a character. It is this unconscious part of the Super-Ego, however, that controls our customs and habits, the taboos of a society as well as its educational methods" (p. 499) - According to Freud, this psychic agency developed from the Ego ideal. It was first defined in his publication *Mass psychology and Ego analysis* (1921). More recently, psychoanalysts, above all Lampl-de Groot (1963), distinguished between two forms of ideal images. The Ego ideal represents the behavioral standards taken over by a child from his parents and other persons serving as a model. This includes all prohibitions and concepts of sin, evil or bad behavior as well as all virtues.

The ideal self on the other hand represents the ideal wishes of a child both in terms of his own self and his imaginary ideal parents. There are close relationships with the concept of narcissism of Heinz Kohut. At this juncture it should also be mentioned that in recent decades, probably as a result of the social development we are discussing here, there has been an increase of narcissistic personality developments, which corresponds to a withdrawal from this world.

The Super-Ego is a summation of identifications, i.e. ,it contains introjections, imaginations and internalizations. It was built out of fear of retaliation or love withdrawal, its organization thus protecting the Ego against the outside world. The Ego adapts itself to avoid punishment, revenge, servitude or love withdrawal.

According to Freud, a more or less fully developed Super-Ego is not possible before the oedipal phase in the latency period, i.e., after the age of six. It reaches its full maturity only after the child's separation from his parents during puberty. There is no doubt, however, especially on the basis of the theories and observations of Melanie Klein and her students, that there are precursors of the Super-Ego going all the way back into the earliest time of object relations. The child's primary need is primary love (as defined by Balint), i.e., the striving after being loved which has no regard for the other person's needs and unshakable trust. During his development, therefore, the child - irrespective of this need - must learn a love which also shows consideration for the other person's needs. This can be done successfully if the parents set a corresponding example. Balint calls the result "fair share" and "mutual concern". Here we can see similarities with the concepts of Kohlberg and Piaget.

In all cases of neuroses, i.e., in cases of masochistic selfpunishment, it is the task of psychotherapy to make the punishing Super-Ego more friendly and tolerant by modifying or nullifying negative introjections and identifications by means of corrective affective experiences within the framework of a transference neurosis. However, it turned out that this causal-psychoanalytic treatment is not always necessary but that a change of dynamics can also be achieved from the periphery so to speak, i.e., by reconditioning within the framework of behavioral therapy.

Speaking of psychoanalytic theory, it should be pointed out that according to Harold Lincke the Super-Ego is essentially a symptom of compromise formation. It is only due to its general spread and acceptance in our civilization that we have failed to pay greater attention to this aspect of the Super-Ego. Simultaneously it includes the final renunciation of the incestuous objects of love and lifelong adherence to them in their introjected form. It seems that our civilization promotes a relatively high level of Ego-Super-Ego tensions. Society tries to exploit the resulting feelings of shame, guilt, and inferiority and to translate them into a high action potential by employing defenses, such as performance, initiative and identification, together with the Super-Ego against them. The Ego, restricted as a result of this identification, resorts to adjustment.

On the basis of his psychoanalytic observations Béla Grunberger (1974) introduces another interesting concept into the discussion, which psycho-analysts have not yet generally accepted, however. He resumes the idea of precursors of the Super-Ego in the very early periods of childhood and develops the concept of a primitive maternal "Über-Ich", which is the result of training by the mother. It is compulsively sadistic and unrelenting and strives for absoluteness. Identification is accompanied by sadistic affects which are projected onto the mother and reintrojected. There is also a secondary identification with the content of training, which can be changed more easily. The views held by the different schools of developmental psychology can thus be summarized as follows: Values are generated as a result of imitation of, and identification with, the immediate environment in childhood." (pp. 33-35)

I feel that the opinion held by Bronfenbrenner is also very important in this context. He holds that in the US (and we, after all, more or less follow this development) there is a "break-down of the processes that make human beings human" due to the fact that children are left to institutions, the media, and peer groups. To ensure the development of a healthy Super-Ego it would be necessary for the generations to move closer together again.

In this context I would like to add that my motivation to deal with ethical questions derives from marriage and family counselling where I was confronted with seriously conflicting interests for the first time and, unlike in individual therapy, did no longer get by with the concepts of neutrality, abstinence, and all-partiality. Professional (philosophical) ethics was no help either. Neither the Ten Commandments nor the Categorical Imperative (to mention only two examples) could really help me on.

Together with my team, therefore, I tried to develop a new concept. The definition we arrived at is admittedly modest but has proved fairly successful: "The goal of our counselling activity is the smallest possible misery to the smallest possible number of people, with special consideration of children."

A psychoanalytically based ethics, of course, is one that draws on psychology. Values, ethics, and moral behavior spring from guilt, shame, and development of the Super-Ego as a result of nature and nurture, with early object relations playing a decisive role. It would take too long to go into detail. Of the modern authors I would like to mention Fairbairn (Guntrip) and Kernberg in particular. I will not discuss the question of "fantasy" mentioned in the title of my book but simply refer to the relevant passages in my book.

Although I am fully aware of the incompleteness of my presentation of a psychoanalytic ethics, I must come to the second part of my paper - an ethics of psychoanalysis. Here, too, there is not much to be found in the literature. Most psychoanalysts seem to assume that, given the precise observation of the technical rule - especially that of abstinence -, there would be no further difficulties. Criticism comes mostly from outside and most often refers to:

1. a lack of social responsibility and commitment (i.e., questions of care, distribution problems and concepts of social justice are not taken into consideration);
2. the role of power in this asymmetric relation, i.e., the fact that the candidate is at the mercy of an incomprehensible machinery, the arbitrariness of a few people, the training analyst, the seminar leaders, and the two or three supervisors;
3. the rigid orthodoxy, the hostility toward the physical, the fear of interaction problems in group and family therapies and the dislike of innovations of any kind.

Adherence to the classical techniques is understandable since an opportunistic adjustment to the needs and circumstances of a given society implies the risk of a dilution and dissolution of the fundamental criteria of psychoanalytic thought and action. With the extension of indications from transference psychoneuroses to character disturbances (Aichhorn), perversions (Stoller), psychosomatic diseases (Weizsäcker, Uexküll and many others including Stephanos) and, above all, psychoses (Rosen, Sechehaye, Benedetti, etc.) a great many technical modifications had to be accepted anyway; of course, this also applies to the extension of psychoanalysis to children and adolescents, which meant the introduction of play technique. Finally, psychoanalytically oriented psychotherapy in the form of focal therapy as well as time-limited therapies (Bellak, Mann) have meant revolutionary changes with all their advantages and disadvantages. As a social psychiatrist and psychoanalyst I myself have again and again experienced the conflict between a patient-centered approach on the one hand, and a technique- and theory-centered approach for the purpose of preserving an important teaching and research method and a therapeutic technique for selected patients on the other hand. I am convinced that the dilemma can be solved if the psychoanalyst as a Balint group leader and supervisor also brings in his special psychosocial knowledge and abilities and if the other side (i.e., social psychiatry) acknowledges the importance of psychoanalysis. I myself have never had any difficulties with this dual function. One simply has to accept being attacked from both sides. However, social responsibility and social justice - ultimately a patient-centered approach - must be an integral part of the psychoanalysts' considerations and actions. I see no fundamental difficulties here.

Let me summarize: Psychoanalytic knowledge about the origin of values, the genesis of ethics and moral standards as well as conforming or contradictory actions, when combined with a consequentialistic ethics with the guiding values of "social responsibility" (Jonas) and "justice" (Rawls), may well become a timely guideline for our behavior which can even be taught in a participatory and anticipatory learning process, predominantly in small groups. Unless we want to resign, however, and continue heading toward disaster, it is urgently necessary to promote suitable activities.

University of Vienna

BIBLIOGRAPHY

Aichhorn, A.: 1969, *Verwahrloste Jugend*, Huber, Bern.
Bellak, L. and Small, L.: *Kurzpsychotherapie und Notfall-Psychotherapie*, Suhrkamp, Frankfurt/Main.
Benedetti, G.: 1980, *Klinische Psychotherapie. Einführung in die Psychotherapie der Psychosen*, Huber, Bern.

Benedict, R.: 1960, *Urformen der Kultur*, Rowohlt, Reinbek.

Bloch, E.: 1959, *Das Prinzip Hoffnung*, Suhrkamp, Frankfurt/Main.

Bloch, S. and Chodoff, R. (eds.): 1981, *Psychiatric Ethics*, Oxford University Press, Oxford.

Brecht, B.: 1968, *Die Dreigroschenoper*, Suhrkamp, Frankfurt/Main.

Bronfenbrenner, U.: 1976, *Ökologische Sozialisationsforschung*, Klett, Stuttgart.

Eicke, D.: 1976, 'Das Über-Ich - eine Distanz, richtungsgebend für unser Handeln' in D. Eicke (ed.): *Freud und die Folgen . Die Psychologie des 20. Jahrhunderts* , Bd. 2, Kindler, Zürich, pp.499-514. Erikson, E.H.: 1966, *Einsicht und Verantwortung*, Klett, Stuttgart.

Fairbairn, W.R.: 1952, *Psychoanalytic Studies of the Personality*, Tavistock, London.

Flugel, J.C.: 1970, *Man, Morals, and Society*, International University Press, New York.

Foucault, M.: 1978, *Von der Subversion des Wissens*, Ullstein, Frankfurt/Main.

Freud, S.: 1968, *Zukunft einer Illusion*, *Gesammelte Werke* Vol. 14, Fischer, Frankfurt/Main.

Fromm, E.: 1954, *Psychoanalyse und Ethik*, 2. Auflage, Diana, Stuttgart.

Gilligan,J.: 1976, 'Beyond Morality: Psychoanalytic Reflections on Shame, Guilt and Love' in Th. Lickona (ed.): *Moral Development and Behavior*, Holt, Rinehart and Winston, New York.

Grunberger, B.: 1974, 'Gedanken zum frühen Über-Ich' in *Psyche* 28, pp. 508-529.

Guntrip, H.S.: 1972, *Psyche und Gesundheit. Stress, Angst, Aggression, Isolation*, Umschau Verl., Frankfurt/Main.

Hartmann, H.: 1973, *Psychoanalyse und moralische Werte*, Stuttgart. Hartmann, H.: 1928, 'Psychoanalyse und Wertproblem' in *Imago* 14, pp.421-440.

Haynal, A.: 1975, 'Freud und Piaget' in *Psyche* 29, pp. 242-272.

Jacobson, E.: 1971, *Depression*, International University Press, New York.

Jonas, H.: 1979, *Prinzip Verantwortung*, Insel-Verlag, Frankfurt/Main.

Kaplan, A.: 1957, 'Freud and Modern Philosophy' in B. Nelson (ed.): *Freud and the 20th Century*, Meridian Books, New York, pp. 209-223.

Kernberg, O.F.: 1978, *Borderline-Störungen und pathologischer Narzißmus*, Suhrkamp, Frankfurt/Main.

Kohlberg, L.: 1974, *Zur kognitiven Entwicklung des Kindes*, Suhrkamp, Frankfurt/Main.

Lampl-de Groot, J.: 1963, 'Ichideal und Überich' in *Psyche* 18, pp.321-332.

Lasch, Ch.: 1982, *Das Zeitalter des Narzißmus*, Bertelsmann, München.

Lickona, Th. (ed.): 1976, *Moral Development and Behavior*, Holt, Rinehart & Winston, New York.
Machiavelli, N.: 1980, *Der Fürst*, Wiesbaden.
Mead, M.: 1959, *Geschlecht und Temperament*, Rowohlt, Reinbek.
Mitscherlich, A. and Mitscherlich, M.: 1979, *Die Unfähigkeit zu trauern. Grundlagen kollektiven Verhaltens*, 11. Auflage, Piper, München.
Nedelmann, C. and Becker, H.: 1983, *Psychoanalyse und Politik*, Suhrkamp, Frankfurt/Main.
Piaget, J.: 1973, *Erkenntnistheorie der Wissenschaften vom Menschen*, Ullstein, Frankfurt, Berlin, Wien.
Piers, G. and Singer, M.B.: 1971, *Shame and Guilt*, Norton, New York.
Rangell, L.: 1976, *Gelassenheit und andere menschliche Möglichkeiten*. Suhrkamp, Frankfurt/Main.
Rawls, J.: 1975, *Eine Theorie der Gerechtigkeit*, Suhrkamp, Frankfurt/Main.
Rosen, J.N.: 1964, *Psychotherapie der Psychosen*, Hippokrates, Stuttgart.
Sandler, J., Dare, Ch. and Holder, A.: 1973, *Grundbegriffe der psychoanalytischen Theorie*. Klett, Stuttgart.
Saussure, R. de: 1975, 'Apprendre et sentir ou de relations de la vie intellectuelle et de la vie affective' in *Revue fr. psychoanal.* 5, pp. 208-219, zitiert in A. Haynal.: 'Freud und Piaget'.
Sechehaye, M.A.: 1973, *Tagebuch eines Schizophrenen*, Suhrkamp, Frankfurt/Main.
Stephanos, S.: 1973, *Analytisch-psychosomatische Therapie*, Huber, Bern.
Stoller, R.J.: 1979, *Perversion*. Rowohlt, Reinbek/Hamburg.
Strotzka, H.: 1983, *Fairneß, Verantwortung, Fantasie*, Deuticke, Wien.
Richter, H.E.: 1979, *Der Gotteskomplex*, Rowohlt, Reinbek/Hamburg.
Uexküll, R.v. (ed.): 1979, *Lehrbuch der psychosomatischen Medizin*, Urban & Schwarzenberg, München.
Weizsäcker, V.v.: 1946, *Der Gestaltkreis*, Thieme, Stuttgart.
Wurmser, L.: 1981, *The Mask of Shame*, John Hopkins Univ. Press, Baltimore.

DISCUSSION

Josef Fuchs SJ, Ann Higgins, Lawrence Kohlberg,
Georg Lind, Heinrich Scholler, Hans Strotzka, Günter Virt,
Paul Weingartner, Thomas E. Wren, Gerhard Zecha

SCHOLLER: I think it is very useful to have this differentiation between shame culture and guilt culture. It is reflected in our notions of conscience. Going back to 'synderesis' is going back to a shame culture, because 'synderesis' is based on the Greek word meaning 'I have seen in me'. The Greeks invented for conscience something they have seen by shame and internalized. Jewish culture has no word for conscience which led to the remark of Treitschke, "Jews have no conscience". But in the Hebrew language we have a lot of words like "heart" or "kidneys" that show we have the guilt culture. So, we have really a mixed culture between shame and guilt.

But I would like to mention another idea. Shame culture is not only found in primitive societies. Asiatic cultures, e.g., the Chinese and Japanese cultures are based on shame culture. But today one of the most pressing conflicts is the Marxist ideology in China, because in Marxist ideology we have a lot of guilt culture, for instance, the well-known profession of guilt, which as part of the Marxist ideology has been introduced into a completely different Asiatic society. We can assure, it will not work; it has to pass away.

You referred to Rawls. In Rawls' *Theory of Justice* we find two different approaches to conscience. He says: Freedom of conscience has to do with secrecy. This would refer to shame culture. And then he mentions in the same section civil disobedience. Civil disobedience is also based on conscience, but more on guilt culture; so he must address himself to the public. So, in Rawls' theory we have again these two different approaches: shame culture and guilt culture in interpreting conscience.

STROTZKA: I am very grateful for your contribution. In my lecture I left out the passages on shame culture and guilt culture, because I had to limit myself. But I'm not quite sure if the concepts of shame culture and guilt culture really work. Cultural anthropology on which the concepts are based empirically is at the moment a little in trouble. I had the pleasure to work with Margret Mead for many years in the World Federation for Mental Health and I have known her well, also personally. I always thought that Mrs. Mead found out in her anthropological studies what she wanted to find. I was not surprised when - I think - two years ago a book came out on Southern Sea populations which just fooled her. I again think that's wrong and unjust, but the concepts of shame culture and guilt culture certainly exist.

The problem of secrecy is, I think, without doubt important, privacy and public also. If you live under social control like in a village where you are observed permanently from all sides then the standard of your role is probably higher, but your suffering is also probably higher. This may be one reason why people tend to the anonymity of urbanism to escape this permanent social control. On the other side, if social control is diminished by anonymity within masses etc., certainly the breaking of rules is increasing. The tendency now to develop always greater institutions and societies is counter-acted by the movement of "Small is Beautiful" where you can participate in decisions. We should develop this movement, because morality can be improved, I think, only in smaller communities where you have a stronger participation in all decisions, also concern in small moral decisions which are so terribly important.

WEINGARTNER: First a short historical remark: I just remind you of what I told you yesterday of the dialogue *Protagoras*. Probably in these old cultures shame was a very important thing. It was Hermes who had to distribute among all the humans shame and justice. So the view was: With these two you can have a basis for ethics and social contract.

Second a more systematic remark: It is connected with the whole paper. The general view of psychoanalysis was always that some human evaluation of a certain patient is explained by some genetic way in the sense that you try to explain to the patient how it came all about or how it developed. Now, my question is the following: What do we want to explain? Does psychoanalysis explain a statement like 'The patient thinks that he hates his friend' or 'The patient is of the opinion that he hates his friend' or is psychoanalysis also interested to find out whether the patient "in fact" hates his friend? There is a big difference, because the second kind I would call 'real value-statements' or 'real norms', whereas the first I would call 'value-like statements'. To me, the question is very important whether the explanation done by psychoanalysis or the task of this scientific approach is such that it really has to explain with a genetic, causal method genuine value-statements or genuine norms or only these value-like statements.

KOHLBERG: My question has to do with this. I was rather impressed by Habermas' distinction between two kinds of developmentally genetic approaches to morality and other phenomena: the psychoanalytic one and the kind of approach that I have tried to use, stressing that they have two different functions. The function of the psychoanalytic explanation in the theory of development is essentially what he calls "emancipatory", that is: In the process of psychoanalysis the patient emancipates himself from false values or distortions of values of one sort. He opposes this sort of developmental understanding. Then we have what he calls a 'rational reconstruction of ontogenesis', that is where there is an assumption that there is some linkage to a justifiable notion of positive values. The methods and the functions of the two approaches to moral development are quite different.

STROTZKA: The first function is emancipatory, the second... ?

KOHLBERG: The second is really both the elaboration of meaning of philosophically or normatively justified value-judgments; an account of development which selects those features which are relevant to the ontogenesis.

STROTZKA: Would you allow me to answer to both in a little wider respect. We have always the problem, 'Is psychoanalysis a science or not?' Popper's explanation was that it is no science, it's a theory which explains everything and it can never be falsified. I think Popper is wrong, because he doesn't understand the psychoanalytical process. What Popper says is quite clear, but you cannot judge a psychoanalytical process from a momentary situation. Because it's a long development and if the interpretation of the patient's utterances has been right or wrong will be shown in the next weeks or months how it develops. So, I think Popper's verdict is wrong, but on the other side the problem of psychoanalysis is that it is both: It is a hermeneutic process and then falsification doesn't mean anything; but it is also a normal behavioral science. The criteria of being scientific are applicable. If Habermas says it has been a scientific misunderstanding, to claim to be a science is only partly true. Both is intended: certainly emancipation and elaboration of the meaning. It's certainly a highly complicated matter.

The other answer to Weingartner is: The therapist in psychotherapy doesn't explain anything to the patient. That's one of the ethical uses of the technique. If anyone explains anything at all, then the patient explains it to the therapist and certainly to himself. When I say, psychoanalysis explains bad or good conscience, the development of values, then I do not mean that this is an explanation for the patient. It gives some insight generally how the system works.

Concerning value-judgments: Most analysts and I myself would say, 'In our therapy, value-judgments do not play any role; people are not thinking about their languages, feelings, ideologies, they are always working with concrete human relations in a very small group-relation framework.' I think nearly always value-like problems are coming up in reality, not values in the stricter sense.

WEINGARTNER: If you say, 'the patient explains', this is not quite clear to me, although I think I understand what you have in mind: The patient expresses after being asked again very important things for the whole process of explanation, but I think only the analyst has the theoretical background (i.e., the theory) to connect these early events with the later ones. This is what an explanation is: He connects the earlier events as initial conditions with his general statements of a theory.

STROTZKA: The answer is again a little away from your question. There has always been the problem, 'What happens to religious beliefs in psychoanalysis?' You know, there are some people who were able to find the integration, some not. In my

discussions with theologians or priests, we agreed more or less
on something which looks a little pragmatic but I think it's
reality. There is a neurotic religious system which is self-de-
structive and destructive for others like scrupulous people or
compulsion-neurotics who have no God. Here the religious attitude is a neurotic symptom. And there are religious people for
whom religion is no problem, which is not even touched in the
analysis. It works relatively well; the trouble is that psychoanalysis is basically and principally a value-critique or ideol--
ogy-critique.

LIND: I was glad that you emphasized that psychoanalysis has a
major emphasis on the clarification of the area between the
unconscious and the conscious motivations. I try to understand
that you want to make sure that the conscience of a person is in
correspondence with his unconsciousness. He is not aware of
his real interests, his real needs. But what you say is, 'Be aware
of your needs, only then you can deal with them in a valuation.'
So actually, I would not agree with you but probably you did
not mean to say that.

I think the developmental and the pyschoanalytic view are
somewhat complementary, but in the lecture you said, "Moral
dilemmas generally constitute exclusive choice situations in
which one person can be helped only if another is hurt". I think
both approaches want to do something different, so that explains the difference of method here. In moral dilemmas the
dilemma is not between two persons but between two values
that are in conflict.

What I wanted to ask you was whether the concept you have
alluded to as conscience, as being a Super-Ego, as an instance
which decides, punishes etc. In your text, Dieter Eicke is quoted: "It is composed of wishes, ideals ... norms and value-
judgments and affects. It punishes, it lives, it gives rise to
qualms of conscience and self-observation, it regulates self-
confidence etc.". I don't know wether I am right but it sounds
rather mechanistic in a way that there is, for instance, no place
for an agent which co-ordinates and reasons about it. I wonder
whether this agent which I think of is rather located in the Ego. I
think Heinz Hartmann has done much work in this direction; we

also suggested actually to consider Piaget's theory of cognitive development for explaining the Ego-functioning.

STROTZKA: If there is a certain harmony between conscious and unconscious, the ambivalence is relatively small. Unconscious tendencies are known and can be handled in a rational manner. This is the concept of mental health.

The passage you mentioned earlier is quoted from Gilligan. Gilligan is rather radical in his formulation, but I quoted him, because radicality is also something that helps to clarify. It's not my point of view, I am a compromising person. The last point you mentioned is very important. Certainly, the structural concept of psychoanalysis looks very mechanistic like the role-theory of Freud. It looks like three homunculi are working within the person and the self, the Id, the Ego and the Super-Ego, and in fact, all of them are constructs. It's a heuristic principle which helps to understand and simplifies also to some extent the dynamics of the personality.

LIND: I think one of the major flaws in psychoanalytic writings is that one separates these three instances: the Ego, the Super-Ego, the Id as homunculi or as different parts in your head which fight against each other, while I have pointed out in a short critical review of this structural approach of psychoanalysis that the Ego cannot at all be conceived as a piece apart from the Super-Ego and the Id, it's rather the cognitive system which relates the Super-Ego and the Id.

STROTZKA: You mentioned Hartmann, because he has the concept of the common matrix which is much closer to the psychic reality.

WREN: Is it the case that value-judgments generate feelings of shame and guilt? This I take to be the position of Rawls, who in his own book has a section discussing shame. He takes issue with Benedict and Mead, who would say in effect, the opposite: namely, that the experience of shame and guilt would generate value-judgments. That is, they have developed the model of the shame- and guilt-feelings generating value-judgments along the lines of an expectancy model. In sum, the contract is that of the classical philosophical position, which says that one is ashamed because one has violated one's value, versus the standard psychological approach that says that one has values to ward off shame. Why are the same terms used in such opposite ways? My thought is that there seem to be two notions of autonomy involved here. In the psychological approach the autonomous agent involved in shame would be some external agent, either a single person or society, whose autonomy confronts and over-rides that of the moral subject in question. In the philosophical approach, which is also embraced by psychologists such as Kohlberg, the story is quite different. Even though "to be ashamed" includes considerable anxiety, its central element for me, the subject, is the realization by me, the autonomous but shameful subject, that I have fallen short of some ideal which I have imposed upon myself. Or someone else might have given me the ideal, but having internalized it as my own, it is I who gives myself the shame. Such is the autonomy involved in the philosophical construal of shame as being ashamed. The contrast with the other sort of autonomy is my way of accounting for what I see to be two totally different models of the relationship between value and moral feelings. The contrast, once again, is between the philosophical model in which value-judgments come first and the shame- and guilt-feelings come later, and the psychological model (I don't differentiate here between psychoanalytic and social learning theory) in which the shame comes first and the values come later.

KOHLBERG: This is what I would see as probably the major distinction between the cognitive developmental theory and the psychoanalytic theory. Let's take guilt, for it is a little clearer than shame. In our discussion of responsibility we said in some sense that guilt comes out of the development of the sense of responsibility rather than that the sense of responsibility comes out of guilt in the usual sense that you have described.

STROTZKA: The problem is the inner world and the outer world and the Außenwelt der Innenwelt und die Innenwelt der Außenwelt. In fact, I think, a child is not violating a value-judgment, it's violating the love and appreciation of the person on which the child is dependent. It's not an abstract problem, but a problem of persons with whom I am connected and interacting. I think this is the difference between philosophical considerations and psychoanalytic considerations.

SCHOLLER: Let me quote a poem from Goethe:

> Was ist außen,
> was ist innen?
> Nichts is außen,
> nichts ist innen,
> denn was draußen ist,
> ist drinnen!

What's outside, what's inside? Nothing is outside, nothing is inside, because what is outside is also inside.

FUCHS: I still want to say something on guilt and shame. There is a very small book written by the Protestant theologian Dorothy Sölle, *Obedience and Fantasy* (exists also in German). This would be quite interesting also for psychologists. It has been written for morality. Obedience and fantasy - this is evidently a very important distinction. Obedience-orientation is a law-orientation. 'Fantasy' means: the orientation to human reality, not only to a norm. 'Norm' is normally an inadequate expression of human reality. Those who look only to laws do not cope with the whole human reality. This is a real difficulty. She tries to overcome this difficulty and insists: You need fantasy, not only a written law. Then maybe you'll find out what you really should do in a concrete human reality.

You mentioned also that our moral behavior should be rather teleological. I do not know whether you who are present here are aware that this is a big, very important tendency. They think they can cope more with human reality than with a deontological norm. Maybe it's quite interesting to notice: terminologically you referred - and you were right - to teleology as a kind of consequentialism. We do not use this word so much on our continent here. But slowly, slowly they eliminate this word and put another there; because they are becoming afraid if we say 'consequentialism' and not 'teleology', then we look only at the consequences and do not see, what we are really doing with the whole reality including the consequences (but not only the consequences). Then they have to find out: What elements are in the whole reality? What is the most important element? Therefore, today in the States, they call it rather 'proportionalism'. Look at the whole reality. Find out what the proportion is of the different elements in it. You cannot avoid everything, you cannot realize everything. You have to be responsible and find out, what is the most important reality to be saved or to be realized. So we call this today in the States 'proportionalism'.

STROTZKA: I am extremely grateful. I have not yet heard of proportionalism, but I easily understand what it is and I would accept it with pleasure. I know Dorothea Sölle personally and I am very glad that she also had this idea, because fantasy is "grobes Denken", it's thinking ahead and we cannot reach progressive innovations, if we do not consider fantasy as an extremely important factor also in ethics.

HIGGINS: I want to make a very general comment on the issue of shame and guilt and the idea of man and woman - man feeling more prone to guilt and woman to shame. I just made the observation that in most cultures throughout history women and children have been treated similarly. I think we can understand why this relation holds, why at least people talk this way and why maybe, in fact, there is some basis to it historically. I don't think that's an explanation that Carol Gilligan would agree with in total, but I think she would agree with me in part.

I also want to talk a little about the therapy-practice and pick up the idea of fantasy. A part of fantasy seems to me also the structure of reasoning. If we take a cognitive developmental perspective, seriously we do talk about structures of reasoning and not only as a heuristic but actually as more than that. There are kind of logical structures in the mind. Some of us have tried to think about how this developmental theory could be useful in therapy. There seems to be a relationship between different kinds of defenses and different structures of reasoning. So, for instance, protection would be a kind of very early defense. And it seems in practice people do make value-judgments. Decline comes in with being unhappy about something. Maybe it is also true that the therapist finds what he/she is interested in, but I found that at least in some cases that what unhappiness seems to stem from is: They've made a value-judgment about their own defenses. They are bothered by the way in which they still act toward other people. So, e.g., either projection or manipulation: They make a negative judgment about this action. So, people do make value-judgments in therapy in regard to their own behavior.

STROTZKA: We are now coming in a rather difficult field. Apparently the therapy of you and your colleagues can be called 'cognitive psychotherapy', right?

HIGGINS: No, because that's, I think, more behavioristic, No, I'm really speaking of structural theory. So you can think of Kohlberg's theory and J. Lovenger's theory. It's a way of respecting the client more; it helps me to have this developmental idea to see the way in which they would like to be. It's a kind of recognizing that because I can see the structure of reasoning. I see some of the normal, positive ways of thinking they have as well as the neurotic.

STROTZKA: The idea strikes me that patients make value-judgments about their own defenses and this may be a mode of neurotic behavior. I have not been aware so much of this, but I can easily understand it. The problem is that I - from my development as a therapist - would think that patients are frequently not aware of their defense mechanism. If projection is one of the most important pathological dynamic forces in a neurotic development, it's of the greatest importance to make the patient aware that he is projecting. Then the value-judgment will change, because he feels that he is not acting with real persons but with persons in whom he projects something and this helps to a great extent.

ZECHA: My question is concerned with the ethical part of your lecture. You say, "A deontological ethics ... can no longer cope with the complex nature of a pluralistic, rapidly changing society". What are examples of a deontological ethics? Examples are Kant's ethics, for instance, another example would be the Golden Rule-ethics. But you say without further justification that such an ethics can no longer cope with the moral problems of our society. I don't see where the short-comings are. On the other hand, I do see what your proposal is. You say to have a modest but nevertheless successful advice: "The goal of our counselling activity is the smallest possible misery to the smallest possible number of people, with special consideration of children".

If I take this as a moral doctrine then it occurs to me to be a dangerous if not terrible moral doctrine, because it is just not enough to avoid misery or to aim at the smallest possible misery. This principle leads directly to abortion and euthanasia because if you abort then there would be no misery for the aborted child; and if you painlessly kill people, then you avoid misery. So, there is a problem, but this problem would not be there, if you stick to one or the other interpretation of the Golden Rule.

STROTZKA: Now the discussion is becoming serious. In my book, I'm talking about the Golden Rule and also Erik Fromm is representing it. I would not include the Golden Rule in this respect when I say, "Deontological ethics does not really help in solving the new moral problems". I would like to give an example: If you think of the embryos or pre-embryos that are the result of extra-corporal fertilization: What happened just now in Australia? What are we doing with the two embryos that are frozen and their parents died - should we kill them, should we use them in another way, should we make experiments with them? The temptation to make experiments with embryos is enormous for scientists, because what one can do with such embryos is unbelievable: monsters could be developed and all terrible things could happen.

According to my understanding we have no precedents in the existent ethics to get along with such problems. We have to develop new concepts of what is bad, of what is right or wrong, of what is allowed or forbidden.

Such are the examples I have in mind; that you need new concepts which nobody has yet, especially for embryos. It is a terrible situation of helplessness. Thinking of the consequences or of the proportions in which all that happens it is terribly necessary to find a useful rule. You cannot use the Golden Rule for all these situations, because I would not know what I would like that it would happen to me, for example. Probably I would prefer to be killed as soon as possible, but I am not sure if this can be generalized. It's very dangerous if you make such a universalization. Really, we are in a totally open situation in many respects, especially through the new technologies. Certainly, to reduce misery by killing is not a new concept, it's a very old concept in many cultures. Newborns have been killed because one felt we cannot feed them; older ones have been killed or spontaneously have chosen to be killed and to die. In the present ethical situation, especially after the Nazi-experience, this solution is a solution which is totally unacceptable for most of us: to make the choice that killing is the best solution to reduce misery. I am rather sure that you dont' want to say this is our goal. But it has certainly to be discussed why this is not acceptable, because there are values. I'm running into troubles, for example, with abortion. I am one of the people in this country who were for the *Fristenlösung* (i.e., the ruling that the termination of pregnancy is legally permitted until a certain number of weeks has elapsed in the pregnancy) and still I am despite of the fact that I am disappointed of the results of the *Fristenlösung*. These are extremely serious problems and we have always to work on them.

VIRT: When you mentioned your goal as the negative version of Jeremy Bentham's formula, 'the greatest happiness for the greatest number', I noticed also that it is a problem when the psychoanalyst approaches ethics. The psychoanalyst comes from negative experiences (mental problems, neurosis etc.), but can we formulate the aim in ethics from a negative point of view? Every judgment about misery implies an opinion of what is good. Therefore I have problems with the negative approach to ethics of the psychoanalyst, especially with Sigmund Freud. A second remark concerning the deontological foundation of norms: We have the problem that very concrete norms make the claim to be absolute under every condition, in every situation. The Golden Rule is a necessary condition for the justification of a concrete ethical norm, e.g.,the prohibition of abortion, it does not, however, provide a sufficient condition. Deontologists have two types of arguments; first by nature (the problem of natural fallacy and all the implications of science) and second that according to the responsibility to human values you have no right to deal with human life. Only God has this right. But one can show that also this second type of argument is false from a theological point of view, because you would put God and man on the same level making them competitors, so to speak. There-fore in theology we have also our problems with deontological ethics. I cannot follow the deontological argumentation.

STROTZKA: That we have chosen a negative formulation comes from the factual situation in such counselling agencies. There are no optimal situations we could find: marriages are broken, children are growing up with terrible consequences for everybody, and so we thought to operate with concepts like "most human" and so on would just give a wrong picture of the real situation.

It is sad, because there is an enormous amount of misery. We can only try to distribute it more or less justly. That's the situation in which I have to work.

KOHLBERG: Just one word to your defense of the formula; one of the first things I learned about Bentham-like utilitarianism is: It's much easier to accept the formulation that human pain and suffering is an evil than it is to accept the proposition that human pleasure is *per se* a good or something like that. There is something to the negative formulation from the philosophic point of view.

ZECHA: I am expected to formulate a final statement. Let me state just one important observation: Through the whole con-ference I had this in mind: We are using 'conscience' in every-day life, we know the term also in various scientific disciplines, in various contexts and if it is not just a word for any feeling, for rhetorical purposes or even without any meaning, then there must be some consensus about some basic value-convictions. I listened carefully to all the contributions and I think I could catch a few indications in that direction. For instance, Prof. Strotzka mentioned, "Just to live" - that's an important guide-line for further analysis. Or yesterday, Prof. Kohlberg said, "Respect for other people" - yes, this is also an element that points to that direction; and similar thoughts were contained in the other papers. This shows that the notion of conscience does have an underlying material content that should be made clear

and should be brought to the awareness of all scientists and people concerned.
Thank you very much to all of you.

End of discussion.

INDEX OF NAMES

INDEX OF SUBJECTS